Outrageous Behavior Modification

OUTRAGEOUS BEHAVIOR MODIFICATION

Handbook of Strategic Interventions for Managing Impossible Students

Second Edition

Barry T. Christian

Illustrations by Jenny Loehr

pro·ed
An International Publisher

8700 Shoal Creek Boulevard
Austin, Texas 78757-6897
800-897-3202   Fax 800-397-7633
www.proedinc.com

© 1997, 2008 by PRO-ED, Inc.
8700 Shoal Creek Boulevard
Austin, Texas 78757-6897
800/897-3202   Fax 800/397-7633
www.proedinc.com

ISBN-13: 1-987-1-4164-0212-1
ISBN-10: 1-4164-0212-8

Art Director: Jason Crosier
Designer: Nancy McKinney-Point
Illustrator: Jenny Loehr
This book is designed in Fairfield LH, Agenda, and Felt Tip Roman

Printed in the United States of America

1 2 3 4 5 6 7 8 9 10 11 10 09 08 07

Contents

Chapter 18
The Gotcha! Game   143
When Students Monitor the Teacher's Enforcement

Chapter 19
Outrageous B-Mod   149
A Few Parting Shots

Preface

Disclaimer:
A Cautionary Note to the Reader

You are holding a revised, expanded, and even more powerful version of our first controversial work. Please note that the unorthodox methods presented in this handbook are offered for instructional and educational purposes only. Each chapter unveils a different group of classroom strategies—and these are frequently illustrated by some of our mostly true war stories. Outrageous behavior modification (OBM) interventions have been developed by eccentric school psychology practitioners and should be applied only after due consideration—and at your own risk! Please be aware that the actual use of these nonstandard techniques may result in temporary confusion and disorientation for your oppositional-defiant students. Also be aware that Benjamin Spock, Carl Rogers, and Oprah would probably not approve of OBM (even though they might grin privately). Some PC educators have even expressed tactful concern that OBM methods may cause stubborn disruptive students to act civil and complete assignments *against their will*. It is you, the reader, who must ultimately decide whether to apply any particular strategy. OBM users must therefore assume full responsibility for their successes. Welcome aboard! Please find your seat. Buckle yourself in securely, and hold on tight.

How To Actually Use This Handbook

Strategic interventions are more difficult to teach and apply than concrete methods. Even though our research suggests that very bright and highly verbal individuals (that's you) will be attracted to the *OBM Handbook*, there is still the challenge of making the ideas approximate reality. You will notice that we have bolstered each chapter with manic but believable application stories. If you aren't quite ready to read a particular chapter, no problem ... we offer a low-carb summary box at the end, which should provide the basics of that particular strategy. Some of the high-functioning folks at PRO-ED, the publisher, have even helped to make the chapter text material more user friendly by inserting thumbnail-size images of the various support materials. All you need to do when you see one of those is leaf back to Appendix G, and there you will find all the full-size reproducible forms, coupons, cards, and protocols. Is that convenient or what? Now you can practically design a little something for Oppositional Eddy while you're strolling down the hall to the copy machine. Enjoy.

The Revised OBM Handbook:
More Blame Throwing

Basically, this revision is offered as a repackaged and manically expanded "best of the best." Of course, with a revision comes some new acknowledgment comments and a nostalgic or even tearful look back at the literary birthing process. These acknowledgment quips are those few defining moments at the awards banquet where we lean in to the microphone, thank *"all those who helped make it possible"* and then tack on an impassioned plea for the rain forest or beached whales.

Just like those rambling podium gratitudes, the *revised OBM Handbook* requires quite a large stack of thank-you notes. Many of the expanded techniques were spawned from the incredible *X-File* experiences of seemingly healthy educators who actually attempted the interventions. These revisions certainly bear the imprint of many classroom practitioners, shocked and baffled administrators, and a cadre of indulgent "related service" personnel. The dubious spotlight of appreciation is also focused on our tireless staff at the OBM Institute, including many contracted liability attorneys, spin doctors, and riot control specialists.

Most educators are mildly amused by OBM strategies. Some readers simply don't get it. A few hardy souls actually understand *and* try out the strategies. This last group includes dozens of folks in the Silver Consolidated Schools (that's in beautiful Silver City, New Mexico); and they are represented by the likes of Debbie Upton, Rudy Quinonez, Kim Hopwood, Barb Stewart, Dolores Maese, Rosella Escobedo, and fearless rooky Luis Alvarado. It's hard to believe that these lucky educators get to live in a story-book western town—and also get paid for working with neat kids. Go figure. Some astute readers are bound to question what kind of school administrators would actually tolerate our nonlinear interventions. Well, we're here to thank our progressive SPED directors, Corrine Weyrich, Pam Gibson, and Pam Fenstamaker. We want to encourage them to keep doing those deep-breathing exercises.

Another, even smaller frontier settlement and a designated OBM field testing site is Reserve, New Mexico. This is a one-street, F-150 town nestled in the mountains of the expansive Gila National Forest. It's my favorite hundred-mile drive to work, on which I sometimes negotiate with obstinate herds of elk crossing the highway and pass under the scrutiny of stoic bald eagles perched in the ponderosas. Yes, it's a rough life peddling these newfangled behavior interventions. But it's worth that bumpy stage ride to consult with pioneer types like Courtenay Schwandner, Barb Pendleton, Jolene Delgado, and Vicki Shriver.

A schedule of OBM training workshops has continued around the Southwest—despite threats and disparaging remarks from those traditional behavior modification guys. From wilderness places with no cell service all the way to teeming urban areas with airport security checks and eight-lane toll booths, the OBM workshops have presented ideas and received valuable feedback from genuine live teachers. Speaking of urban workshops, special thanks goes to Ivan Vance, a senior consultant with the nearly world famous Region X Educational Service Center deep in the heart of Texas. Mr. Vance is a school psychology veteran who has been there, done that, and escaped many consequences of his own strategic interventions.

During the revision process, there was much talk in the hallways of the OBM Institute about doing a worldwide talent search for a top-notch professional illustrator. The response to our job-opening announcement on *Jay Leno* was phenomenal, with literally hundreds of enthusiastic applicants seeking to work on the handbook. Scores of talented cartoonists camped (in orderly lines) at the front entrance to the institute, each hoping for a chance at graphic arts immortality. Eventually, our search committee discovered Jenny Loehr, and you will understand why her spirited illustrations were selected for the revised handbook.

One special drawing (page 9) was saved from the first edition of the book. This was done a few years ago by a fourth-grade student who managed to capture in a single sketch the defiant attitude of our oppositional student customers. Special thanks to Erika Jayne Christian, who somehow grew up Ritalin free in our mostly normal family.

Finally, there's my confidential list of strong-willed, factory-wired oppositional students, who could fill an auditorium (or an IEP circus tent). You kids have definitely added some salsa to my career. This expanded edition of the *OBM Handbook* is dedicated to you ... and we all trust that you will not read any of these strategies until long after your graduation!

Fractured Acknowledgments from the First Edition, 1997

The present handbook represents a small step in the post–behavior modification journey. The author has been a compiler and systematizer of methods, but many outstanding school psychologists and classroom instructors should share recognition and reasonable blame for their contributions. From the early days of experimentation in the field, Phyllis Crawford, MA; Cliff Jones, PhD; Barbara Fishgrab, MA (and a smiling newbie PsyD); and Frank Amadeo, MA (no-needa PhD) have critiqued and shaped the actual strategies presented in this book.

This intrepid (now historic) team of counselors has provided effective psychological services to the Gallup-McKinley County Schools (in New Mexico), one of the largest geographic school districts in North America. Our fearless counseling staff could pull together like a MASH team for crisis intervention or work independently as unseen Lone Rangers in far-flung desert schools. These professionals have taught me more in our "outrageous" Friday staff meetings and through their counseling successes than I have ever imparted to them. Hey, it doesn't matter what anyone thinks, you all deserve to keep your counseling licenses. Thanks, guys!

Finally, the author is personally indebted to hundreds of teachers, administrators, and guidance counselors who have attended his in-service training workshops across New Mexico and Arizona. These classroom practitioners have helped to refine the various wacky interventions and keep them almost grounded in reality. For the behavior management work you do every day in our schools, this *OBM Handbook* is really dedicated to you!

1 Introduction to Strategic Management

Our Start-Up Chapter for Wide-Eyed Wannabes

What's So "Outrageous" About It?

Many of the methods presented in this handbook are "strategic" in nature. That is, they tend to avoid direct power confrontations with resistant students and instead use preplanned interactions that confuse and erode the difficult behaviors. These strategic methods include not only the learning principles of more traditional behavior modification techniques, but also many hypnotic principles and psycholinguistic concepts that address the student's resistance at a deeper "personality level." Over the years of teacher consultation, workshop training programs, and real-world practice, this rather unorthodox approach has come to be affectionately known as Outrageous B-Mod (or simply "OBM" for those savvy folks on the inside).

Some OBM methods make use of planned confusion or disruptive word pictures. Others incorporate double-bind requests and offbeat "psychobabble" interpretations. Among our favorites are the straight-faced paradoxic assignments that appear to encourage the problem behaviors—while gently disrupting and fogging them. The real beauty of OBM methods is that they skillfully make use of the student's own stubbornness and rigid style to fuel the desired changes. We've sometimes described it as "programmatic judo" because the resistance energy is strategically used to defeat the misbehavior. Therefore, the more oppositional a student is, the better these methods seem to work. Hey, what a deal.

Lt. Columbo in the Classroom

We have found that OBM methods are partly an arsenal of outlandish strategies and partly a playful, engaging attitude. It has also become apparent that this approach is geared more to micromanagement situations (i.e., those predictable face-to-face power struggles) in the classroom, than toward district-level behavior policies. OBM interventions are not intended to replace the foundational management principles by which most of the daily classroom routine is organized. Rather, our methods are offered for those critical situations in which power-thirsty students "reflexively" defy limits and boldly go where no students have gone before in usurping authority.

Think of our OBM materials and classroom management in comparison to a big-city police department. For directing traffic and citing speeders, we have our general police force. Sure, from time to time they also have to bust the crooks or break up domestic disputes, but the daily beat is usually predictable and characterized by standard procedure. Occupational pressures include choosing between glazed and chocolate-covered and keeping up with the weekly ticket quotas.

Sometimes a really bad egg starts to operate in a city, and he does his evil deeds secretly, repeatedly, and with no remorse. Such cases are assigned to special cops who are just as sneaky as the bad eggs. The detective-type cops are still doing law enforcement, but they use different methods because they're not dealing with average-citizen slipups. Some of these special sleuths get so close to the criminals that they become loud, foul-mouthed, amoral types (not like us), but others are the unassuming near-genius types like our man on the case, Lt. Columbo (OBM approved).

Okay, let's see who's along for the metaphorical ride. The general traffic-cop work is broad-spectrum "macro" management, right? We like to compare this to directing the daily classroom routines, expectations, and learning activities. This is general social control. For the hard-case encounters (i.e., with oppositional-defiant students), we bring out our slick, near-genius OBM methods and do some face-to-face "micro" management to bring things back to baseline. Of course, even with educators, there's the problem of choosing between glazed and chocolate-covered.

Although nearly every teacher, administrator, and counselor can make some use of OBM methods, we have found that certain folks are "naturals." These gifted educators are the special sleuths who respond well to resistant students. We try to pick them out of our workshop crowd early in the day. These folks have the innate capacity to simultaneously follow an OBM workshop lecture and also drift away in their own private thought world to actually plan half a dozen creative interventions. A few teacher trainees have been heard to spontaneously laugh right out loud during a workshop— and then snap out of their trance with grinning embarrassment. Having read only the first few paragraphs of our handbook, you may already have an idea of whether OBM is for you. We hope it is!

Depending on your own personality style, closeness to retirement, and medication level, you may find yourself strangely amused by the possibilities of OBM . . . or not. As you move further into the handbook, keep in mind that many of the classroom interventions have multiple levels of meaning.

Consider the way our Lt. Columbo interrogates his prime suspects. One observer may see a bumbling detective wandering about in a rumpled trench coat. This inept guy seems to be a sorry excuse for a detective. He misses obvious clues, gets distracted with trivial conversation, and seems to misinterpret the key facts. Of course, the rest of us look on with little worry for the gifted gumshoe. To us, his subtle interviews are like a 3-D chess game and may even rank as a classic art form. The unassuming questions crafted by this sleuth reveal a quiet genius going about his life's work. There are many parallels here with master educators.

Hopefully, you'll discover some of the same Lt. Columbo artistry in this strategic approach to behavior management. Keep in mind that any tokens, charts, and rewards included in our classroom methods are only "props" and not the real substance. Welcome to the emerging technology of Outrageous B-Mod!

Who Are These Oppositional-Defiant Students?

In case you didn't catch it the first time around, let us say it one—more—time: The interventions presented in this handbook are not offered for "general" classroom management. It will become obvious that these specialized OBM methods are best suited for a type of student we call "oppositional defiant." In fact, the psychiatric community has included this category as a "Disorder of Childhood or Adolescence" in the *DSM-IV* (and following) diagnostic code books. The shrinks have recognized this type of kid for years . . . but classroom teachers have known them since Aristotle opened his first outdoor seminars.

It is interesting that this particular category is distinguished from dozens of other conduct, emotional, and developmental disorders. In general, these difficult young people are easily identified by their inordinate thirst for power and conquest. They are wired to question authority and lust after control. They don't back down or change mental sets easily. It seems that they come to us preprogrammed at the factory to resist any limits placed upon them. They are not considered "disturbed" so much as they are "disturbing."

One conclusion we might draw from these traits is that these are "kids with an attitude." They may not be mugging little old ladies or struggling with deep depression, but they do have a commanding presence in any classroom. Sooner or later they will come into conflict with the established hierarchy of authority. Too bad for you if you happen to represent that authority.

Sound like some students you've met? Keep in mind that they are not necessarily gang bangers or juvenile offenders (although they can be). They are not necessarily emotionally disturbed (although they can be). And they are not necessarily attention-deficit kids (although, heaven help us, they can be). Think for a second about one of your most impossible students. Mentally insert his name in the form in Figure 1.1 and consider each of the diagnostic criteria. Do you have a certifiable case on your hands?

The Lighter Side of Classroom Tyrants

Since my uncommon staff of school psychology types will never let well enough alone, we have moved beyond that stuffy *DSM-IV* diagnosis with some real-world descriptors of our own. Below are a few of our *Calvin and Hobbes*–inspired traits of oppositional-defiant students:

1. While completing a career preference worksheet, he asks you for the proper spelling of *despot*.
2. In explaining today's playground altercation, the little fellow confidently asserts that it was the other students who forced his wrath—because they were too slow in obeying his commands.
3. He is able to methodically list dozens of exception clauses to each of your class rules. Given an opportunity, he can also do a convincing F. Lee Bailey defense of any infractions.

4. You find yourself *not* making reasonable requests of him, just to avoid that whining song and dance.

5. You present him with one of the most valuable and coveted classroom rewards ever given to a student, and he looks up to ask, "Is this all?"

6. You learn that he holds the distinction of having frustrated the combined efforts of Dr. Phil, Dr. Laura, Dr. Dobson, and Dr. Seuss. It's some kind of record.

7. You receive a curt, businesslike memo from this student informing you that his social studies grade needs to go up on the next report card. It's labeled in bold type, *"Re: Just a friendly reminder."*

8. Before meeting any of the parents, you are able to pick his haggard mother out of the crowd. She inquires hopefully about an extended school year.

9. You arrive at your classroom to find him relaxing in your chair, heels on the desk, "smoking" one of your flair pens, and demanding to know what kind of reward the class will get on Friday.

10. You find yourself rediscovering your earlier zest for teaching—and then realize he's been absent for two days.

Okay, now you get it. These are the truly oppositional-defiant students—and we OBM practitioners just love to see them shuffling into class. This handbook is especially designed to help these kids get with the program and keep teachers in control of the festivities.

There is a classic story told of the Roaring 20s in Chicago. A new gangster recruit has arrived in the Windy City and is being shown around by his criminal mentor. "What about the cops?" the new crook asks. And the sagelike reply is, "Well, around

---

Oppositional-Defiant Disorder

My Student: _____

Certifiable Banana? _____ Yes _____ No _____ Most Likely

The American Psychiatric Association's *DSM-IV* diagnostic criteria for good ole "313.81" Oppositional Defiant Disorder indicates that these children show a long-term pattern of negativistic, hostile, and defiant behaviors that include at least *four* of the disgusting traits listed below:

_____ 1. Often loses temper

_____ 2. Often argues with adults

_____ 3. Often actively defies or refuses to comply with adults' requests or rules

_____ 4. Often deliberately annoys people

_____ 5. Often blames others for his or her mistakes or misbehavior

_____ 6. Is often touchy or easily annoyed by others

_____ 7. Is often angry and resentful

_____ 8. Is often spiteful or vindictive

Figure 1.1. Oppositional-Defiant Disorder

here the cops are not the enemy—they're either our employees or just some minor competition."

And what a slick metaphor to introduce classroom OBM! In our classrooms the oppositional-defiant students are not at all viewed as a personal threat. These poor waifs are either "acquired" by our company or simply provide some entertaining competition. Their rigid style is just incorporated into the daily program, and we may even grant them some artificial power from time to time. I hope you are enticed to read on.

Using the Male Pronoun

You have probably noticed that our student examples so far use the male gender. Chances are this doesn't bother you much at all, especially if you have just worked your way through some politically correct text where the author kept switching back and forth at random between the gender pronouns. We're reasonable down-home folks, and we do believe that both boys and girls should generally be used in educational examples. However, in the present handbook, you will find exclusive use of the male gender when OBM techniques are described. Aside from continuity, we have an empirical basis for this presentation. Year after year, we have conducted a gender-frequency count on our own student caseloads. It may be no surprise to you, but we have consistently discovered that over 85% of our oppositional kids wore blue booties in the crib. Having said that, it's also only fair to warn that when your class roster includes a high-powered oppositional-defiant kid of the female persuasion (especially when she has determined to take over a mid-school classroom), it's probably a good time to review your mental health insurance benefits.

Yes, we did see that raised hand way in the back row of our reader audience. The question was about our use of the female pronoun for our cool and witty OBM teacher. Well, the teacher population numbers are still with us on that call, and there's the added benefit of simple clarity throughout the handbook. You're really going to like our OBM teacher. And, since it seems we have no more reader questions just now, we're going to move along with some more introductory material.

Principles of OBM: *Just a Bit of Uncommon Sense*

Number One: If it ain't broke ... don't fix it!

OBM methods are unique, strategic, relational, and sometimes labor intensive to get off the ground. If your regular classroom management procedures are sufficient, why change? Why use a fancy dynamite charge to lift your petunias when the old garden spade works just fine?

I am reminded here of a staff consultation meeting where a notoriously difficult student was being discussed. (You've been in these meetings, right?) One teacher had just reported some pretty awful disruptive behaviors, and (because I was invited there as the "consultant") I found myself beginning to mentally arrange some respectable inquiries that would guide the design of a behavior intervention plan: *"Hmm ... Wonder if her time-out consequence is too weak? ... Maybe there's some uncontrolled social reinforcement that's supporting this behavior cycle? ... Should we define some target behaviors and get started with a functional behavior assessment? ... Uh, isn't it about time for lunch?"*

Meanwhile, the next person to report on this student was a no-nonsense veteran teacher who acknowledged that some of the same evil, nasty disruptions had occurred in her class. I recall one of our newbie counselors saying something like, "Wow, that sounds pretty serious ... " Without blinking, the veteran teacher responded, "Not really, I just told him to cut it out and get back to the spelling list." (It worked.) Her method was direct, nontechnical, and effective. The moral of the story? Many situations don't require our fancy strategies. If you already "have the power," just use it.

Once again, with feeling: *"If it ain't broke ... don't fix it!"*

Number Two: If it isn't working ... stop running it into the ground.

Has anyone figured out why some teachers live out decades of their professional career recycling their "Plan A" behavior management strategy that flat-out doesn't work? Because oppositional-defiant students have the propensity to test the limits of our endurance, it is important that we be willing to let go of the old standbys. We may need to shut down our tired old methods of rational explanation and tactful redirection. From time to time we may even have to give up such classic tools as happy stickers, notes sent home, and raging threats of imminent destruction. Sure, these may work for other students, but they only bring a slight smile to the face of the hard-core oppositional student. To rephrase this important OBM principle: When your standard procedure doesn't work, stop whining and do something different.

Number Three: Work smarter ... not harder.

A teacher with a creative, unconventional arsenal of management strategies is more suited to educate a strong-willed student. We feel only sympathy for those well-meaning teachers who wear an *Avis* button and endure more unfruitful grief. And yes, there is a certain gleam of empowerment in the eye of that teacher who has discovered some effective OBM strategies. It's always a joy to behold the enthusiasm of workshop participants who have had some lights go on and can't wait for Monday morning. We hope this handbook will put a fearless gleam in many weary eyes!

Number Four: The next best thing to compliance ... is confusion.

Think about this: It's hard to be rebellious *and* confused at the same time. In managing resistant students, some use should be planned for strategically generated bewilderment, distraction, free-floating anxiety, and mental disorientation. Moving targets are harder to hit, and the teacher who is known to be occasionally unpredictable (i.e., *like a fox*) is less likely to be prey for the power-crazed oppositional student. Many of the OBM methods presented in this handbook are meant to deliberately confuse nefarious agendas and get our difficult students back to the learning process.

Number Five: Transform "problems" into educational projects.

As you journey through this unorthodox handbook, you may notice the absence of direct blame or assignment of fault for misbehaviors. Despite some bad press lately, many of us psychologist types do still believe that individuals bear responsibility for their conduct. However, we are also aware that oppositional-defiant students have made an art form out of denial and rationalization. Because of their intense chemistry and lifelong habit of resistance, these students are caught in their own personal prison. All they know is the resistance game. So ... because we would rather work smarter, we tend to avoid the barricaded front door and slip quietly through a side window.

Essentially, the OBM teacher develops temporary blindness to whatever disgusting resistance is playing itself out this afternoon. Instead of a no-win confrontation, she finds a way to make a helpful project out of it. Our smiling OBM teacher enters the classroom armed with a plan for transforming that disruptive target behavior into some "necessary" and respected educational project. This will make much more sense later. Meanwhile, your assignment is to watch five of the old Mister Magoo cartoons and ponder the applications of "strategic myopia."

Number Six: OBM doesn't fit every teacher.

We have found that some teachers are temperamentally predisposed to instant success with OBM technology. Others are not. That's life. In most cases, our consultation meetings have been colored by honest laughter, the sharing of classic war stories about "oppositional students we have known," and some very productive "possibility thinking." Our consultees generally leave with a packet of strategies under their arm, new resolve to lead their classrooms, and a dangerous plan for Monday morning. By the way, any teacher with a plan should automatically be considered dangerous.

On the other hand, we have found some rare allergic reactions to OBM stealth. I recall one extreme negative case with a hyperassertive male teacher who sat to the rear of an elementary in-service workshop. With each new principle or strategy presented to the faculty, his hand would immediately go up. He would then pronounce an argumentative "Yeah but" question that highlighted some instance in which a given method probably would not work. As his unsolicited comments became less rational and intensified into red-faced anger, I came to realize that the deeper strategic nature of some OBM methods may trigger unpredicted emotions in certain individuals.

We were never able to convert that guy. I eventually asked him to *help us out* by trying to think of at least two practical problems for each new intervention that was introduced. He promptly *refused*, folded his arms across his chest, and sulked quietly. Our empathetic workshop staff later decided that the steaming 40-year-old heckler was probably an adult version of the kind of student we were discussing.

There is a lighter side to this compatibility thing. I recall some workshop evaluation forms with such insightful comments as:

"You guys ought to be locked up somewhere, for your own good."

"I'm just glad there were some good refreshments at this training."

"I've got an MEd in behavior disorders and we never studied these things in graduate school."

"Do you OBM guys recommend some kind of extra liability insurance?"

"I'd require a five-day waiting period before allowing your OBM trainees back into real classrooms."

"I arrived at the OBM registration table in the morning ... and the next thing I remember, I'm grinning like a lunatic and climbing in my car to go home ... What happened? ... I really need to talk to somebody."

"My principal said we can't use any of your stuff in civilized classrooms ... but I do have some good news ... I was able to save a ton of money on my own child's therapy by switching to OBM Chapter 7. Thanks guys!"

Number Seven: If you can't extinguish it ... license, tax, and regulate the joy right out of it.

Some strains of nuisance behavior are quite resistant to total extinction. Not to worry. Instead of fighting them (which we never do in OBM practice), why not find a creative bureaucratic way to regulate them to death? In the daily business of managing oppo-

---

Introduction to OBM

A Summary of Uncommon Sense

1. **If It Ain't Broke ... Don't Fix It!**
   Some situations don't require fancy strategies. If you already "have the power," just use it.

2. **If It Isn't Working ... Stop Running It into the Ground.**
   When your "standard procedure" doesn't work, stop whining and do something different.

3. **Work Smarter ... Not Harder.**
   In many instances a good strategy may work better than red-faced confrontation.

4. **The Next Best Thing to Compliance ... Is Confusion.**
   It's difficult to be oppositional *and* confused at the same time.

5. **Transform "Problems" into Educational Projects.**
   Consider welcoming the oppositional behavior as a pretext for some wonderful learning activity.

6. **OBM Doesn't Fit Every Teacher.**
   Most teachers have hidden OBM talent, but, some rare allergic reactions to OBM stealth have been observed.

7. **If You Can't Extinguish It ... License, Tax, and Regulate the Joy Right Out of It.**
   Attach the burden of a bureaucratic "paper chase" to challenging behaviors.

Figure 1.2. Introduction to OBM: A Summary of Uncommon Sense

sitional students, it may be just as important to "appear" to have control as to actually have control. In these cases, the teacher appears to accommodate the evil behavior but adds the onerous burden of ridiculous applications, permits, required procedures, inspections, and regulatory paperwork. Big Brother already knows this one.

It's Time To Assess Your Own Compatibility with OBM Methods

After lecturing and consulting with hordes of educators, I am increasingly convinced that our self-assessment exercise in Appendix A is still a useful predictor of how any given teacher will "mesh" with strategic methods. Okay, so it's not psychometrically sophisticated. And yes, it may seem a bit goofy (*understatement*). But it does speak volumes about an individual's OBM compatibility.

In addition to the contrived raw score, the informal attitudes and spontaneous reactions generated during this little exercise have pretty much reflected just how well a teacher will be able to understand, enjoy, and apply the OBM methods. By the way, we believe that enjoyment of OBM is a prerequisite to successful application. Anyway, we like to hand out this assessment sheet and then just stand back and listen to the chuckling or ice-cold bewilderment. In just a few minutes we can identify those workshop participants who will excel … and those who may need crisis intervention. If you have not yet done so, remove all books and papers from your desk, turn to Appendix A, and begin the test. You are on your honor. Good luck!

Here, for your amusement, is our favorite fourth-grade drawing of a very stubborn student who won't listen to the teacher and who never does what he is told.

"Could You *Pretend* To Be a Real Jerk?"

The Classic OBM Paradigm

When Resistance Is Compliance

This is the one that started it all. When set up correctly, the teacher takes almost immediate control of the problem behavior, no matter how the student chooses to respond. This intervention is built on a paradoxic request (i.e., *"Could you please help me out by pretending to be a difficult student?"*). There is also an embedded double-bind contingency. That is, the student becomes compliant when he performs the disgusting target behavior—or else the student becomes compliant by refusing to perform the disgusting target behavior. Is this elegant or what? There are some required techniques to get it off the ground, but this one can show results the very first day. If you only buy into one OBM strategy this year, why not take this little puppy home?

In the early days of OBM development, we used some of the confidence game lingo that we vaguely remembered from the Redford and Newman movie *The Sting*. Our early workshop demonstration video was also the theatrical debut of one of the special education counselors, who later morphed into Dr. Cliff Jones, school psych guy. He originated the role of Oppositional Eddy for our unlikely demonstration. This strong-willed class wrecker took much pride in his defiance, had his own rap song to boast of "being bad," and even carved notches in his desk to keep track of how many of his teachers resigned during the year—or had to be committed. Our mild-mannered, first-year, rookie teacher should have been easy pickings for Eddy. Instead, Eddy became the focus of an OBM intervention that was narrated through such fanciful steps as Choosing the Mark, The Setup, The Sting, and Cooling the Mark. Even though these steps were lifted from *The Sting*, they were found to describe Eddy's treatment plan quite well. Our not-ready-for-prime-time video production showed helpless Eddy through his stages of metamorphosis. This student's proud career as the in-house problem child was largely neutralized and replaced with some semblance of classroom compliance. The OBM "treatment" didn't change his stubborn personality, but it did rechannel his energies. A summary of the four steps required for pulling off this powerful classroom intervention follows.

Choosing the Mark

Not every student is a candidate for this particular intervention. We have found that the more deeply ingrained the defiance, and the more rigid the personality of the student, the better this method works. Don't look for some easy student to practice on. Rather, be encouraged to boldly target the most disruptive and defiant student in the class. After all, if that one student's behavior were to mellow out, wouldn't everything else in class go a lot smoother?

The Setup

This is a critical part of the intervention. Quietly ask your Oppositional Eddy to remain behind after class when there will be ample time to visit. In this brief private meeting, announce that you are working on developing some of your teaching skills (e.g., student motivation, classroom management) and would really appreciate some help. See the sample scripts, which have been tailored to specific problem behaviors in Figure 2.1 a–d. Once you get the idea, any one of the scripts can be adapted to fit a special target behavior. Take some time now and imagine yourself (with a straight face and innocent eyes) using one of the following scripts with your most oppositional student.

Polishing Your Presentation

Some busy teachers may be tempted to slack off on their setup spiel. After all, this is just for a student, right? This isn't some dangerous gangland kingpin. Nobody's life, career, or new auto paint job is at risk. Well, we hope it's all in good spirit here, but the enlistment monologue is the heart of the *Pretend Jerk* ploy. Here are a few guidelines to help you craft that important first-contact proposal:

1. Describe a straightforward business deal.
2. Point out the win-win benefits for both parties.
3. Ask for help and creative input from the student.
4. Maintain an atmosphere of collusion and semi-secrecy.
5. Avoid cumbersome or confusing requests–simplicity is strength.

Okay, you've picked up the general idea. Keep in mind that the setup phase of this intervention is critical for creating the expectation of a mutual conspiracy. Frequently, the

---

Sample Setup Spiel #1

Excessive Talking in Class:

"I'm trying to practice my skill of handling students who talk too much in class. Is it possible that you might be willing to help me out during the next week or so? All I need is a student who would pretend to be a big-time talker in third and fourth hours. If you could help me, all you would need to do is remember to talk way too much and chatter away during these hours—so I can practice how to do effective warnings and reminders ... And so I can make up tough consequences and stuff. Don't worry, if we run this thing right, you won't really get into any big trouble. You'll be working for me "undercover," and so if you get some kind of punishment, just grumble under your breath and act all upset, as usual. It will be our secret, and I'll see to it that you get released from it ... like if you had to go to the office or something. In exchange for your help, I'll keep track of the days you're on duty and that should earn you a pretty nice reward. [Explain a possible earned privilege, benefit, freedom, or even some cool bonus points.]"

Figure 2.1a. Sample Setup Spiel #1

Sample Setup Spiel #2

Being Slow To Start Work Assignments:

"Thanks for staying after class a few moments. Here's what's happening. This semester I'm supposed to be working on developing some good classroom management skills. You know, us teachers are always supposed to be working on something. Anyway, I was wondering if I could count on you for a little extra help during English class for the next couple of weeks. I need to find a student who would pretend to work very slow, so I can practice some motivational ideas. If you could help out, all you would need to do is be sure you are the very last student to start the written assignments … and then keep an eye on everyone else so you are always behind the rest of the class. Just keep creeping along like a snail. This would give me the opportunity to give you stern warnings and reminders—and maybe some kind of punishments. Oh, don't worry too much about the consequences. We'll make sure that you get out of them somehow when no one else is watching. It would be a personal favor to me, but I would also keep track of the days you help out and give you a pretty nice reward. [Discuss possibilities.] Well, is it a deal? Can we start on Monday?"

Figure 2.1b. Sample Setup Spiel #2

Sample Setup Spiel #3

Resisting Class Rules and Teacher Instructions:

"I know how busy you are, so I'll keep this short. This semester I'll be working on developing advanced classroom management skills. I need a really sharp student who would be willing to help me with my practice of enforcing the rules and controlling the class. In order to be effective, this would have to be a secret deal. I thought you might be willing to help out. All you would have to do is pretend to resist certain class rules and also pretend to resist certain things I ask you to do. [Here the teacher suggests possible rules or requests that might be resisted.] Of course my job would be to give the usual warnings and try to get you to behave. You would make sure that none of my efforts work, even when I assign serious penalties. I'll check with you once in a while to see if my practice looks real enough. For each day that you help out I'll keep track and later slip you some nice reward. I'd like to work on my skills especially during the afternoon, but maybe some practice could be done in the morning if we could agree on a convenient time."

Figure 2.1c. Sample Setup Spiel #3

oppositional student will not be all that excited about helping the teacher "practice skills." The student who feels silly performing any misbehaviors might be reminded that the deal is totally confidential. Of course, it's always good for a few private chuckles to hear your disruptive student backing down and complaining that he would feel embarrassed to act like a total jerk in front of his peers. Nevertheless, it is important to stifle that smirk and keep up the straight sales pitch. You might also suggest a prompting signal (or use some secret gesture or common phrase) to alert a shy helper that it's time to do his thing. More on this later.

Sample Setup Spiel #4

Whining, Grumbling, and Complaining:

"I'm trying to practice my skills of handling student behavior problems in class. I really need to find one student who would pretend to grumble and carry on about the hard work or unfair rules ... especially during first and second hours. If you could help me, all you would need to do is whine and gripe loud enough for others to hear you. Of course, it would have to look like real grumbling, so that no one would know that it was just for training purposes. Then I would pretend to get on your case and would be able to practice my get-tough skills. Don't worry, you wouldn't get into any real trouble. In fact, if you do a good job, I'll give you a pretty nice reward for your efforts. Is it a deal?"

Figure 2.1d. Sample Setup Spiel #4

Yes, It Gets Even Better!

I've never had a student totally refuse to "help me out" with some pretend misbehavior. Maybe this is due to my undiscovered charisma (not) ... or most likely it's those incredible rewards (i.e., special-privilege coupons) I offer as a payoff. My experience with such refusals is mostly limited to marriage and family therapy situations in which one member of the family system adamantly rejects my ridiculous "assignment" of pretending to have a symptom. No matter the reason for the refusal (e.g., embarrassment, denial that the symptom is a real issue, more jockeying for power), I usually plant the following "suggestion":

> "Maybe this assignment isn't quite right for the situation ... or maybe it is. I'm not real sure. Let's just leave it this way: Go back into your world and live out some more days. If the assignment is right, your emotions and body will signal you to go through with it. If this assignment is actually important to do, you will know by the sudden realization that you have automatically jumped right into the behavior without even thinking about it. If you find yourself doing the 'pretend' symptom behaviors, then just continue and do a good job. It means the assignment was right for you. If this never happens, we can work on other things ... "

Get the idea? It's just a friendly door-opener invitation, and then I go on to other matters. When my client families are dealing with some deeply ingrained habit or behavior quirk (e.g., the suspicious and possessive spouse, the phobic client, the hypochondriac, the codependent, the "rage-a-holic"), it's only a matter of time before that nasty cycle kicks in and repeats itself—planning or no planning. It's pretty safe to plant the "maybe" suggestion and then just watch the situation ripen.

In an OBM classroom intervention, I might apply the principle this way:

> "Hey, Ruben, I understand that this assignment is pretty difficult. It might even be embarrassing for some kids to pretend to do those problem behaviors. But I still really do need to practice my class management skills. Tell you what, let's just leave it this way for the coming week. You don't have to do any of the behaviors we discussed. But, if for some reason your mind sends down a message like 'Why not just pretend and help out?'—if you get that kind of thought in your head, and it feels right to get into the behavior, then just go ahead and do a good pretending job. I'll pick up on it right away and begin practicing my class management skills. Later, I'll check back with

you privately and see if you want to keep helping. Sound okay? . . . So if I see you do some good problem behaviors that look real, I'll know you decided it was all right to help out."

The Sting

After a successful setup phase, the oppositional student will most likely offer some feeble efforts to "practice" the selected behaviors—or flat-out "forget" to perform the evil deeds. At this point, it is important for the OBM practitioner to keep a straight face while dutifully "prompting" the student to get busy with some daily practice cycles.

The teacher should now actively build more private collusion with the student. To do so will help to transform those disgusting little behaviors from cold, harsh reality to an "as if" level of fantasy and pretend . . . and even (choke on the word) cooperation! After all, isn't the disruptive tyrant now serving as an associate or secret operative for the teacher?

In order to foster a "this is our little secret" attitude toward the project, the OBM teacher might use candid winks or other secret signals to smoothly remind the student to perform his stubborn or disruptive behaviors. For example, one teacher ran the daily sting by tapping the chalk on the board a couple of times. It seemed like just a nervous habit or a way of emphasizing a point. Of course, the oppositional student was well aware that "two taps" was the agreed upon cue to let go with his usual disruptive routine.

Teachers who have used the *Pretend Jerk* intervention have stressed the need to choose your signal wisely. When you find yourself in the fog of real-world classroom dynamics, that well-chosen secret signal may be your only link to the problem kid. If he falls off the deep end, spaces out, wimps out, or goes ballistic with a real problem display, your signal may be the only lifeline to pull him back into the "pretending" mind-set.

Remember, if this thing goes down wrong, *"The SPED secretary will disavow any knowledge of your activities . . . Good luck, Jim . . . "*

Secret Signals

You may recall a stylish signal used by the con artists in the movie. One of the guys would smile at his accomplice across the busy casino lobby, place his index finger beside his nose, and do sort of a casual salute . . . and then disappear into the crowd. Sorry, that gesture is already taken. However, just about any other kind of secret prompting method might be employed in your classroom operation. Be sure to rehearse the signal until your student can easily recognize it amid the background static of regular classroom discourse. Consider some of these ideas:

- How about that nervous chalk-tapping noise that we already mentioned or —

  An unobtrusive "clearing of the throat"–type noise

  A stifled yawn . . . (no, these may be too common in class)

  A pleasant smile or nod of the head directed toward the student

  Placing a board eraser at some designated corner of your desk . . . perhaps "aiming" it at your helper

  Casually walking by and touching the target student's desk (very slick)

- Why not try some commonly heard teacher talk, such as "How much time do we have now?" or "Are there any questions?" *Or how 'bout—*

  "Class, what planet are we on right now?"

  "Can anyone tell me why I'm employed here?"

  "What's the basic difference between a duck?"

  "About how long is a short road?"

- Maybe you could hold up a giant Nike poster that reads, "Just do it!" (or maybe not)

Prompt Payment for Services Rendered

So what about reinforcers? The OBM teacher should consider using attractive daily or weekly payoff coupons to reward those semiwonderful practice efforts. Personal question: Did you ever dream that you might be lavishly rewarding a defiant student for performing such target behaviors? Well, after all, it is hard work resisting, disrupting, and pretending to be a difficult student. To get those creative juices flowing, the teacher might consult Chapter 11, which discusses the use of *wacky coupons and behavior permits.* You may also find some fairly nontraditional rewards in our "Student Reinforcement Inventory," which is really a manic sampling of OBM payoffs, presented in Appendix D. Some kids would walk over hot coals for these silly things.

On the other hand, some more astute kids may require designer jewelry, Caribbean cruise packages, major appliances, or stacks of unmarked bills as reinforcers. Be reasonable, but consider how many weeks are left in the semester, and what some basic control is worth to you. One teacher weighed the cost of a few rewards against her HMO co-pay for stress management sessions. At any rate, this is not the time to be cheap with solid reinforcement. It is recommended that some more-than-minimal reward be offered to energize this strategic intervention. Your reward may not cost a dime, but it needs to be valuable. It will send an important message to the oppositional student that the "pretend" behaviors are sincerely appreciated and important.

A Look at "Subtle Transformations"

We have found that, in order for this particular OBM intervention to be successful, it is important that the requested practice behaviors be slightly altered from their "raw form." The teacher must take some early control from the power-crazed oppositional student by requiring slight shifts (almost "token changes") in the pretended annoying behaviors. You will want to check out Appendix C, which includes a summary of our *"OBM Guide to Subtle Transformations."* If it is your intent to change the course of a mighty river (especially a rushing, defiant one), you need to start early with some strategic erosion of the soft muddy banks. Be sure to read this material! We put it in the appendix section of the handbook so it would receive the special attention it deserves and not get lost in the text.

Beginning with your setup and continuing throughout the sting phase, it is important to combine an ardent request for the defiant or disruptive behavior with a good dose of subtle transformation. For example, it is not enough for Ms. Smiley to request that Oppositional Eddy pretend to whine about the hard work. Hey, that would be *identical* to what he already does every day. Rather, Ms. Smiley should select Eddy for her intervention, have her private setup visit, and then add the subtle transformation—almost as an afterthought: *"Oh, yes, and could you remember to always whine and complain <u>a lot more</u> during reading class?"* Or perhaps, *"Oh, by the way, could you try to make your voice <u>sound more angry</u> when you tattle on some from lunch recess?"*

This early introduction of subtle transformations will accomplish two important goals. First, it quietly attaches some "busy work" (read: "boundaries") to those annoying behaviors that have always flowed reflexively from your oppositional student. Second, for our frazzled teacher, there is some early sense of control or empowerment added to the daily classroom situation. A request for even the smallest limits or a token change tends to offer the early "hope" that some eventual control is possible. It's satisfying to hear a teacher report, "Well, he's still a royal pain, but at least he's doing it on my terms!" That's just the beginning of OBM control.

During the sting phase, more and more subtle changes gradually become "necessary" or "helpful," and that raging river of disruptive behavior is eventually channeled into some benign direction. As the small changes are requested, the original disgusting behavior is distorted and remolded into a completely different pattern.

At this point, some gentle soul may be thinking, "Oh, I get it, I'll just ask the little fella if he would pretend to be a bit more civil and compliant during math class—yes! and oh, how wonderful it will be . . . oh, joy!" Well, sorry, Polly, that's not quite how we run our subtle transformations. Actually, the OBM classroom is farther down the hall toward Realityville. We often ask for *more of the bad*—before we stumble into a *less of the bad* request. And then there are other times when we dream up some nonlinear, deep-left-field unusual requests for small changes (not better or worse behavior)—just out of deep respect for our naturally suspicious helper.

Just remember this about subtle transformations: Almost any change in the original behavior moves the student away from his power position. It begins to extinguish the early raw form of problem behavior, and it reinforces a new brand of "collaboration" compliance. You might call it "team building" . . . almost.

Some folks look at our subtle transformation component and claim to see some kind of *operant shaping* going on. Yes, it does sound pretty clean and behavioral. However, our field reports indicate that it would actually take hours of interrogation and grilling under hot lights before a trained OBM operative would break down and admit to using *successive approximation.*

Cooling the Mark

The final phase of this particular OBM intervention is a graceful disengagement from the requested pretend behaviors. After all, we don't want to keep requesting resistance and defiance once the strong-willed student is ready to give them up. In the old-time confidence rackets, they referred to "cooling the mark" as the phase where the slick operatives split the cash and left town on different trains, while the high-roller target guy never knew what hit him.

In more humane terms, we define a successful OBM intervention as one in which the stubborn defiant student is helped to let go of some disruptive behaviors and return to (or begin) some productive learning activities. He should continue to have a close working relationship with the grinning OBM teacher and not be burdened with any alienation or resentment. Have you ever tried to untangle a panicked or hyperactive pup from his chain? You know he needs the help, but he really can't e-mail a rational request for "chain untangling." With all of our fancy strategic planning, *let's not forget that we really are trying to help untangle the rigid oppositional student,* even if he doesn't realize such help is needed.

Sometimes this final phase of cooling the mark is accomplished almost automatically in a single day. Other times it is necessary to plan a quiet disengagement from the business of reinforcing all those silly pretended behaviors.

Some Slick Disengagement Ploys
Below are a few suggestions for bowing out of the OBM game:

• Begin to complain that your schedule is getting so downright busy that it's sometimes difficult to keep up with your skill practice—hence the student's wonderful pretend behaviors might be wasted on those difficult days. Or, for you fiscal conservatives, simply explain that you can't pay full price (i.e., the points or rewards) for the pretend behaviors … especially on those busy days when you just can't use them. It will logically follow, of course, that the student will either have to "donate" those days or "save" the disruptive behaviors for days when he is on payroll.

• Suggest that the pretend misbehaviors be performed "only for a couple minutes" at the beginning or end of class. These are gradually cast as obligatory acts, required by some teacher training protocol, that must be gotten out of the way each day. Those stuffy professional development plans can be such a drag.

• Secretly conspire with the problem student to "skip" some practice days. After all, who will ever know? You might even allow the student helper to choose which days he wants to skip the disgusting routine. Assure him that you will not consider him to be a lazy lowlife when he skips a day of disruptive whining or whatever.

• Ask the student to double up on his pretend behaviors, so that the two of you can take a break from practicing for a couple days. Sometimes even oppositional-defiant kids need to take a vacation from their rigid style. Later, get him to talk about how he enjoyed the time off.

• Offer a "forced choice" dilemma to the strong-willed student: "Would you rather practice more often or less often this week?"

• Apologize to the student for placing such a burden on his shoulders for so long. Ask if he feels that you have finally mastered the necessary classroom management skills. If so, termination of his pretend behaviors would be a natural decision.

• Here's another mind-bending favorite that is similar to the first one in this list. Explain the concept of budgetary austerity. Then complain that the line-item allocation for "secret rewards" is running out sooner than expected. Add something like, *We need to do our best work this week, because I won't be able to pay for your help after that.* Suggest that, after this week, the oppositional student may have to be a pretend jerk for free. Maybe it's time for your reinforcement-wealthy student to "give back" to the classroom community, kind of like a community service? This will allow you both to semiretire the project.

No doubt you have already thought out some of your own variations on cooling the mark. Anything goes here as long as a good respectful reason is supplied for terminating practice. You get extra credit as an OBM practitioner if your disengagement chatter makes you grin every time you remember it.

Rewards for a Good Relapse

We all know that your feisty student is going to "relapse" sooner or later. After all, he's had years to hone his intrusive personality style. No problemo, cousin Remo. In fact, future relapses of the target behavior should be predicted and preapproved. Most of all, this new cooperative relationship with the teacher needs to be preserved and celebrated. As a way of cooling the mark, suggest an ultimate "next phase" of your skills practice. In this phase, the regularly scheduled daily performance of misbehavior is suspended. Instead, the student agrees to "surprise" the teacher sometime in the near future with a classic misbehavior that *looks very real*. This disengagement scenario allows the teacher to automatically place a benign interpretation on any future relapses—and even thank the student for remembering to help out. (I see you smiling.) Now, imagine this relapse scenario:

> *The student reflexively blurts out some defiant comment while you are passing out the science worksheets. You respond with a stern warning and a curt redirect, then turn to some other activity without further comment. The lunch bell rings and students begin to exit the classroom. As your target student passes by, you smile and slap a bonus points coupon in his greedy but surprised little hand. You then cautiously whisper, "That was a great surprise behavior ... and it looked soooo real! Maybe try it again this afternoon, and let me know if I'm acting tough enough" (wink, nod, etc.).*

Retirement Benefits

Just think, someday in the future, while you're enjoying those fat Social Security checks, your most oppositional student might be strolling by with his own hyperactive Little Rocky. Imagine him pointing to you as you rock, semiconscious, on your front porch. You hear him proudly comment, "See that ancient burned-out–looking teacher up there? When I was younger, I helped to train her in handling problem kids." You can almost feel the civic pride well up inside him as your defiant student recalls how he *pretended to be a jerk* ... for a real good cause. Can OBM get any better than that?

More Goodies on the Bottom Shelf

The following pages contain even more unnecessary resource materials that could further spoil you with this particular strategy. At the end of this chapter is a summary of the planning and implementation steps for the *Pretend Jerk* intervention. Sure, you hardly need those steps, either, but we've been feeling rather codependent today.

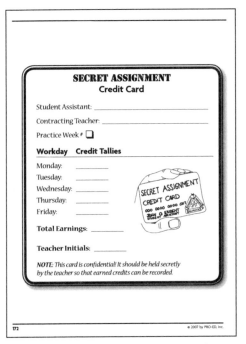

Figure 2.2. Secret Assignment: Credit Card

Superfluous Filler Comments

I am cleverly adding some unnecessary explanatory text here. It will help keep this part of the page from looking so bleak and bare. Actually, anyone this far into the handbook would probably recognize right away how this credit card thing should be filled out and used. Nevertheless—for each weekday we have provided ample space for multiple credit entries. That's assuming the little character will agree to practice the target behavior more than once per day.

Free Legal Advice

Sometimes I find myself sitting in a tense IEP meeting with a suspicious parent who is pondering what devious things the school district may be up to. Sensing the parent's concern, one teacher may explain that an OHI label won't necessarily keep the child out of Harvard; then someone else adds that our optional ED label, with some swimming lessons, might even set him up for the Navy SEALS. If all this encouragement fails, I like to add the smiling reminder: *"Besides, we work for the government, and we know what's best for Junior ..."* (Your results may vary.)

Rave Reviews for Authentic-Looking Behaviors

Here's a card to add a little spice to daily "practice" efforts. Why not give Oscar-winning recognition to an incredibly "real"-looking performance? These bonus coupons help to highlight the pretend nature of the assigned behaviors. These cards are given in addition to the regular earned points that you are already recording on the *Secret Assignment*

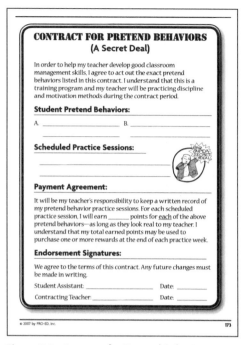

Figure 2.3. Contract for Pretend Behaviors: A Secret Deal

Credit Card. Who knows, you might also convince your fledgling tyrant that if his "take over the world" plan falls through, he might have a future in the entertainment business.

Surprise Relapse Coupons

After you have launched into your *disengagement phase* and that reluctant helper is now a veteran employee, it may be time to give him a couple of the coupons in Figure 2.5.

Figure 2.4. 50 Bonus Points

Figure 2.5. Surprise

Describe them as a little retirement bonus. These *Surprise* coupons give your student an official means of alerting you to a relapse behavior (in case you miss it). The next time he falls back into one of his reflexive oppositional behaviors, he can easily "save face" by slipping you one of his coupons and claiming it was all part of his promised surprise testing behaviors. *"Well, excuuuse me!... that one was only pretend ..."* Since we never label a relapse as a failure, the coupon thing allows you to give some helpful critique on how authentic his behavior looks. You might even suggest some offbeat subtle transformation for the *next* surprise. Be sure to award a few bonus points—but only if he remembered to slap down a coupon. If you feel a need to reprimand some slippage into defiant behavior, channel your energies into chastising him for failing to use his *Surprise* card and getting you all confused. Good relapses (with "save face" re-coveries) are actually a sign of progress. They help keep the cooperative conspiracy alive but low key. Why do I love this stuff?

Could You *Pretend* To Be a Real Jerk?

Summary of Steps

1. **Choosing the Mark:**
   Be sure you are dealing with a factory-wired, card-carrying, oppositional-defiant student. No other kind will do here.

2. **The Setup:**
   - Arrange for a brief private visit (e.g., after class, in the hallway, during a bomb threat).
   - *"Would you help me practice my class management skills by pretending to act out some problem behaviors?"*
   - This isn't just a favor, it's a business deal.
   - Discuss one or more fabulous rewards that could be earned. (See Appendix D.)
   - Be prepared for special handling of the "refusal to be a jerk." (Review details within Chapter 2.)

3. **The Sting:**
   This is the part where your hired assistant performs the pretend misbehavior.
   - Complete your **Contract for Pretend Behaviors.**
   - Do a brief role-play of the target behavior (optional, reduces surprises).
   - Mutually decide on a "secret signal" for prompting.
   - Keep track of earned credits on the **Secret Assignment Credit Card.**
   - Maintain a "mutual conspiracy" climate with the student.
   - Include **Subtle Transformation** requests to distort or erode the "raw behavior":
     "Oh, and by the way, could you do the pretend behavior just a bit differently this time . . ."

4. **Cooling the Mark:**
   - Most teachers don't want to do this silly pretend behavior thing forever. It's time to close up shop when the defiant behavior is no longer meaningful for the student.
   - Use a slick disengagement ploy to fade out the pretend misbehavior.
   - Offer a reward for a near-future surprise "relapse" that looks genuine. (You know it's coming . . . better to be prepared and smiling.)
   - Leave the door open for possible future training projects.
   - Show gratitude for the excellent training help you have received.

Figure 2.6. Could You *Pretend* To Be a Real Jerk? Summary of Steps

Dear OBM Guys:

I'm still not sure why Ms. Stewart is making me write this letter. Okay, here goes. About two weeks ago I said that Social Studies class was a joke. The next thing I know, the teacher gets all worried and concerned, and she wants me to help her test out a bunch of new motivational ideas. I told her I was too busy hating Social Studies and didn't want any extra work. (Besides, everybody knows I'm sure not one of her "favorites.") Anyway, Ms. Stewart then offers me some free bonus points if I would help her try out some new teaching methods. So I thought about it—and what the hey, I said yes. My part of the deal is to pretend I'm a 10th-grade lowlife who wants to drop out of school. This gives Ms. Stewart a chance to practice her pep-talk ideas right there in the classroom. All I have to do is listen to her for a while . . . and then I can just go back to my regular work. She tries out something new almost every day, and with those extra points, I'll probably end up passing this class. By helping Ms. Stewart, I sometimes feel like I'm giving back to the school.

—Lisa, grade 10

Editor's note: Lisa ended up with a 70% in social studies. She later tried to promote a similar deal with a bewildered language arts teacher who had never read the *OBM Handbook*.

Figure 2.7. Dear OBM Guys

3

Rent-a-Thug

Placing the Perpetrator on Payroll

Employers Have More Clout Than Victims

Here's a good one for the "perpetually put upon" student who complains a bit too much of mistreatment and unbearable teasing. We have found that it works equally well for the nice little kid who *really has* been targeted for classroom or playground harassment. This strategy is not intended, of course, for cases of real physical threats, but it can be slick with those chronic mild situations. Similar to other OBM interventions, this one makes a ridiculous project out of a disruptive symptom. Someone has observed that the Rent-a-Thug strategy takes a genuine subway mugging and turns it into a stilted choreography number from *West Side Story*. It carries some of the flavor of Chapter 2, but not quite. Here we will find our victim student hiring local muscle to "pretend" to hassle him—but it's all for a good cause. This strategy shows how being an employer has its advantages.

Setting the Stage

In a brief private meeting with the victim student, debrief on the latest problem episode and then ask the following question:

> *"How would you like it if each time that bully teased you or called you a bad name, it would make you richer and richer?"*

This kind of out-of-the-blue question is intended to shock and disorient the victim student and make him open to suggestions. A more extended "possibility discussion" I have had with professional victims (and real victims) goes like this:

> *"How might you handle it if for each insult you got on the playground, or for each time someone teased you, a hired secretary of mine would stroll right up and hand you a sealed envelope with a $10 bill inside? Just like our very own reality TV show. Each time a student said anything unkind to you—oh oh, here comes my smiling secretary (who looks a lot like a middle-aged Vanna White) to hand you another envelope with some cash. I'm just wondering how many of those envelopes you might be holding by the end of one recess period? How 'bout by the end of the school day? And how many insults and teasings*

might it take before you would have enough money collected in those envelopes to buy a new mountain bike? ... I'm just wondering if you would be willing to ride that shiny new 15-speed bike, even though you earned it by collecting dreadful gross insults at school?"

It's Hard To Find Good Help These Days

During the private OBM interview with the student, I often lament the fact that the school cannot give out envelopes with small amounts of cash inside just for coming to school every day and putting up with a lot of grief. (Well, actually they do—they're called faculty paychecks.) Anyway, it might be a good idea, I say, but that kind of "soothing" and "victim reparation" for mental suffering just isn't written into the budget.

From this offbeat scenario I move on to suggest the *Rent-a-Thug* project. The "reality TV" theme works well here. I explain that this show allows one lucky "victimized" student to earn token credits by secretly recording tally marks on an index card for each insult received during the entire school day. *It's actually better than that, because the victim student is also required to enlist one or two of the current bad guys to tease or insult him each day!* When enough tally marks are collected and turned in, the industrious victim student wins some special benefit, freedom, or classroom privilege. Sure, it's not like winning a TV prize package, but it's still reinforcing. Depending on how suggestible your student is, you might be glancing around the classroom and at the ceiling and asking yourself, "Hmmm, I wonder where they put the secret television cameras for this show?"

Here's a suggested OBM script the victim might use to recruit the "help" of the top name-calling bad guys in class. Each one can be approached privately and individually (after first checking to make sure the bully isn't busy plundering or pillaging)—or your professional victims may consult the whole bunch—with the following spiel:

> *"I'm working on a new program with the teacher [or counselor, principal, etc.], and I really could use your help. I'm studying about ways to handle feelings of anger or frustration that can happen when kids call me names or tease me here at school. I need to find a student who would be willing to call me names like _____ and _____ at least five times per day.*
>
> *"The way it works is that I'll record my 'helper's' initials on a secret card and turn it in each day. The teacher then talks to me about what makes students say mean things to others, and how to handle any angry feelings. For each set of initials I mark on the card, I'll get 100 points! If I collect enough insults for the week, then I'll win a pretty nice prize on Friday ... Can I count on you to call me some of those names at least five times each day so I can start working toward the prize?"*

Of course, the victim student is coached to be very positive and to keep smiling while trying to enlist his Neanderthal thugs. This is not the time to vent sarcasm on the huge, green-tinted, bully student. In order to prepare the sales pitch, a few private role-play scenarios are usually helpful. They need not take more than 45 seconds each. During this brief visit, the student and teacher might also reverse roles just to highlight both sides of an expected conversation. Remember, the tone must be wide-eyed innocence throughout the enlistment pitch. Everything must be optimistic and upbeat. Even if the bewildered bad guys refuse to cooperate (What? Withhold insults?), the victim should be prepped to keep smiling and leave them with a double-bind "open door" request:

> *"I know it sounds stupid to ask for insults. But at least now you know why they're so valuable to me. If you change your mind during the next couple of weeks, just go ahead and call me some of the usual names. I'll know you've just decided to help me earn some points toward my prize."*

Later, when that same old reflexive name calling mars an otherwise idyllic noontime dining experience, the victim student can flash a knowing smile of gratitude and quietly record the event on his card! At last, the sting of ridicule is replaced with the joy of cooperation.

Some Unnecessary Modifications

1. Give me your best shot!

The victim student might suggest (or insist upon) a specific list of the hottest derogatory names (which, of course, are already being thrown at him daily). It might be explained to the rented thug that only the most insulting names will do for this serious assignment. *"How else can a kid learn about the cruel world out there?"*

2. Tipping is permitted.

The victim is earning big points for each insult, right? Why not suggest that he offer to share part of the reward with his rented thug. It might be a tactful thank you for helping out with this difficult assignment.

3. Practice makes perfect.

The victim student could also invite the name-calling kid to one of the pseudo counseling sessions so the teasing and verbal insults could be further roleplayed and practiced more correctly. One part of this joint session might be a role-reversal exercise in which the victim momentarily takes on the thug's role so as to demonstrate the proper intensity of the names he needs to be called. When the original roles are resumed, the thug is expected to be more sensitive and educated in just how to deliver those ego-searing insults. The victim is then ready to critique the thug's performance. The moderating OBM teacher should also be sure to praise good approximations of the "critical skill"(get it?) in both students.

4. Recovery work.

Eventually, the victim student and a carefully selected team of name callers might be enlisted to develop a guidance counseling demonstration of "how to handle teasing," which is then presented to classes of younger students. Who knows, maybe the team could go on to offer a support group for students who are struggling to overcome the stigma and codependency of verbal-insult cycles? Both codependent victims and penitent perpetrators might be solicited for the group. By the way, what do you think has happened to the original name-calling problem that we started with?

5. Consciousness-raising committee.

Your newly formed recovery group might also be assigned the task of designing and producing a counseling poster display that points out the evils of name calling. Some fabulous reward or special privilege might be earned for the production of a good poster. Of course, much recognition should be given to the victim and recovering perpetrator(s); the poster might even be displayed somewhere in the school. Ambitious or workaholic teachers might want to go ahead and start writing that grant to fund a district-wide demonstration project, start selling those logo T-shirts, and raising money for the trip to Washington ... No, no! Stop! There's now effective medication available for manic-cycling OBM practitioners when things get that far out of hand.

Okay, settle down. At the heart of OBM methods is a playful reframing of the problem into an educational project. Notice that no one was punished or ridiculed in the Rent-a-Thug strategy. The victim student was never labeled as a powerless underdog who needed protection. Likewise, the name-calling nemesis of the playground or hall-way was never acknowledged as anything but a voluntary helper. The OBM assignment made by the teacher or counselor allowed everyone to be approached with open innocent intentions. Eventually, the long-standing cycle of verbal harassment and emotional fall-out was programmed into a benign charade. However, despite our noteworthy success stories with the index-card recording ploy, I still like the idea of giving insult-contingent $10 bills in plain white envelopes. But that's just me.

OBM Legends

You've now endured three chapters of OBM strategy planning, and there are many to follow. Perhaps you have discovered how easily these compelling stories might be spawned by the *Far Side* culture surrounding OBM interventions. Over the years, small bands of teachers huddled around coffee pots in cold, desolate lounges have found some encouragement in these tales. Many of our OBM success stories have now been retold countless times as an educator's oral tradition. Perhaps some of the original de-tails have been lost in the hallway mists, but those "uncommon sense" principles (e.g., reframing, distraction, and planned bewilderment) are forever with us. Read on.

Doing the Paper Work

Sure, a simple index card might work just fine. But here's our OBM sample of an *Insult Collection Card,* which might look good copied to your neon blue card stock. It's designed to transform our perpetual victim into a cheerful recipient of painless affronts. As we've suggested elsewhere, instead of simply marking a row of Xs for teasing events, it might help to have your playground trash collector record the initials of his "helpers" who provide those valuable insults. Make sure you've identified some great backup reinforcers to sweeten the deal. You might even take a gander at Appendix D to help stimulate your creative thinking.

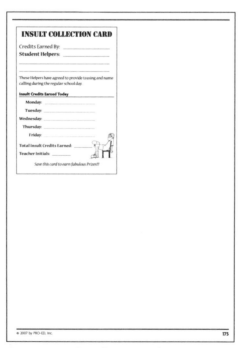

Figure 3.1. Insult: Collection Card

More Program Options

This *Rent-a-Thug* program is obviously intended for deflating and taming verbal insults, but it's not quite appropriate for kids who are being threatened with knives, guns, and chainsaws. (OBM readers are a notch brighter than most, so we're counting on everyone out there for a good measure of propriety.)

Let's agree that some kids are indeed being teased too much, and that some others may be finding too much joy in tattling and whining about their dose of teasing. This strategy may work at different levels for both of those troubled groups. Sometimes the target student may be guided to enlist only one nemesis; other times there's an entire stage crew of insult throwers to hit up for help. In order to reduce overhead expenses, it's also quite possible for your hassled student to do the mental-anguish recording project *secretly* without any formal enlistments. Some classroom practitioners have suggested that recording student initials instead of tally marks would provide a good indication of exactly which kids out there are most involved in the classroom teasing business. Hey, with that kind of data, you could easily upgrade the whole thing into a functional behavior assessment . . . or maybe not.

Rent-a-Thug

Our Bare-Bones Summary

1. **Qualify the situation.**
   Do we have an excessive whiner among us? Or is there some genuine mild bugging going on?

2. **Set up one of those OBM "private visits" with the victim.**
   - Introduce the concept of profiting from each teasing or bugging episode.
   - Explain the need for the victim to enlist an "experienced" helper.

3. **Explain the insult (or bugging) record card.**
   Suggest a cool reward if enough tally marks are obtained for all those practice insults.

4. **Role-play the deal.**
   - Do some mild bugging (teacher acting as the hired perpetrator).
   - Do more mild bugging (student acting as the hired perpetrator).
   - Practice some enlistment spiels that the victim might actually use to hire his helper.

5. **Send little Reginald out into the cruel playground world to cut a deal with his arch nemesis.**
   (This might be a good time for prayer in the schools.)

6. **If something gets started—read the chapter for alternatives.**
   However, if the favorite perpetrator refuses to help out . . . well, we can all live with that too.

Figure 3.2. Rent-a-Thug: Our Bare-Bones Summary

Dear OBM Guys:

I'm a mid-school SPED teacher, and I was forced to attend one of your rather unusual workshops a few years ago—before you were rich and famous. I thought the Rent-a-Thug ploy, like most of your stuff, was totally inane ... the product of your cartoon mentality. Anyway, recently one of my young ladies with mild MR was escorted in from lunch break with a third write-up for fighting (I mean the real slap, scratch, and hair-pulling kind of brawl.) I found out that one of my other girls was constantly teasing this student without mercy. I got so fed up that I found myself stooping to use one of those OBM ideas. My student was too low-functioning and angry to do one of your wacky enlistment talks, so we skipped that part. I just gave her an index card and told her to carry it in her pocket all day. Whenever any of the other girls called her a name, instead of hitting, she was to take out her card and mark down a "J" (for Jenna) or a couple of other possible name letters. She started doing this task quite seriously, and now she brings her card to me for debriefings and some praise of her "grown-up" self-control. I've been rewarding her for marking on the card—which seems to really upset her tormentors. At least, we have a disruption in the old routine. Well, thanks. And keep taking your meds.

—(Name withheld as simple retribution)

Figure 3.3. Dear OBM Guys

Our Top Ten Strategic Responses

To Vile, Profane, and Gross Behaviors

Some Near-Genius Rejoinders

Remember the concept of micromanagement that we mentioned in Chapter 2? What we are talking about here is the micromanagement of specific face-to-face confrontations with the oppositional student that are orchestrated so that the teacher retains some semblance of leadership and implicit control. As with the other OBM strategies, our *Top Ten Responses* were obviously not designed for general classroom management. They were never intended to keep a busy group of students on task. Rather, the gifted responses assembled in this chapter are intended for those difficult times when you really need something smooth and pithy to say. These classic comebacks are engineered to help the beleaguered teacher maintain control of the moment, instead of being caught flat-footed and speechless.

Teachers often report that they do private mental reviews of difficult classroom situations (e.g., "How well did I handle little Bruno's tirade this morning?"). While this drive-home exercise may resemble a post-trauma flashback for some teachers, it could also be a time of productive reflection on the day. We have all worked through one of these critical reviews and concluded, "I sure wish I had said something really clear and elegant. I never seem to have the right words when I need them!" Sound familiar? Well, not to worry. We're here to take care of you. This chapter is intended to get you rolling with some strategic responses that will keep you in control when other teachers might get worked up, red faced, and confrontational or (worse yet) scared and sick, retreating into their "wimp zone." Wouldn't it be pleasant to review today's problem episode with little Bruno and have a faint grin slip across your face? Wouldn't we all rather enjoy the replay and conclude, "Those were the perfect words for that situation! I love it! Just wish I had that one on video tape!" Welcome once again to the strategic world of OBM.

Think of it this way. Most of us take pains to avoid dark alleys, late-night parking lots, and certain notorious streets in town. We don't like the feeling of vulnerability, and we prefer to keep our adrenaline stored in some visceral gland, where it belongs. Place us in the generic mugging situation and we'd feel helpless, angry, and distressed. Compare our intense anxiety with a soft-spoken kung fu master who has somehow wandered into that same space. He may not want any trouble, either, but he has at his command a vast repertoire of speeded precise movements that would neutralize the mugger and a half dozen of his goofball accomplices. Despite an equal expenditure of adrenaline, our mild-mannered Jackie Chan–type fellow would probably have fewer post-trauma symptoms than we would.

Likewise, when the classroom teacher is suddenly confronted with vile, profane, or gross behaviors, there is something akin to an assault going on. These confrontive episodes represent a direct challenge to the leadership of the learning environment. We hope that you will find one or more of our strategic verbal rejoinders to fit your style, and that you will feel much more comfortable dealing with your oppositional students. A quick OBM review may be in order before we go down to the dojo. Read on, grasshopper.

Okay, Once More: The Big Three . . .

1. Classic Reframes

Reframing methods are found not only in our present chapter but throughout this manual. These are a way to take the raw behavioral event and reinterpret it in other terms. It's like taking a painting and enhancing the mood it creates by replacing the original low-budget plastic frame with one that is gilded mahogany and much more complementary. Fictional characters such as Mister Magoo and Inspector Clouseau are also adept at misinterpreting key events that are right in their face. If they did this intentionally and strategically, we might credit them with some pioneering work in Outrageous B-Mod.

Consider the myopic Mister Magoo cartoon character. In one story segment we are shown a gnarly-looking brute sneaking up behind Magoo. The thug has a bat or club raised and ready to clobber our hero. Magoo turns around and chatters something like "Oh, you must be the gardener. Well, you're late, sir! And that rake you brought is much too short for all this work . . . yak, yak, yak . . ." The dumbfounded villain blinks helplessly at the audience as Magoo hustles him off to the garden—still rattling on with several more absentminded work instructions. We hope you find yourself smiling and considering that strategic "blindness" and creative "misinterpretations" can be useful (and even fun!) in the classroom. You'll find some interesting examples in the collection of strategies below.

2. Stealthy Distractions

Distraction methods take the spotlight off the "real" problem and place attention on some totally unrelated item. We've already mentioned Lt. Columbo's shrewd ability to "misinterpret" obvious clues in order to distract and draw out his sophisticated suspects. Beyond that, we all remember tense movie scenes where the bad guys seem to have the upper hand and unexpectedly our clear-thinking heroine feigns a faint (say that fast several times). Anyway, that momentary distraction pulls all attention to a different level of reality (e.g., a minor medical crisis) and away from that ugly black revolver aimed at our protagonists. At that point Napoleon Solo, or Thomas Magnum, or James West is poised to seize the moment and turn the tables. Some of our strategic verbal responses act in the same way to defuse a tense moment and regain classroom control.

3. Planned Bewilderment

Beyond specific distraction episodes are broader global periods of deliberate confusion. At this point you may be drifting back to recall an earlier part of this manual where we announced that "The next best thing to compliance is confusion." Some of our workshop teachers have raised their hand to confess that their classroom is *always* confused, with no controlling effect on the resident power monger. To this we must reply that all forms of confusion are not created equal. We are suggesting *planned* confusion that is purposefully orchestrated to achieve control in otherwise hopeless interactions. It's hard to be rebellious and disruptive when you are downright bewildered and disoriented. Even the most demanding and strong-willed students will tend to mellow out when they are lost in a *Twilight Zone* rerun.

Hypnotists have used this planned confusion gag for years in breaking down mental resistance and creating their famous daydream states. The mind can tolerate only a limited number of incompatible thoughts at one time before it starts to glitch and freeze up. Try to picture your most oppositional student looking up at you, his mouth hanging open and a confused, sick-cow expression plastered across his face. This product of planned confusion may be your preferred low-stress alternative to the usual classroom confrontations. We hope you will find some fertile inspiration among this chapter's sampling of strategic responses.

David Letterman, Move Over

Okay, heeeere we go. Out of literally scores of witty entries gathered over the years, here is our top-ten list of favorite strategic responses to vile, profane, and gross student behaviors. Since we don't have the stage band set up, and our drummer is in time-out again—let's just move along and put some of our favorites ones right up front:

1. Hey man, that looks soooo real!

The approving teacher, obviously overcome with amazement and pedagogic pride: *"How do you make it look soooo real? You know, if a stranger were to walk in here right now and see your performance, he'd probably swear you were really upset about something!"* [The doting teacher walks on, talking to herself.] *"I'll never cease to be amazed with this class ... There's more talent here than on most TV shows."* This is a great one for defusing such states as pouting, intimidating rage episodes, phony alligator tears, and those hysterical reactions to a scraped knee. (Implicit message: You can't be serious.)

Now that you get the idea, let's slide on into some real zingers.

2. Come on now ... Don't be so hard on yourself! I'm sure you're doing just as well as anyone could expect!

This is a "crazy maker" for defiant students who are geared up for mortal combat. Right smack in the middle of a heated tirade aimed at destroying the teacher's leadership, our overly supportive OBM instructor gushes some canned lines of syrupy encouragement. Here is a study in both distraction and benign reframing. Notice that the teacher seems oblivious to the challenge and instead takes up the role of a sympathetic coach who rushes to the aid of a favorite player. Perhaps we may even get the sense of a wise mentor offering support to a gifted student protégé who is wallowing in self-criticism.

By the way, we could do another entire handbook for working with oppositional parents who storm into school meetings with rumblings of the Tasmanian devil. This "supportive" response helps to tame down the Taz factor and leaves those tactless, disturbing folks standing there, mouth hanging open, blinking wide-eyed into the camera, and uncertain how to proceed. Meanwhile, notice that our mild-mannered OBM teacher remains totally supportive, smiling warmly, and no ill will has been projected. All other consultation options remain wide open, since no offense has been created. *Hey don't be so hard on yourself!*

Hint: Why not tape this one to the candy machine in the faculty lounge.

3. This is great! Well, at last you're able to get in touch with those deeper emotions!

In this case, let's suppose that Oppositional Eddy has just lost his composure when his obviously superior health poster was not chosen for the special hallway bulletin board. In the midst of his blustering and protesting, we see our proud OBM teacher smiling and obviously overcome with admiration. At last this complex student has found a measure of self-actualization—right there in the classroom! Our emotionally constipated rebel has now been enlightened by gaining access to those deep primal emotions. The teacher might enhance the approbation with something like: *"I'm really proud of you today, Eddy! You know, sometimes a student has to risk looking like a total fool in order to bravely discover his true feelings. Your courage here today can be a model for all of us to follow."*

Here most OBM teachers would begin to disengage and prepare to shift focus back to the learning activities. But, like some of us who can't let well enough alone, this teacher just has to make a few more laudatory comments. Try to picture Eddy's bewildered expression as our OBM teacher shovels on more praise:

"Those health posters on the wall will all come down in the future, Eddy, but your personal victory here today will remain as a mighty classroom monument to a brave pioneer who showed us all how we can contact that screaming baby deep within ... how we can really loosen up and embrace our infantile feelings ... yak, yak, yak ... Yes, I'm so proud ... and the next time you feel cheated or unappreciated around here ... please don't hesitate to let that red-faced inner child just scream like a banshee ... yessiree ... that's what we need around here, kids who can get in contact ... yak, yak, yak ..."

4. I don't care what everyone else may be thinking about you right now ...

Teacher glancing around as if to survey the peer group: *"Nope, I'm just glad that you're finally able to express those embarrassing ugly feelings so well—right here in front of everyone. This is great! Is there anything more you need to say out loud?"*

Here we catch a glimpse of a reality-bending technique in which the teacher implies a special knowledge of the hidden thoughts of all others in the classroom. The unstated message is that "everyone" in class is watching with disdain and condemnation. As students approach the adolescent era, they become even more vulnerable to that imaginary (and often quite critical) peer audience.

You may note that this implied knowledge helps to set up a double-bind message. On the one hand, the OBM teacher is showing benign support and encouragement of the acting-out behaviors ("Go ahead and cathart all over the place!"). On the other sneaky hand, she is sending the message: *"By the way, everyone here thinks you're a real geek when you act like this."* So, do you like this one? Keep in mind that it's also a no-lose request. If the oppositional student insists on more time to blow smoke and noise, the teacher wins (i.e., he's complying with her invitation and instructions). Of course, if our defiant scholar refuses to continue, the teacher could also live with the silence. Think this one through carefully and work on your presentation. Why not practice on a grumbling faculty member who hasn't read the handbook?

5. *It's truly refreshing to see how well you control yourself during these difficult times!*

Here's one of our favorites for those special moments when a student (or attitudinally challenged colleague) is in the middle of a temper display. Following the model of our myopic Mister Magoo, the teacher becomes strategically blind to the disruptive tantrum and heaps praise on the red-faced, angry student for showing such *relative* strength, control, and obvious restraint. The follow-up chatter might go something like. *"You know, a lot of other kids would probably lose it if they had to put up with the same grief you get here every day! How do you manage to stay so cool in the face of adversity? I mean do you have some secret words you say to yourself? or something really special you were taught to do?"* As you can see, this one's a clever reframe that offers a benign distortion of the facts. It gives the teacher some implied control of the situation and an opportunity to keep teaching. After all, it's easier to give praise than correction.

True confessions: I unashamedly use this approach with irate parents who are looking for blood. In such cases, I try to separate myself from the school establishment (always a good idea when you sense heat) and commiserate with the frustrated parents. Some of the parent talk might go like this: *"You guys must be real saints! Even with all this stuff* [name the problem] *you just keep on cooperating with the school. I know a lot of parents who would have given up long ago. What's so different about you folks?"* Usually, at this point the angry parents seem to recover a bit and take their finger off the launch button. They most often accept my evaluation of their long-term forbearance and then openly discuss how much they have suffered at the hands of the school district. Our informal conversations usually take place before the "real" meeting. During these upbeat visits I describe them as incredibly flexible, creative, and good willed. We then collude on possible solutions that the parents might present at the table when those real educators finally show up for the meeting. Have you noticed the absence of confrontation?

6. *Hey there, why don't you go a little easier on your mom!*

Here's one for splitting the spoiled troublemaker from an indulgent parent. This is a distraction method that includes confusion along with an off-the-wall interpretation of the most recent misbehavior. The assumption is that the OBM teacher knows the "real" roots of the student's oppositional posturing. She then artfully directs the spotlight away from the objective problem behavior to the struggling mom, dad, custodial grandparent, or other major player. The standard dialogue continues with pedantic finger wagging and sympathy seeking for the parent: *"Don't be so hard on your mother! I'm sure she's doing the very best she can. C'mon, cut her some slack. It's not easy being a parent these days ... yak, yak, yak ... In fact, every time I see you getting into this kind of trouble* [i.e., like for the millionth time this week] *I know there's still a lot of 'thank yous' and 'I'm sorry's' that you need to send home to your dear old mom ..."*

Oddly enough, our competent but burned-out mothers of genuine oppositional-defiant kids don't seem to mind the use of this ploy. Also, from time to time it might be a good idea to assign a letter-writing consequence, so that the student can begin to balance the ledger of long-overdue sentiments to his mom. Notice how the focus has changed from the defiant episodes to the trumped-up solution of showing more gratitude to a parent? I use this one only when I'm sure there isn't any gross abuse or neglect at home. Most often, that isn't the issue with our classic oppositional-defiant students. On the other hand, I could understand why some good-but-frustrated moms might be tempted to lean a bit in that direction.

7. Hey, everyone, stop laughing! Maybe this kid can't help it! I've seen cases like this before.

Notice the many implications here. First, the OBM teacher's comments suggest that "everyone" of the peers is laughing at our strong-willed student, either openly or (worse) privately. Second, the diagnosis of some unknown clinical syndrome and lost volitional control is offered as an explanation for that last crying or cussing or book-slamming episode. After feigning to hush up the class, the teacher might turn supportively to the troubled student and add, *"Do you want me to try and explain your situation to these other kids while you calm down? ... Or is it just none of their business?"* This forced-choice question suggests that the classroom tyrant actually wants to calm down now. It is also skewed in the direction of the student admitting to having some strange unspeakable problem, while insisting it is no one else's business. Oh, the joys of strategic language crafting!

Of course, there's still the risk that a gifted oppositional student might call your bluff and have you explain his unique clinical syndrome. In that case, it might be best to act embarrassed for the student, cover your mouth suddenly, and turn away. Hesitantly suggest you really don't know a lot about it, but there are specialists who study the syndrome. Mention that you know of a doctor who might be willing to visit the class and explain the problem ... so there will be no teasing. On the other hand, if you're feeling a bit feisty, you might rattle off a few of the key symptoms: swollen earlobes that draw fluid off the brain resulting in a mental vacuum, for example, the irresistible impulse to flap the gums, denial of having any problems, and bad breath. *"Yes, there are several more telltale symptoms, but they would be just too embarrassing to announce in public. Besides, the clinical research remains inconclusive."* At this point, if you feel a need for more "psychobabble" fogging, you have top-level clearance to skip ahead to Chapter 6.

8. Are you okay? You don't look too good at all.

This strategic response is similar to #7 except the concern is for medical wellness rather than some unknown mental health problem. Supportive, gushy, codependent teachers should be especially adept at this one. Here again, the teacher ignores the negative behavior and diverts attention to something else—the student's apparent illness (which might be causing the problem behavior).

The concerned teacher might extend the monologue with: *"Oh, my, you are getting sick ... Do these spells happen often? Would you like to see the nurse or maybe lie down for a while?* [The teacher maintains a concerned and bewildered expression.] *Are you supposed to be wearing one of those medical bracelets? Maybe there's a phone number I should call when these episodes happen?* [The teacher then hastily scans the class for a wastebasket.] *You're not going to barf on the floor, are you?"* Hopefully, these caring inquiries are enough to break up the gross behavior episode and also put the teacher back in control of the classroom.

By the way, this is also a great distraction strategy for haggard principals who must deal—one more time—with that malcontent teacher at the end of the hall. It works even better if you have two or three staff members standing nearby—who immediately agree with the principal and offer to dial 911.

9. Aren't you afraid you might risk damaging someone's fragile self-esteem when you say those kinds of things?

This one could be worth some confusion and shock effect—especially with oppositional kids who maintain some vestige of social morality. Here the OBM teacher holds forth the highest expectations for the moral sensitivity and sterling character of our defiant student. She presents surprise and disbelief that this student would ever remotely consider demeaning the personhood of another human being. The implication is that this must be some mistake: *"This just isn't like you ... I'm shocked and saddened that something has pushed you so far ... I know it would have to be very serious ... because some of those comments might be possibly construed as hurtful by people who heard them."* Essentially, this strategy is based on the production of "cognitive dissonance" in the student (i.e., creating internal conflict by pointing out the difference between his exemplary character and this confusing sample of actual behavior).

10. Okay, which one of you guys is making my friend Bill here say these crude things?

Here's another wonderful distraction: Blame some classroom peers for the problem behavior episode! *"Who is it that's making a good student like Bill feel so lousy that he has to say these rude and crude things?"* The teacher pensively scans the classroom, considering who might be the sleazy perpetrator of Bill's pain.

First, the OBM teacher could fault one or two students who are totally uninvolved. She might wonder out loud whether these apparently innocent-looking characters might actually be perpetrating some kind of mind-control conspiracy: *"Hmm ... yes, that might be it ... some kind of dark experiment. And poor Bill is the guinea pig. But what could be the purpose of making Bill lose his dignity and vent obscenities in class ... and how does the whole thing work? Well, I'm going to be watching you two very closely for any monkey business. This class is not the place for mind-control experiments ..."*

A second daring option is to vehemently blame one of Bill's own gang! This opens up the *divide-and-conquer* ploy that will be discussed extensively later on in the handbook. The OBM teacher might split Bill away from his oppositional associates with such banter as: *"Look, we all know that Bill is not the problem student here. You guys are always trying to set him up for trouble. I'm surprised he even hangs out with you anymore. For your information* [directed at the tough-guy circle] *most of the teachers in this school really like Bill and are impressed with all the improvement he's shown this year. We know he gets tagged for stuff you other guys are doing ... and we're all watching very close these days. Bill, you don't have to rat on your friends. I know it's not really you who wants to say these gross things in class. I ought to bust these other clowns right now, but I won't ... just out of respect for all you've been putting up with this year."* Kinda brings a tear to the eye, doesn't it?

Another Parting Shot

Okay, some of these rejoinders may be far fetched (*understatement*). We just hope you found one or two that will help you save your leadership credibility when little Rocky cuts loose next time. Keep in mind one of the key OBM principles discussed earlier: *The next best thing to compliance is confusion.*

Strategic Responses to Vile, Profane, and Gross Behaviors

Summary of Those Witty OBM Techniques

1. **Reframes**
   Take the raw behavioral event and reinterpret the intended meaning so as to disarm the aggressor. If the vile behavior was intended to embarrass, intimidate, or disrupt the teacher, find some way to welcome it as a sincere compliment, a sign of educational progress, or some latent talent.

2. **Distraction**
   Offer a quick rejoinder that changes the focus from the "real" problem to some totally unrelated or harmless topic. Find ways to ignore the malevolent intent of a defiant or gross behavior and focus instead on the teacher's concern for untied sneakers, bad grammar, or emerging flu symptoms.

3. **Planned Bewilderment**
   Upon detecting the first signs of defiance, use preemptive distractions to generate mental confusion in the problem student. Use deliberate "crazy-maker" statements, shocking announcements, and baffling questions to stifle that rebellious mental energy. *"... See what I mean? Those nearly unspoken comments were all part of a sick Canadian hacker conspiracy to discredit our local skaters ... So tell me ... what three hopeless things have you already not done about it?"*

Figure 4.1. Stategic Responses to Vile, Profane, and Gross Behaviors: Summary of Those Witty OBM Techniques

Dear OBM Guys:

Chapter 4 has already saved me untold grief. I expect that readers are authorized to use these comebacks outside of the classroom, right? My high school reunion is coming up, and I was already starting to dread the tacky "compliments" I get from a certain person. When I thought about two of the OBM strategic responses I could use, it almost brought on a grin! Now I'm actually looking forward to the reunion. Thanks!

—Ms. J.

Figure 4.2. Dear OBM Guys

5 Gripes and Excuses Some Kids Use

Memory Enhancement Work for Malcontents

More Fun with Oppositional Students

Have you ever been totally fed up with the endless alibis and lame excuses generated by your strong-willed students? Some kids can be caught red-handed before a host of witnesses and video-taped from three angles performing their misdeed and *still* come up with a list of self-vindicating excuses. These are incredible reasoning skills! We can also agree that oppositional students do have extreme difficulty acknowledging their weaknesses, and it seems that meaningful apologies just get stuck in their throat. Their ingenious rationalizations and smoke-screen complaints about injustice could rival almost any media-driven courtroom rhetoric. Some kids have to work at it, but others are naturals with excuses. This chapter is focused on managing those few innately gifted excuse makers found in many classrooms.

Since you are now with us into Chapter 5, you are already savvy enough to expect a different reaction to the chronic excuse makers. We will not be recommending that you jump into the ring with your champion whiner and try to spar with something as crude as logic and reasoning. Rather, we are going to discuss a way to commiserate and collaborate with your strong-willed student in lamenting his sorry plight. Just think of all the rotten, boring things he has to do, isn't allowed to do, or has to put up with! It's enough to make a kid qualify for the "attitudinally challenged" class.

Yes, there are so many bad things happening all the time that it's easy to forget some of them. It's our suggestion that you help your oppositional student keep his sarcasm and stubborn resistance well organized and properly focused. To accomplish this humane goal, we recommend that you join with your difficult student and assign some daily list-making "opportunities."

List Making ... Ad Nauseam

As with our other OBM strategies, you will need a good cover story to get things rolling. Following are three lines of reasoning that might allow the straight-faced teacher to justify an outrageous list-making ordeal:

Phony premise #1: Sometimes an oppositional student might become nervous and overwrought due to an unconscious fear of forgetting or overlooking some of the bad things in his world. To some obsessive-compulsive students, keeping a personal list of frustrations is almost like "controlling" those same frustrations. Great volumes of psychic distress might be generated if the afflicted student were to lose track of his many gripes and they were allowed to become free floating within his character structure. Huh? What we're suggesting to our uptight whiner is that if he doesn't write them down, they will get lost and hunt him down ... and that won't be pretty.

Phony premise #2: One teacher explained to Middle-School Mike that his classroom adjustment problems stemmed from "poor cognitive organization" of the many sources of threat to his self-esteem. Somehow, poor recall of his many life stressors was linked to having bad luck, getting pimples, and making painful decisions. Mike simply needed a helpful assignment ... which would be forthcoming.

Phony premise #3: Some unfortunate students are hypersensitive to the multiple social and emotional irritants in the classroom environment. Just like having an allergic reaction, these students tend to internalize almost every source of frustration around them ... and then start showing those dreadful symptoms. Eventually, the pressures of everyday life just build up in your oppositional student like a vigorously shaken bottle of Dr. Pepper. All it takes is one twist of the cap and everything sprays all over the countertop and onto his "No Fear" T-shirt. The solution to this messy plight is to allow for frequent controlled catharsis (e.g., OBM list-making work). Sure, that sounds credible enough.

So, there you have it. A list of plausible "reasons" for list making: (1) As a benign support for keeping one's mental world organized; (2) as a reinforcement of specialized memory skills; or (3) as a catharsis opportunity for the hypersensitive types among us. Our impossible student is simply asked to spend 5 minutes *at the beginning* of each day brainstorming lists of those frustrating life events. *Note:* This assignment might also be completed in lieu of some detention consequence—especially if he's been busted recently.

Depending on his miserable and disturbing life experiences, he might be required to generate a compelling inventory of unfair situations, angry feelings, or even his own "private stock" inventory of classic excuses. Previous days' lists might be reviewed in order to keep those negative items fresh in mind (of course, earlier items could not be recycled on future days' lists). This helpful assignment has been a real growth experience for many contrary-natured students. Hey, it must be helpful, as it does cast the teacher in a leadership role.

Our OBM teachers also seem to get a kick out of the assignment. When a full week of list making is completed, a copy of the resulting master inventory can be kept for both teacher and student reference. As our subject student eventually drifts back to his old complaining habits, the teacher can offer to record a baseline of "preferred excuses" or "favorite gripes" simply by placing tally marks by his favorite items. This will allow her to keep track of which bellyaches, excuses, or symptoms of stress seem to come up most often.

These helpful lists also allow OBM teachers to give meaningful feedback to their whining students. We have heard such comments as, *"Looks like old #12 is most popular again today!"* or even, *"Whatever happened to #5 and #17? We haven't heard them for days in first-hour class."* Remember, next to being compliant, our oppositional students hate to be considered predictable or analyzable. To be "understood" is a sign of weakness. To be "figured out" suggests a chink in the armor, and that must be resisted at all costs. I have actually seen hard-core stubborn kids give up a major (i.e., favorite) disruptive excuse simply because it was pointed out that they were "like, totally predictable."

The Setup

Usually, we start out with a presentation of one of the three phony premises for the assignment. But why stop there? You can include the obvious need for handwriting practice, long-term memory support, resolution of deeper existential angst, or even some fancy keyboarding exercise. Basically, just give the student some plausible reason that the list making is necessary. He is then required to sit at a certain desk each day until he has brainstormed three to five new items for his master list. Often the assignment goes on for a full week or until an undisclosed total number of items are generated (say, two or three thousand?).

Overly conscientious OBM teachers have been known to keep a few of these classic titles (i.e., prepared blanks) in a folder and ready for use when needed. By the way, is it really an underhanded threat to suggest that the student's folder of whining topics and pet excuses might be passed on to next year's teacher? What about reviewing them at an IEP team meeting? Of course, OBM teachers are not above "supportive" blackmail, especially when it's used strategically to enhance the learning process.

You could print the assigned topic of concern at the top of a page and number spaces for the daily quota of list items. You may need to remind students that they can't repeat any item, regardless of how good and juicy a particular one may seem. To stimulate your imagination, we've included a list of common topics for your thoughtful consideration. At the end of the chapter you will also find that a few of these have been transferred to worksheets for a week-long brainstorming assignment. These particular forms have already seen action with some of those perpetual whiners and excuse-making buffs among us.

Sample List-Making Topics

1. More examples of why life isn't fair in this class
2. Immature and annoying things that some other kids do
3. Reasons why I always get blamed for things
4. Some lifelong benefits of quitting this stupid school
5. Serious emotional traumas I have suffered in this class
6. Inhumane class rules and how I would change them
7. Honest-sounding reasons why homework might not get done
8. Violations of student dignity I have witnessed around here
9. Some benefits and frustrations of arguing for your rights
10. Rude behaviors I have endured from geeks, nerds, and punks
11. Secret methods I've used to stay awake in this boring class
12. Some ways this class reminds me of a prison

Some Lifelong Benefits of Quitting This Stupid School

Your assignment is to create a list of personal benefits to you for taking the bold step of becoming a school dropout. Use your knowledge of older dropouts—from last year—to help you think of all the real benefits.

Student:_____

Class: _____

Monday: **Thursday:**
1._____   1._____
2._____   2._____
3._____   3._____

Tuesday: **Friday:**
1._____   1._____
2._____   2._____
3._____   3._____

Wednesday:
1._____
2._____
3._____

Figure 5.1. Some Lifelong Benefits of Quitting This Stupid School

Some Honest Reasons Homework Might Not Get Done

Your assignment is to create a list of really good excuses for incomplete homework. Use your own observations and painful experiences in this difficult class to help you think of answers.

Student:_____

Class: _____

Monday: **Thursday:**
1._____   1._____
2._____   2._____
3._____   3._____

Tuesday: **Friday:**
1._____   1._____
2._____   2._____
3._____   3._____

Wednesday:
1._____
2._____
3._____

Figure 5.2. Some Honest Reasons Homework Might Not Get Done

How I Would Change the Unfair Rules in This Sorry Class

Your assignment is to create a list of immediate changes you would make in the rules for this dark, oppressive classroom. Use your own bad experiences here to help you think of as many humane changes as possible.

Student:_____

Class: _____

Monday: **Thursday:**
1._____   1._____
2._____   2._____
3._____   3._____

Tuesday: **Friday:**
1._____   1._____
2._____   2._____
3._____   3._____

Wednesday:
1._____
2._____
3._____

Figure 5.3. How I Would Change the Unfair Rules in This Sorry Class

Rude Behaviors I Have Endured from Geeks, Nerds, and Punks

Your assignment is to create a list of the most 'crude and disgusting' behaviors you have witnessed in the cultural wasteland of this classroom. Try to recall your very worst social encounters and your most humiliating memories to record below.

Student:_____

Class: _____

Monday: **Thursday:**
1._____   1._____
2._____   2._____
3._____   3._____

Tuesday: **Friday:**
1._____   1._____
2._____   2._____
3._____   3._____

Wednesday:
1._____
2._____
3._____

Figure 5.4. Rude Behaviors I Have Endured from Geeks, Nerds, and Punks

**A Few of the Reasons
I Always Get Blamed for Things!**

Your assignment is to create a list of believable reasons for
the unfair accusations thrown at you in this oppressive
classroom. Use your own miserable life experiences here to
help you think of as many false charges as possible.

Student:_____

Class: _____

Monday: Thursday:
1._____   1._____
2._____   2._____
3._____   3._____

Tuesday: Friday:
1._____   1._____
2._____   2._____
3._____   3._____

Wednesday:
1._____
2._____
3._____

180   © 2007 by PRO-ED, Inc.

Figure 5.5. A Few of the Reasons I Always Get
Blamed for Things

**More Examples of Why Life Isn't
Jolly in This Miserable Class**

Your assignment is to create a list of the inhumane
conditions endured by students in this class. Use your own
rotten experiences here to help you think of as many
answers as possible.

Student:_____

Class: _____

Monday: Thursday:
1._____   1._____
2._____   2._____
3._____   3._____

Tuesday: Friday:
1._____   1._____
2._____   2._____
3._____   3._____

Wednesday:
1._____
2._____
3._____

© 2007 by PRO-ED, Inc.   181

Figure 5.6. More Examples of Why Life Isn't Jolly
in This Miserable Class

Gripes and Excuses

Summary Points

This is a handy little exercise to use (or threaten to use) with chronic whiners and your
typical song-and-dance excuse makers:

1. **Select a target student:**
   Only the classic malcontent will do here.

2. **Present a plausible rationale:**
   You need to supply a good reason for this assignment. Keep a poker face while
   explaining the need. Review our optional phony premise spiels. I like #3, but that's
   just me.

3. **Run the assignment:**
   Collect at least one school week of list entries. Thank the student for the brilliant
   ideas.

4. **Follow-up support:**
   Offer to repeat the assignment as needed ... *until some student benefit is evident.*

Figure 5.7. Gripes and Excuses: Summary Points

Dear OBM Guys:

I was with a busload of teachers who toured the OBM Institute last semester. When they gave out sample materials, I ended up with some of the list-making forms. I've just finished one week with one of your "Suffer Fools Gladly" list-making exercises. It perfectly fit one of my bright oppositional students. This poor kid sees himself as perpetually enduring gross ignorance among his classroom peers. His lists of complaints were impressive, but I think he may be running out of steam. I can hardly wait to use my "Is this all?" line. Maybe by next week? . . . And thanks for the great refreshments at the institute cafeteria.

—Sharon B.

Figure 5.8. Dear OBM Guys

Playing Sigmund Freud in the Classroom

The Force Can Be Strong on Oppositional Minds

Your Crash Course in Psychoanalysis

Just as you can learn all you really need to know about life in kindergarten, so too your life quota of psychoanalytic skills can come from a few classic movies. Honest. If you have seen *Psycho, The Three Faces of Eve*, and maybe *Dr. Jekyll and Mr. Hyde,* you have all the fundamental concepts for success in your classroom psychoanalytic practice. Well, okay, there must be a few deeper principles not covered in those movies, but you'll get enough from them (and perhaps an afternoon of network talk shows) to sound credible in your OBM work.

Basically, psychoanalytic thinking has done a thorough job of convincing our culture that nothing is (really) as it appears to be. All human behavior is the product of swirling shadowy unseen psychological forces battling each other for expression. No one ever performs an asocial act simply because he intended to do something bad. There is no "bad" anything for which one might be culpable. We are all victims of unresolved "conflicts" or malevolent social pressures. Freud and his followers could see primitive sexual drives, parental enmeshment, fixated development, and a host of shadowy complexes and neuroses in even the simplest of behaviors.

... And now you, too, can start seeing these deeper forces in everyday contacts with your most difficult students! Keep in mind that these rigid, demanding, strong-willed students are also quite brittle. Power is their game, and they do not want to reveal anything "personal" that could possibly be exploited. Oppositional kids loath the idea of "being understood" or being "read like a book." When our fledgling OBM teachers arrive on the scene with their supposed deeper understanding of the student's developmental plight, it can be a real threat to the power agenda. And that is just what the classroom doctor ordered.

Hanging Out Your Shingle

If you hale from a much earlier, kinder, and gentler decade, you may recall the Ricky Nelson song that declared that "fools rush in where angels fear to tread." (I only know this one from the oldies station. Honest.) Anyway, that lyric may offer some food for thought before hanging out your OBM shingle with jolly old Sigmund. We are suggesting that teachers can gain some control of the oppositional student by making off-the-wall interpretations of his classroom behavior. We are not suggesting that actual—perhaps real and painful— material be mirrored to the student as an explanation of his problem behaviors. As the song states, only a fool rushes in (and breaks open Pandora's box). The physician's first rule is "do no harm," but that doesn't exclude a bit of strategic hassling from time to time.

So, how does the OBM teacher draw the line? My first response is that the teachers who should use this particular strategy are those of you *who already know* where to draw the line. You have an intuitive sense of fair play, of close enough but not cruel, of witty but not damaging. More on the ethics of OBM in a later chapter. From a more pragmatic perspective, you don't have to dig up *real* dirt on your impossible student. We have found that crazy, confusing, and unlikely interpretations of behavior seem to work just fine.

In the pioneer days of OBM I had some favorite scripts of canned interpretations—primarily for the vulnerable but impossible middle-school tough guys. Some have asked why the fabled analytic scripts were not kept secure within the massive OBM Institute. Well, those handwritten manuscripts were targeted long before the meteoric ascension of OBM technology. In the early years of development, it seems that some body-pierced burglars or alternative school gangsters somehow managed to breach multiple levels of custodians, Title I aides, and secretaries. They successfully broke into my broom-closet office at Harrison H. Schmitt Elementary School and (oddly enough) stole just those classic scripts. That's an indication of how valuable they were reputed to be just for their hypnotic effects. But not to worry. This part of the chapter could blossom out of fond memories alone.

Using "Assumed Knowledge"

Oppositional students come in different packages. Some are a royal pain (*in the* ...) but have other redeeming qualities that endear them to you. Dave fit that description. He was a tall, blond kid with a high verbal IQ, some kind of a learning disability, and a deeply felt mandate to argue any issue from pro sports to student rights. I still liked him. He also had a dozen entertaining explanations for any of his classroom disruptions. In my weekly counseling work and classroom visits, it became apparent that Dave was slightly paranoid and highly suggestible. This helped a lot when I started digging around in my ideas bag to select an OBM strategy.

One week I met with Dave prepared to ask a series of meaningless interview questions. (Picture this mentally besieged oppositional student trying to figure out what was cooking.) As the "interview" progressed, he became more and more insistent that I tell him why these questions were significant for him and that I let him know if he had the "right" answers. Every time I paused and mumbled something to myself, his suspicious style seemed to double in intensity.

Here are just a few of the items from the contrived "developmental trajectory" interview designed to give me a truckload of fresh-smelling "assumed knowledge" about Dave:

"Just try to relax . . . or maybe let yourself enjoy being somewhat tense. I'll be assessing your developmental trajectory today." (He showed some indication of the usual boredom mixed with a hint of suspicion regarding this new concept.)

"So . . . what's your actual exact age right now?" (I then computed some cryptic numbers on paper while mumbling privately: *"Uh huh, just add the algebraic weights and the level III correction factors . . . Uh hmmm, just as I thought."*)

"I really need to ask you this before we continue the interview: Have you had any unusual dreams lately—that you can't remember too well?"

"How about some thoughts popping into your mind—that don't make any sense?"

"And I'll guess you may have also noticed some very small things happening during the day that you can't remember too clearly?"

"Do you sometimes get the impression that things aren't real? Like maybe the world isn't really real? Hmmm."

"Have you noticed that your stomach sometimes growls or gurgles when you sit toward the front of a classroom?" (I knew his seat placement in the class just before lunch.).

"Now . . . I need you to think carefully about this one before you answer. Have you noticed any times recently in the hallway when (for no apparent reason) some other kids may have looked at you with just a very slight—almost unnoticeable—expression on their face?"

"Over the past 2 weeks have you lost some small items at school (like a pen, or comb, or a small plastic object) that nobody else remembers seeing?"

"Have you noticed recently that the metal door handles seem unusually cold, especially when you reach for them with your left hand?" (I knew he was left handed. The cold feeling was just a guess.)

"Is it possible for a kid at your critical stage of development to lose something and not remember it at all?" (Just as he repeated his reflexive denial, I handed him his own chewed-down Bic pen, which I had lifted a few minutes before the interview—all without comment.)

Okay, you get the general idea. Actually, I had a much longer list of two dozen unusual inquiries that helped me develop a supposed psychological "profile" of Dave's precarious developmental trajectory. While maintaining some detached clinical objectivity, I sketched out a two-axis graph and zigzagged a line across a dozen unnamed scales. I then commented to my oppositional adolescent that such a profile might be useful in predicting *"irresistible future changes"* in his behavior. As you might guess, this stubborn, slightly paranoid student was immediately interested in what the forthcoming "irresistible" predictions might be. At the same time, he tried to muster some skepticism and arguments that such predictions just wouldn't work for him.

Polymorphous Adolescent Development Test

Let's suppose you're just too busy to dream up a bunch of shadowy interview questions like the ones I used with my stubborn middle-school client. There are other ways to quickly generate half a dumpster full of "assumed knowledge," all aimed at that willful adolescent's fragile psyche. You might use a venerated psychoanalytic test such as the *Draw a Moody Cloud* or the family systems assessment instrument *Draw-Your-Family-Coming-Home-from-Wal-Mart Test*. Maybe you would prefer my old projective favorite *Draw a Microwave Oven*. If you're in a pinch, just take a clean paper towel and wipe down a table in the teachers' lounge (preferably after a rich pasta lunch). Carefully spread out the dried Rorschach Inkblot Paper Towel before the bewildered student and ask him to free-associate to all the unusual colors, designs, and smells. Take careful notes, do a few clarifications, and suddenly you have a wealth of knowledge about his complex developmental crisis.

If you prefer a paper-and-pencil written exercise, we submit the *Polymorphous Adolescent Development Test* for your thoughtful consideration. Our committee of *Far Side* scientists generated this cryptic instrument just for you. It is presented here in its entirety for your amusement and possible use. This test has absolutely no psychological meaning. It is merely a collection of vague items that may hold some face validity for those students caught in the thralls of adolescence angst.

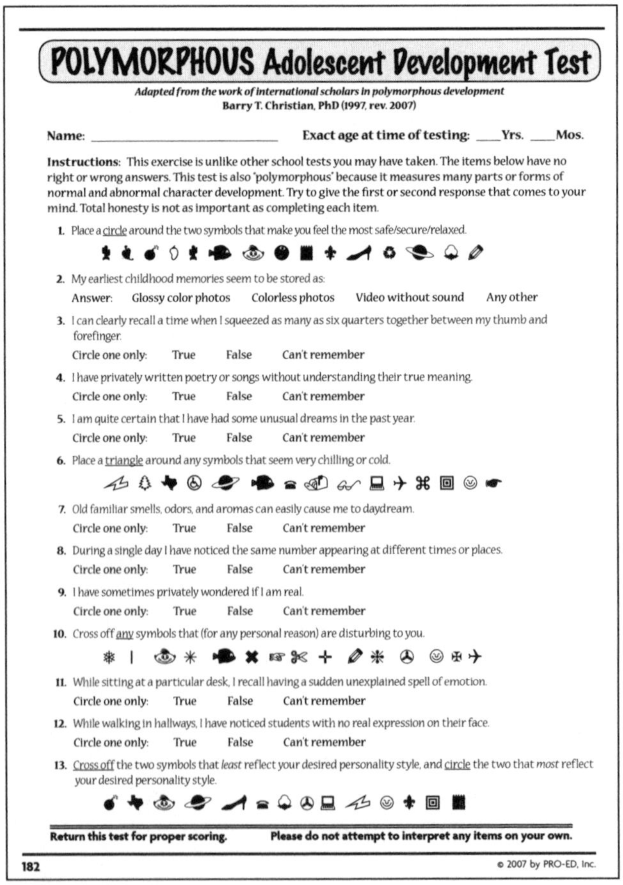

Figure 6.1. Polymorphous: Adolescent Development Test

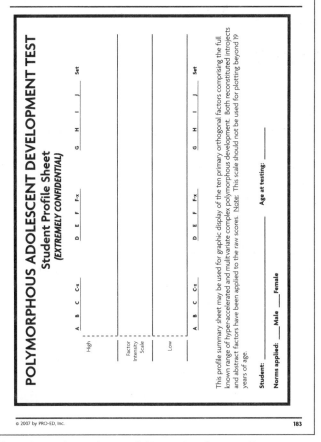

Figure 6.2. Polymorphous: Adolescent Development Test

Test Administration Hints

If you choose to administer this test, always do so with a flair of cool clinical objectivity. Assure the student that this instrument will generate information helpful in planning his personal and school life. Stress that the results will be kept strictly confidential and that he will be fully debriefed once the elaborate scoring and interpretation process has been completed. Although this isn't a real test of anything, our OBM staff has been diligent in seeking counsel on its proper use. We have been assured by the A. E. Neuman consulting firm that our "polymorphous" measure of development ranks with many other classics carried in those tabloids "for inquiring minds."

Cryptic Interpretations

These are the rare moments a teacher should relish. Why hurry to give Dave (or your own strong-willed counterpart) a lot more information? Why jump too soon into diagnostic explanations, cryptic predictions, or those helpful "therapeutic" assignments? Sometimes we need to just let our bird stew a while longer before serving.

Our homemade "profile" should be vague enough to support just about any interpretation. The best ones will be as nebulous as a tabloid horoscope or a psychic hotline script ... no specifics, just things that sound specific. Once you have plotted the data and eyeballed the student's profile, it's time to stare pensively into space, stroke your beard (optional, if you have one), and then offer some deep OBM insight.

Below are a few sample interpretations you might consider. Notice that none of them involves any mean-spirited labeling or direct confrontation about the *real* classroom problems. You won't see any objective diagnoses (e.g., "You talk back too much," "You never start working on time," or "You're basically a pain to deal with each day"). Remember OBM Principle #3: *Work smarter, not harder.* These sample interpretations show how you can get past that tough oppositional armor and closer to that soft, insecure (flabby) underbelly. To do that we create a problem or "issue" that is totally off in left field. Now that you have the benefit of "deeper insights" from your contrived interview or fabricated test scores, these oddball clinical ramblings can be presented with the confidence and authority of a *Verbal Advantage* graduate.

In the items below, watch for (and savor) the empathetic mood tone of the OBM interpretations. Here we see the teacher as a warm, knowledgeable sage who is simply offering our suspicious student the benefit of seasoned insight and guidance.

Try some of these debriefings on for size:

> *"You seem to be entering a stage of punctuated psychological equilibrium. In fact, this profile suggests maybe two or three levels of personality metamorphism. Look here at the angle on these triad factors. Hmmm … That's truly amazing."*

> *"You're definitely well into Stage IV of neurosocial confabulation. That's really a critical phase that will demand a lot of your energy. Especially at this grade level. Of course, there are always some special cautions and concerns at this stage. Have you ever read any of the neo-analytic writers?"*

> *"Looks like you've successfully negotiated the two fundamental adolescent crises of attitudinal cathexis and early identity lamination. These are both latent developmental milestones that are essential to future archetypal disposition. Wow, and you're only 13 years old!"*

> *"This profile shows the classic lines of both the retentive and expulsive prototaxic modes. See the difference here between these highs and lows? No doubt a full sublimation of object-choice transference. I'm not easily impressed, but this is exemplary."*

Psychobabble Verbiage Generator

So this looks intriguing or maybe just entertaining, but you couldn't possibly dream up all that psychoanalytic verbiage. Besides, the defiant kid you're presently thinking about would need more than the proverbial "snow job"—he'd require some kind of a blizzard to get him confused. Again, not to worry. Don't wimp out and go back to happy stickers. All you need is some convincing terminology to craft your "interpretation" of student behavior. Check out our verbiage generator. Along with that venerated polymorphous test, it's another great support tool for OBM practitioners. As always, we're here to take care of you.

Psychobabble ... Verbiage ... Generator

Feeling a little slow on the draw with those phony psychiatric terms? Join the club. What you need is a whole new menu of psychoanalytic excuses for human behavior. Just choose three random numbers from 1 to 9. Find the corresponding word in each column. Simply link your words together, state them with confidence and authority ... and you have generated a psychodynamic interpretation for oppositional student behavior. Is this cool or what? Let's try a couple for fun. Suppose you tend to perseverate a lot and just chose 8-8-8. This would yield the term *"Precocious Intrapsychic Detachment."* How about 1-3-6, which gets you *"Archetypal Character Sublimation."* If one description doesn't seem quite right, don't lose your grin! Just pick three more numbers and create a totally different cryptic term. While you're at it, why not drop a few of these gems at your next parent conference or IEP meeting? And what an ideal way to explain your last chocolate binge? Our crack team of OBM scientists have calculated that you can generate 729 psychobabble terms from this list. *Let it snow, let it snow, let it snow ...*

1. Archetypal	1. Personality	1. Fixation
2. Dysfunctional	2. Oedipal	2. Orientation
3. Existential	3. Character	3. Cathexis
4. Polymorphous	4. Narcissism	4. Transference
5. Intrusive	5. Mastery	5. Displacement
6. Retentive	6. Fantasy	6. Sublimation
7. Punctuated	7. Object-choice	7. Ambivalence
8. Precocious	8. Intrapsychic	8. Detachment
9. Unconscious	9. Autonomy	9. Striving

Some Personal Favorites

Go ahead, you're dying to try it out! Make up some lucky numbers. Create a few pet terms and record them below for future snow-blinding interpretations!

_____	_____	_____
_____	_____	_____
_____	_____	_____

Figure 6.3. Psychobabble ... Verbiage ... Generator

Irresistible Future Changes

While novelty and interest are running high and the OBM teacher still holds all the cards, it's easy to move into some convincing predictions about the target student. At this point we like to introduce an element of confusion and curiosity that opens even the iron-willed student (who may be feigning a lack of interest) to some of your wonderful prognostications. Here are three guidelines for crafting your predictions of irresistible future change:

1. Predict irresistible behaviors that are really just thinly veiled replicas of the ones he *already* performs in a daily habitual manner.

"Yes, this stage of adolescent development has always been a puzzle to me. Your profile here is quite unusual. Note the juxtaposition of these three points. The classic analytic theorists would have a good time with this one. I'd guess that sometime today … probably not right now but later … you're going to find yourself walking down a crowded hallway somewhere and thinking out loud in your mind about a restriction in your life—probably one of the school rules. I don't know which one it will be. At about that time, your subconscious mind will tell you something about your polymorphous personality profile that could be very useful. Like maybe some insights on your stronger traits … that could give you a chance for survival down in Ms. Joyless's class. Now you've even got me curious as to what you're going to discover. This should really be a fascinating day!"

"What we've got here is a very unique adolescent profile. See how these points cluster together while the other ones are scattered? This profile seems to suggest you will sometimes find yourself starting out with a lot of hope in something but not finishing it. I'm not real sure what all that means…. Maybe like trying to stay out of trouble for a day but having bad luck … or perhaps trying to get started on some work but getting distracted. I guess we'll just have to wait and find out…. There are also some other indicators, but let's take them one at a time…"

"Hmmm … this is a special profile … Notice the peaks on some of these energy scales. There's some indication of restlessness or even agitation … that may be displayed in your daily life. You may begin to find yourself walking into situations where you do the exact opposite of what someone tells you to do … or possibly feel an overwhelming need to argue about some minor issue you really don't even care about. I just wonder if this is a long-term 'fixed' style or just a blip on the screen. Is it possible that you'll have no choice but to follow that demanding and punishing life script? Or maybe these scores won't really dictate your future? This should be a very fascinating day. Let me know what you discover."

2. Predict behaviors that are *unavoidable* to any student, but which now can be explained as internally driven and purposeful.

"Sometime today or maybe this week you're going to find yourself resting in a comfortable condition—in an uncomfortable location. You'll be resting … even when you don't really feel tired at all. See these two points … very far apart. Let's see, mentally, you'll be clear and reflective (see this scale here). Hmmm … I just wish we had more students with this profile…. Anyway, when you find yourself resting and reflecting, you may want to listen for any positive message coming out of your subconscious mind…. It seems you're about ready to move through some important developmental milestones … or do something really important. This seated-and-resting thing may be your body's way of slowing you down in order to listen better."

"This profile suggests you may be moving into a period when your thoughts will come so fast that you could say some things without thinking. There may actually be a flood of ideas that you will feel compelled to speak about…. Maybe later, all this running off at the mouth should make sense. Let's both listen to see what pops out of your head today. Perhaps there will be some deeper meaning to discover."

3. Predict "either/or" behaviors that are self-fulfilling whether he resists them or performs them.

These are great for setting up the difficult student for your "knowing look," which lets him know how well you understand his developmental plight. Remember, oppositional kids hate to be understood or figured out. If you're lowdown, mean, rotten, you can also plan for some reverse-control statements such as "Hmmm, just as we predicted." I've known stubborn kids who actually refused to perform the predicted misbehaviors, just to keep from hearing those all-knowing comments from the OBM teacher.

"This brief phase of development is always curious to me. It seems to happen a lot in this grade. See how these scales—which are usually equal—are moving apart? Basically, you can expect to find yourself somewhere in the confusion of the school day ... and faced with a frozen moment in time where some decision is needed. Everything in your mind will get very clear and focused. Some kids who have been through this experience say that things may go into 'slow motion' for a while, just like in the Matrix *movie. You will then find yourself making some conscious decision to do something important ... or resist doing something. Wonder what all that means? It's different for each kid. Guess we'll just have to wait and find out."*

"This is a very unusual profile. Seems you'll soon be walking a pathway where your inner drives will demand some kind of positive life changes. Wonder if you will reap all the benefits of those changes ... or if some part of you will resist or sabotage your inner drives. This is often an exciting but confusing stage. Benefits or sabotage? ... which inner voices are the strongest? It should be educational for both of us to watch how the battle turns out in the days ahead."

As you might guess, the fire-breathing oppositional student will actively seek to thwart any simple direct predictions about his behavior. Remember, this is just how they are wired. But also remember that OBM strategies are made to flourish best with this kind of knee-jerk resistance. Any teacher who can come up with the kind of nonsense interpretations discussed earlier should also be more than capable of spinning predictions of unavoidable behaviors that are equally vague.

Just as an aside, we have sometimes considered whether there should be a 24-hour OBM hotline set up for teachers to call in and get help in crafting outrageous interpretations and predictions. We've also thought of a free Web site for spin doctor consults. However, our favorite dot-com address has been passed among a series of other more impressive entities like Okeechobee Business Machines, Off-Broadway Musicians, and the esteemed Ohio Board of Morticians. Enough already, let's get you set up with the last function of the Sigmund Freud ploy in your classroom. Here's the payoff.

Offer a Slick Behavioral Prescription

Let's suppose you have already planted the seeds of some wacky profile interpretations. We'll also assume you have choked back some smirks while dropping in a double-bind prediction about unavoidable near future behavior. Wonderful! Now is your golden opportunity to carry the whole thing to new heights of strategically planned bewilderment by attaching a helpful therapeutic prescription. After all, what good is that fancy diagnosis without supportive intervention?

Your prescription is a helpful therapeutic assignment offered to the student as a means of resolving his deep-seated intrapsychic conflict. Alternatively, it might be offered quite humbly as a last-ditch, desperate means of breaking him free from an overwhelming habit or pathologic character trait. Well-designed behavior prescriptions, offered with a straight face and clinical detachment, allow your oppositional student to resist (as usual!) or comply with equal effectiveness. In fact, he can be successful or an abject failure—and still be framed as fully cooperative.

Better yet, the stubborn student who resists your prescription (what's new?) can be cast as the hapless victim of some primitive urge or some developmental drive that only the teacher fully understands. Remember, knowledge is power. And even assumed knowledge carries some clout. Once your prescription has been set in motion, you will have some days of blissful classroom interactions where knowing looks and understanding nods show deep empathy for the student's heroic struggle with "that problem."

Okay, let's think seriously for a moment about a good workable prescription for your oppositional student. First off, what's the surest thing you might expect from any suggestion you dream up? That's right: *Resistance*! If a student rushed off and dutifully performed one of my OBM prescriptions, I'd have to seriously doubt whether he was truly oppositional. These students are preprogrammed to resist, challenge, and subvert authority. Why should they comply with some silly directive from me, even if it's supposed to help with "that problem"?

Just like our earlier trance-inducing predictions about near-future behavior, the prescribed treatment for a contrived problem must be crafted so that just about *any* behavior (or even nonbehavior) is seen as praiseworthy compliance. No matter how the student comes in to class tomorrow, I've got to have some logical reason to smile and congratulate him for his monumental effort. I've got to take on the persona of myopic Mister Magoo and "see" some evidence of my student's Herculean effort to work through his problem or forbear under his extreme inner pressures. This kid's cast as a hero, no matter what he does!

Let's cut to the chase and look at some canned OBM prescriptions. Yes, it may be necessary to practice these in front of a mirror—or during staff meetings—until you can do them without grinning:

1. For the student who dominates the class by arguing and talking out.

Let's assume he has already been given some psychobabble interpretation of his situation (suppose a 5-3-6, or even a 4-9-7) that has to do with passing through a "critical stage of growth."

"Thanks for stopping by, Jim. No doubt you've had more time to reflect on that interesting personality profile we discussed last week. Isn't it amazing how some thoughts and behaviors can almost be predicted to happen exactly when your development requires them? I've sure noticed some of these things coming out over the past few days. Isn't it great? (The empathetic teacher flashes a grand Ultrabrite smile.) Remember, this is one of those difficult stages to get through. Some kids get lost in the middle of this maze and never seem to find their way out.

"If I could offer only one suggestion during this trying time of personality reorganization, it would be this: When confusing thoughts buzz into your head, try to focus your eyes on one nearby object—something with an earth-tone color—and stare hard at it... until everything in your head settles down. In fact, when you get good at

staring, you can even pretend to do it in your head while you keep chattering away in class in the usual way. No one needs to know what you're really up to. Well, that's just a suggestion. Let me know how things turn out..."

Notice how this prescribed behavior allows for either/or responses. He can actually stare at an object or just pretend to stare while continuing to talk out as usual. Either way, the OBM teacher has set up just a bit of collusion... and is perhaps also taking some early implicit control of poor Jim. I can hear you asking, "So when does Jim actually learn to shut up in class?" Patience, grasshopper. First comes the setup and then the sting. Meanwhile, let's look at another common script for an OBM prescription. This one was found recently among the lost sticky notes way in the back of Dr. Freud's old wooden desk.

2. For the student who argues and mumbles threats under his breath.

"Howdy, Bruno. I just needed a moment or two to say how pleased I was to review your psychological development profile. [Here the teacher may review some of the cryptic findings or maybe mention some of the recent irresistible behaviors connected with his developmental condition.]

"It might be important for you to know that the next couple of weeks could be critical in this stage of your development. If the test results are accurate, you may be able to pull all of these free-floating thoughts and impulses together at the right time. If so, you'll move easily right into the next stage. I have just one suggestion. During the next couple of weeks, you might need to follow your first impulses ... like to argue in class or whisper defiant comments under your breath. You might need to follow those impulses as they surge up from your younger infantile character structure ... even if they do cost you some punishment or severe ridicule from your peers. You might even need to do more than those childhood impulses would demand, just to get through the transition. Sometimes you have to risk being slapped with some disciplinary consequences in order to follow a psychological crisis through to completion.

"I know it will be a struggle, and you may have some kids thinking you're a jerk or something ... But it will be well worth the pain and humiliation, don't you think? Of course, there's the chance you might beat all the odds and move suddenly and effortlessly into the more advanced stage without wrestling with all those infantile forces. You might find yourself quietly sitting in your desk and working away and all that stress just evaporates on its own. Well, either way, I'll be watching to see how the next weeks go. It should be a very interesting study in developmental psychology!"

As an experiment (with a required term paper?) the teacher might offer to allow Bruno to retake the *Polymorphous Test*—on the other side of his developmental transition. Who knows, a comparison of the pre- and post-ordeal intrapsychic profiles might be educational for all of us.

3. For the hard-core resistor who's lost somewhere in Denialville.

Some kids are more "clinically" oppositional than others. There is a breed of extremely rigid (and perhaps lower-functioning) students who really can't get into the psychobabble developmental stuff. They simply resist everything with no shame ... and certainly no insight. For those uptight, hard-bitten, defiant types, we offer a slightly different soup menu. Here's a helpful OBM prescription that sets up a kind of obsessive-compulsive challenge—which is quite impossible for anyone to follow (and that's the idea).

"Greetings, Dominic. I'll bet you haven't had a good chance to think about that developmental crisis stuff. That situation we discussed may look scary, even impossible. Maybe so—but desperate times require desperate action. There may be a way to get through this stage and into some peace and quiet ... but it's not going to be easy. In fact, I don't know if you can pull it off. If you're ever going to tame those deep psychological impulses and anxieties in your head, you're going to have to fight on their turf. It's time to take control! You're going to have to deprive your mind of sleep ... maybe just survive on two or three hours a night ... and you're going to have to start totally controlling and occupying your mind by counting all kinds of things, like tiles in the ceiling, cracks in the sidewalk, lockers in the hallway—anything you can find that will force your mind to be under your control.

"You'll probably have to starve your mind of sleep and then make it a slave to some intense task in order to wear down those developmental impulses ... maybe even have to start counting more and more things like the exact total number of steps you take in a day ... or the number of breaths you take in a week, or even how many times you swallow during a meal—until you are at last able to break free and climb into the next peaceful stage. I've even heard of kids in your situation who wore a thick rubber band on their wrist and gave themselves a snap every time they forgot to count the step they just took ... and they kept it going all day long. Well, it sure is a major psychological battle that you're facing here. Let me know what you plan to do ..."

If this oppositional kid is really worth his salt, he'll flatly reject your stupid ordeal, but there will also be the sense that he backed down from the OBM teacher's prescription (read: *challenge*). The idea is to beat this student to the proverbial punch by describing an impossible task that he could never really accomplish (and then let him reject it). After the setup, the teacher may conclude with, *"I know it's mighty tough for you right now ... I only wish we could think of some easier way."*

After this bombshell, just let the dust settle around the impossible student for a few days. From time to time you might point out some of the "unavoidable behaviors" that he struggles with right there in the classroom. You could explain these as the telltale symptoms of his raging developmental crisis. Of course, these "symptoms" are just the same old daily resistance and disruptions the teacher has already endured for most of the semester. Yes, but now the teacher is wearing the hat of an empathetic mentor who can lament the plight of the struggling preadolescent (even if he doesn't necessarily want his plight lamented!).

Wait a day or so until the student reflexively does some more of his resistance routines. Work up a sympathetic knowing look and say something like:

"Well, Dominic, you can see it's going to be quite a roller coaster ride ... full speed ... with no breaks. Meanwhile, just brace yourself the best you can. The test data suggest that you can expect more of these powerful impulses and wild urges and free-floating anxieties.... You know what I mean, like making bad decisions, or having some problem words slip out at the wrong times ... or even getting yourself busted for things you really didn't want to do ..."

504 Plan for Pain-in-the-Butt

This entire last scenario is offered as a response to the toughest cases. Perhaps the best outcome we might hope for is simply preserving the teacher's authority position in the face-to-face relationship. The teacher continues to have "deeper insights" than the student would like her to have, and the whole wornout resistance routine is reframed as a relentless intrapsychic struggle ... that is, the student's perilous journey into adolescence. Think about it. By diagnosing a developmental crisis, the teacher has actually transformed her oppositional headache student into an emotional cripple who needs "accommodations," understanding, and support. The OBM teacher can now get real busy hovering over the bewildered student with excessive, controlling, "smother love." We all know this as a power trip in some families (so why not use it strategically in the classroom?). There you go smiling again.

Anyway, if things mellow out in the weeks ahead, the teacher might announce that she had a brainstorm and came up with some easier way for the poor student to crash through that developmental barrier. She might suggest that he try making a tight fist and squeezing the blood out of his hand (and back up to his brain) whenever stupid urges are detected. This easier prescription would also allow the teacher to continue the psychoanalytic interpretations and be a supportive guide to the student for the remainder of the semester. And look who keeps the power! Sure it's classic codependence, but with a delightful OBM twist.

But Can It Fly, Wilbur?

You've worked through quite a piece of the *OBM Handbook*. I've checked with the front office staff, and everyone thinks you've earned the right to some closure on *playing Sigmund Freud* in the classroom. So, just how do we pull all this slick talk together into an understandable, workable strategy? In response to that vexing question, the night-shift R&D crew at the institute has compiled a nice summary page for your inspection.

Playing Sigmund Freud in the Classroom

Summary of Those Wild OBM Procedures

1. **Gather Your Diagnostic Data:**
   Dream up a developmental transition crisis (psychoanalysis is a fertile field for digging up all manner of developmental problems). It might even help to administer our ***Polymorphous Adolescent Development Test*** (or just assemble some odd bits of life information), display your "data" on a homemade profile chart, and assign a psychobabble diagnostic term to describe the student's present psychological crisis.

2. **Make Your Grim Prognosis (describe the nontreatment option):**
   Strengthen your sagelike credibility by predicting some irresistible behaviors or "symptoms" that the student can expect to encounter as he wrestles with his turbulent developmental crisis. These predictions of unavoidable self-sabotage should be thinly veiled replicas of his current disgusting misbehaviors (e.g., an irresistible impulse to make excuses). Also point out some of the penalties, punishments, and negative social consequences that he will probably have to endure. You might want to cruise back through the chapter and review some of our cool examples.

3. **Write the Prescription:**
   In a follow-up meeting, offer a "behavioral ordeal" designed to help the student transition through this difficult stage of development. Generally, the prescription is a **Subtle Transformation** that *requires* the oppositional student to *intensify or keep doing* a problem behavior—but in a slightly different way from its "raw form." Your official prescribed behaviors might include both public and private efforts. If the student resists the outward behaviors, the teacher can still *infer* that much private mental effort is being expended (and therefore give buckets of daily praise and admiration for all that unseen internal work).

4. **Define and Protect the Relationship:**
   The diagnosis and prescription should cast the teacher as a wise mentor who is just trying to help the student through a developmental crisis. There must be no hint of antagonism.

5. **Strategic Follow-Up Care:**
   If blatant defiance and resistance are expected from the student, the first prescription should be an impossible task or some extreme ordeal described as *"the only way out for you."* This allows for the expected rejection of the task. The supportive OBM teacher should then commiserate with the student and lament his plight (e.g., *"Looks like you're really stuck at this impasse … I wish the solution were easier"*). The teacher can either enjoy watching the oppositional power leak out—and then smother-love the cripple she has created—or simply offer an easier prescription.

6. **Signs of Recovery:**
   Once any compliance is established, begin to let the next prescribed behaviors *drift* toward more benign (i.e., tolerable) symptoms. There is an art form to this, but the OBM team believes you're ready! Do some window shopping for just the right **Subtle Transformations** in Appendix C.

Figure 6.4. Playing Sigmund Freud in the Classroom: Summary of Those Wild OBM Procedures

Dear OBM Guys:

Your cheap mental-testing stuff sure never worked on me. The only reason I'm writing this letter is because I'm earning a one-level advance in our classroom program. All I know is that Ms. Murdock had us take your stupid *Polymorphous Test* so we could learn about our personality. It said I was like totally stuck in some developmental stage and that I would be unable to shut up in class for about a month. What a crock! I haven't said two words in this class in almost a week! Looks like your test doesn't work on us "difficult" kids. Keep trying!

—(Seventh grader, name withheld)

Figure 6.5. Dear OBM Guys

7

Practice Tantrum Sessions

Do Them Right ... or Not at All

Terrorist Demands and Negative Reinforcement

Here's a good one for explosive elementary kids who are in training for major conduct problems in mid school. We're talking about the resistant and defiant students who punish their teacher with red-faced, out-of-breath screaming fits. These are always entertaining to watch in someone else's classroom. Perhaps unknown to these terrorist practitioners, the learning principle working in their control strategy is "negative reinforcement." That is, they are willing to terminate an aversive stimuli (i.e., their infantile tantrum) as a means of reinforcing the teacher for complying with their demands. You may also recall seeing this negative reinforcement strategy practiced by tearful children with loud voices and reaching hands at the Wal-Mart checkout displays. As usual, there are many settings for the same strategy: "Meet my demands, and I'll turn off your misery."

Hostile Takeovers

I recall a wonderful parody of the hard-driving MicroSoft Corporation during the glory days of the high-tech boom. We are presented a scene with thousands of nerdlike employees busy laboring away at their 14-hour shifts. Suddenly, the company sends out a news ticker at the bottom of everyone's computer screen. It glibly announces: *"Alert: Terrorists have broken into Building C and are taking hostages.... Continue working."* Some minutes later the anxious employees receive another news ticker: *"Alert: Terrorists in Building C are threatening to blow up the entire complex ... company negotiators have been sent in ... Continue working."* People become more tense in the cubicles. Finally, a third news ticker appears on the screen: *"Alert: The Microsoft Corporation is pleased to announce that we have acquired the terrorists.... Continue working."* We'd like to think that maybe the Silicon Valley giants had been reading up on our OBM strategies. This chapter reveals another powerful strategy for dealing with oppositional-defiant types in our classroom, neighborhood, department . . . and, uh, perhaps in our marriages?

Quick and Uncommon Intervention

First, let's back up a bit and talk practicality. A good front line of intervention to any of these situations might be the application of direct authority: *"Hey, you! Listen up! Stop doing that—and do this instead."* As pointed out in Chapter 1, why use some fancy complex intervention when you have total control and overwhelming decisive power? Well, a fact of the teaching business is that we often have far less raw power in the classroom than we think. We don't work with court restraining orders, traffic citations, or cruise missiles. Besides, when we lose our cool and "go ballistic" on these classroom insurgents, they'll just take hostages somewhere else. We just don't have enough real power to make power ploys a good option. Instead, let's try to think out of the crate. Imagine the unconventional OBM teacher as a highly trained "lone commando"—maybe like Rambo, Norris, or Lara Croft. This quirky operative must go into the classroom jungle on a special mission where other teachers and counselors have repeatedly failed. The task is to get in without arousing defenses, make radical changes in the student's behavior, and then get out before he can muster the usual defenses . . . or even before he knows what happened.

Good News for Tantrum Sufferers!

We have found that the assignment of "practice tantrum sessions" has generated quick (almost immediate) deceleration of the problematic behavior. These little training sessions have also enhanced the teacher's sense of confidence and have even preserved the fragile student-teacher relationship. As usual, this OBM strategy avoids any heated confrontations with the terrorist kindergartner or the hostage-taking second grader. You may recall the Israeli government policy: "We don't negotiate with terrorists." Well, rather than confront or negotiate, the OBM teacher *hires* the oppositional student and immediately embarks on a course of supportive "training" for stress management.

I was consulting in a small K–12 school in an isolated high-desert community where you would expect to find an abundance of harmony with the environment and inner tranquility. Not so. A new teacher at that school was about ready to surrender and seek out more peaceful work at a prison or trauma center. Her career doubts were due to one extremely disruptive third grader who was virtually holding the resource classroom hostage with daily tantrums. After observing one of little Sergio's fits, I was already considering residential treatment options. This kid rejected any imposed structure (e.g., "do this worksheet") and would flash-storm into sudden violent tantrums in which he would dump work materials, tear up his paper, and throw himself on the floor kicking and crying. Remember, this was a third grader, not a preschooler. He also had a habit of screaming, "I hate you! I hate you!" at the top of his lungs while barricading himself under a table (i.e., where no one could reach him!) and even doing some impressive head banging if he had an audience.

Our Clinical Studies Show ...

Fast forward a bit: After only about one week, Sergio's daily tantrums had been totally extinguished and he was freed up to develop some more civilized means of resistance. Our neophyte teacher proved to be one of the brighter lights on the tree. She was one of those OBM naturals who received only a few minutes of consultation on the "practice tantrums" thing and promptly orchestrated some major changes in a student's life. Below are the general steps that have been repeatedly applied in school settings.

How To Do the "Practice Tantrums" Intervention

1. Reframe the problem:

Instead of focusing on Sergio's resistance and tantrums, the teacher expressed to him her concern that he had "too much pressure inside," just like a shaken bottle of cherry cola. She then tactfully explained that all his mental pressure was probably the reason for those inconvenient explosive episodes. (Yes, an idea lifted—with permission—from Chapter 6.) She may have gone on to declare that little Sergio "was being way too hard on himself" (Chapter 4, item 2 of the Big Three), which would have allowed even more empathetic concern.

2. Prescribe the solution:

Whenever there is too much pressure bottled up in your 2-litre psyche, it's a good idea to find some controlled "release" for that pressure. The teacher told Sergio that she would allow him "pressure release" practice time each day for one full week. Because it seemed there were already some behaviors that worked for him (i.e., the tantrums), why not use them to help solve the problem? In short, Sergio was told he would be given some practice tantrum sessions each day.

3. Design the curriculum:

The teacher didn't have any of our convenient materials, so she sat down with a ruler and felt-tip marker and worked out a practice chart. This grid listed several necessary practice behaviors that were slightly diluted versions of the real thing:

Making and holding a mean facial expression, tearing up a piece of junk mail and throwing it forcefully into a waste basket, while screaming "I hate you" in a loud voice ten times; next, lying on the floor and kicking the cement block wall ten times; and then sitting under a work table and hitting himself on the head with a rolled-up piece of newspaper while crying out like there was terrific pain. (Hey, sounds to me like the mosh pit at a punk rock concert.)

Anyway, for each target behavior, Sergio would receive an evaluation (and point credits) according to how "real" his performance looked. There was even the offer of some bonus points if he could add a little something extra or spicy into the practice behaviors. At the end of the week, his points would be tallied and he could use them to purchase some fantastic reward (well, sort of fantastic). And of course, the whole program could be "held over" for additional days if more of that gastric pressure needed to be released.

4. Operate the program:

As part of his next counseling session, I arranged for the regular classroom to be empty and invited Sergio's teacher to help us with a "planning session." After reviewing his need for a pressure release, we explained the target behaviors and briefly demonstrated each one. We then had bewildered Sergio role-play one entire practice tantrum! Some of his efforts were heartily praised, and others were critiqued. He was also reminded of the really cool reward he might be able to earn. Note to advertising rookies: If you convince a kid that some agreed upon reward is "really cool," it becomes "really cool."

During the following week, this somewhat confused little kid reluctantly practiced his tantrums for part of the morning recess period. Almost magically, his spontaneous "real" tantrums declined on the first day. I arrived at his school the week after for the next counseling session and was told that Sergio had performed no real tantrums for 2 days. He was also refusing to do his prescribed practice session.

5. Terminate the program with an "open door":

Somewhere in the middle of the first week, Sergio began to resist doing his practice tantrums. *(Note: He claimed that they looked foolish and wasted his work time!)* The OBM teacher feigned some concern that the pressure-release plan might fail if not carried out properly for the full week. She then made a private deal with Sergio to allow him to skip his regular practice sessions if he didn't feel "in the mood" and would rather just go out to recess. However, in exchange, he must promise to do some "excellent" practicing in the regular class setting if the right kind of mood came over him. The teacher worked out a secret signal (Remember Chapter 2?) for Sergio to give her if he felt the urge to do some "practicing." It was also decided that whenever Sergio began to look upset, angry, or nervous, the teacher would find the checklist and could call for some immediate pressure-release practice.

Long-Term Recovery Work for the Ex-Tantrumer

Notice how smooth this termination is? We all know that "old habits die slowly," and it was just a matter of time before little Sergio got the itch to tantrum again. When that happened several days later, our OBM teacher just pulled out the clipboard with the evaluation grid. She quietly approached Sergio and whispered for him to "do a really excellent job on this one" so he could earn the maximum credits for each listed behavior on her homemade chart. Interestingly, the teacher also coached Sergio to make sure he was "really in the mood" before attempting a classroom tantrum. If his mood wasn't full blown, she suggested that he delay the tantrum until he could do it justice.

One Day at a Time

As luck would have it, I walked into the classroom sometime later and found Sergio backslid to his old ways. He was under the table again, and the teacher was looking for the clipboard. I popped my head under the table and asked if he was in the mood to do a "serious" tantrum. In his own oppositional manner, he shouted, *"No!"* and returned to thumping the back of his head against the table leg. I agreed with him. *"You're right about that. You're still in too good a mood for this. Do you want to wait ... or just go ahead and try one anyway?"* He still said nothing but just sat there with a grim, contorted expression. I waited awhile and then added, *"The teacher can still give you a couple of points even if it's just a wimpy job ... but we've got to get it done now, before the bell."* Poor Sergio kicked out at a table leg, folded his arms across his chest, and slumped back against the wall. The kid was still stubborn and oppositional, but he was coming to see himself as a tantruming has-been, an 8-year-old failure in the fit-throwing business. I guess all that pressure got leaked out somehow. Anyway, Sergio refused to talk. We suggested that he just sit there under the table for a while and try to work up a genuine angry mood. The class returned to other matters. Some minutes later, the bell rang and Sergio climbed out from under the table and lined up for the cafeteria. We thought this might be a good time to use "planned ignoring."

In follow-up consultations with the OBM teacher I learned that Sergio was nominally compliant during the remainder of the semester. Our rookie teacher was smiling again and back in control of the classroom. To my knowledge she never turned in her Peace Corps application and may still be teaching in some blissful desert community. Following are a few suggestions left with this heroic educator for maintaining Sergio's gains:

Enhancing Your Practice Sessions

1. Daily prognostications and friendly wagers:

In the morning, ask the student to make a prediction as to whether he will "get in the mood" for a good spontaneous practice session. You might suggest a friendly wager, and always bet against the student's prediction.

2. Audio- or videotapes:

Do all the permission stuff ahead of time and then inform the student that you intend to tape his next efforts at practicing a spontaneous tantrum in class. You might pave the way by also taping some of his private practice sessions during recess. I prefer videotapes because they make a wonderful graduation present when you pull them out of storage in a few years. You might even send one in to *America's Funniest Home Videos*. Better yet, save some of them until your oppositional student grows up, becomes a highly visible political figure, and might be motivated to buy them back. (Of course, there's also a good chance he'll grow up to become a Mafia leader. That could make the sell-back negotiations more delicate.)

Anyway, these tapes can always be reviewed and further critiqued in a future counseling session. Some of the "classics" can also be sent home and the parent asked to rate how "real" the episode appeared to be. Audiotapes are also good for send-home reviews.

3. Peer review panel:

Assemble a panel of classmates to observe a live demonstration tantrum (i.e., like the ones they have endured all year) and vote on whether it should earn any credits for authenticity. Consider a show-of-hands vote right in the classroom.

4. Peer demonstration role-plays:

During the introductory phase, ask one or more peers to role-play how the target student typically "does" his tantrum thing. This may be even more revealing than a teacher demonstration. Ask the oppositional student to comment on how well the other classmates were able to capture the style and essence of his genuine tantrums. As usual, the teacher should avoid any spells of hysterical laughter.

5. Tantrum permits:

Check out Chapter 11 for some hints on how to sell time-limited permits for "doing" various classroom disruptions. These flashy permits also make great stocking stuffers and party favors!

Final Thought

Any time you have a student who throws a classic temper tantrum, you have a brittle and vulnerable kid. These guys are both spoiled and neglected at the same time. Such a kid is crying out for someone to care enough to set some limits and boundaries ... or even a practice program. This is a great place to start your OBM career! To help get things rolling, we've provided a Practice Tantrums evaluation chart. Simply list some safe but doable tantrum behaviors, and you are well on your way to the OBM practice field.

PRACTICE TANTRUMS!

Student: _____   Start date: _____

Practice times: _____   _____

Behaviors	Monday	Tuesday	Wednesday	Thursday	Friday
1.					
2.					
3.					
4.					
5.					
Totals:					

Daily Rating Codes:

S = 10 points: Satisfactory (looks & sounds real!)

S– = 5 points: Wimpy job, but acceptable

U = 0 points: Unsatisfactory (not believable)

Teacher Comments:

184   © 2007 by PRO-ED, Inc.

Figure 7.1. Practice Tantrums!

Practice Tantrums

Quick Summary Notes

1. **Reframe the Problem:**
   Provide some working metaphor that explains why a problem behavior occurs. I like the soda bottle pressure idea.

2. **Prescribe a Solution:**
   In our chapter example, the solution is "pressure release" work. You may think of other practice justifications (e.g., trying to get in touch with that frustrated inner child of the past).

3. **Design a Curriculum:**
   Use our convenient form (Figure 7.1) or make up your own. The items on this checklist should be similar to the components of tantrums usually seen in the classroom.

4. **Operate the Program:**
   Better start with a teacher demonstration and some guided role-playing to help clarify each tantrum item. How about some softening of the more disruptive elements ... Hey, it's your call. Then just run the practice trials (privately) like any other individual learning activity.

5. **Terminate the Training:**
   Better review the details of various terminations. Every situation is different. You might decide on a gala graduation party, a private decision to gradually quit, or even a secret signal to do helpful follow-up work.

Figure 7.2. Practice Tantrums: Quick Summary Notes

[This is a note received in the classroom mail drop.]

Dear Ms. Martinez:

Well, it happened again during lunch break. Lucy and her friends started in on me and my anger went up to about 8 or 9. Thanks to your quick angry-feelings practice session in the gym, the pressure dropped off (to about 4) and I didn't get in any trouble ... and best of all, I didn't get any warts on my ears like you were afraid I might get! These new practice sessions are sure working, and I just wanted you to know. Also, I don't think you are strange or weird, honest.

—(Name withheld)

Figure 7.3. Dear Ms. Martinez

8 Zero Tolerance Policies

Getting Impossibly Tough—on Incredibly Small Behaviors

For those smiling faces among us who are permanent residents in the concrete operational stage, the whole idea of "zero tolerance," or ZT, may seem very standard and predictable. Such gentle folks no doubt pair ZT with the standard school district policy that lists all those really, really bad behaviors that sure enough need to be squelched. The resulting mental images may include elements such as sirens, handcuffs, and the Miranda Act. For our special education jockeys, there may be additional imagery, such as a joyful gathering called a Manifestation Determination or perhaps a spirited discussion of a 45-day "interim alternative" place of suffering for the violator. After all, any zero-tolerance policies must be set up to bust the very worst offenders among us, right?

Well, yes and no. As usual, this being OBM, we like to put a slightly different spin on things. If anyone is listening, we like to remind them that OBM methods are specifically intended for managing the chronic resistance of oppositionally impaired students. We're always glad to let the SWAT team do whatever they do with their customers. We just like to do our thing where it applies.

Distraction Methods and Trickle-Down Management

The OBM brand of zero tolerance works in two ways, and we need to have you listen up here, because it gets kind of deep (or not):

1. Basic distraction: One powerful item in our bag of old Jedi mind tricks (Appendix F) is something called "mental distraction." While ordinary school district ZT policies are intended for straightforward behavior control, ours are actually designed to relentlessly target a few tolerable, even easily ignorable, behaviors in the classroom. And why do that, you ask? Answer: By becoming incredibly tough on some quirky little social foible, the OBM teacher strategically takes control of many other expected normal activities (like class work). Instead of demanding rule compliance or harping on work production, the teacher goes ballistic on proper posture, clean fingernails, or use of blue ink only. The confused students are lectured mercilessly, reminded and hassled, prompted and monitored—all about some insignificant left-field behavior. This distraction ploy may actually generate some useful neurotic symptoms as the whole "difficult" class finds itself busy avoiding some little behavior and becoming a bit paranoid about the mild consequences attached to it. Of course, there's also less energy and time remaining for your challenging students to do their usual resistance of the bigger stuff.

2. Trickle-down behavior management: Okay, so everyone is up to speed on distraction. But there's something else in the package. Our ZT strategy can actually help target some of your pet-peeve behaviors. You don't have to make up strange target behaviors—just look deep inside and discover which of those student quirks offend you the most. Sure, you'd like to maintain general civility and productivity in class. If you are blessed with a bunch of oppositional types, you'd also like to reduce the excuse making, whining, and sour attitudes. But don't be seduced with those obvious goals. Remember, first seize total control of something small, and then let your iron-fisted command of the minuscule trickle down to other more worthy behaviors. Let's suppose you are mildly offended with paper trash on the floor, unbridled yawning in class, or even ragged edges of notebook paper. One or more of these could easily become your ZT goal. Somewhere within the vast spectrum of student imperfection lie many potential nit-picky target behaviors. *Hmm ... what to do ... what to do ...*

Choosing a Low-End Target Behavior

Let's stay with the trickle-down idea for a while. You need to choose a good start-up behavior for your program. Major disruptions certainly command our attention, but those lesser irritants slip in and out of awareness like a demented mosquito loose in the RV. Only when we get buzzed again, do we remember how very much we are bothered. Only when we are having our own bad hair day, do we vow vengeance on the mildly disgusting behaviors. These stressful times cause us to lapse into a brief paranoid episode. We remind ourselves that those students who cultivate such repertoires of vile little quirks are the same caste of self-willed individuals who may be bent on seizing control of our class! For an afternoon, we declare total war on nail biting, pencil tapping, messy desks, and those whine-aholics.... Ah, but then tomorrow comes, and the grass is growing and the birds are tweeting, and it's payday. We call a truce with the mild aggravations of the classroom and let them drone on in peace. And so it goes until that headache returns.

Values Clarification

Okay, so we're not talking about those big-time conduct problems that demand a fancy functional behavior assessment. Our down-home response to the roller coaster of tolerance and irritation begins with some quick values clarification. What's important to me? What's worth the energy of confrontation? How much can I live with and still remain a semirational person? How much of the semester is left? It will have to be your call. You have to decide where to draw a line in the sand. Is Weird Harold's tall-tale telling a genuine disruption to the learning process? Do little Ernie's unsolicited jokes and sick comments trample your leadership? When you decide that some bothersome student behavior is your own "issue," then simply let it go. In fact, you might want to box up all your dark "personal issues" and Fed Ex the lot of 'em to Dr. Phil or even John Bradshaw. Alternatively, when you are convinced that certain high-frequency behaviors are beyond normal toleration, you might be ready to make your formal zero tolerance declaration.

Because this particular strategy was aimed at small, unwanted, and highly visible irritations, it was proposed that we code our procedure as the ZIT (Zero Infraction Tolerance Program). To make a long story bearable, our first public use of the ZIT treatment methods generated a massive outcry from the Association of Cosmetically Challenged National Educators. We were virtually forced to modify the name to its present form.

Back to Zero Tolerance

Remember those *Miami Vice* guys waging war on the Colombian drug lords? Back then, I recall some effort to establish a zero-tolerance drug policy for all incoming vessels and vehicles. As I understand it, the deal was that *any amount* of illegal drugs discovered on a yacht or airplane could result in immediate seizure of that fancy piece of hardware. The intended message was: Don't bring any of that stuff to our shores. Small amounts would be treated as large amounts. No warnings or second chances would be given. Monitoring and enforcement would be consistent, and stiff penalties would be handed down like predictable clockwork. You know this idea was too rational and simple to last very long. But if it had, we can bet there would have been some serious behavior modification at all levels of the dope business.

Teachers who declare and consistently use zero tolerance almost always make some waves, take heat, and maybe even survive to see changes in class behavior. In fact, I have seen local schools where certain disruptive behaviors are routinely winked at in all classrooms except one. Somewhere, there is that one teacher who tenaciously defends a personal policy that prohibits "gross behavior X," which is probably her pet peeve. As students navigate through the day, they automatically delete that gross behavior in only one classroom. Now *that's* discrimination learning. Following are some items to consider when selecting a ZT policy:

1. Choose worthy target behaviors
As always, you should submit the intended target behavior to personal tests of practicality. Can you live with it? Does it prevent learning? Does it erode your leadership? Does it give you the creeps? Remember to start with some mild behaviors and watch for the distraction and trickle-down effects.

2. Consider alternative interventions
Some very worthy target behaviors may not be appropriate for this particular strategy. Even though they are relatively mild, they just aren't public enough to fit a classroom-wide ZT plan. Hopefully, we have convinced you that there are dozens of other creative strategies for managing oppositional behavior. If not, keep turning the pages to find a better strategy.

3. Define ZT behaviors that can't be easily disputed
This gets back to the old "observability" requirement from the days when you used to be more conscientious in writing your instructional

objectives. A ZT policy for "bad attitude" or "gross noises" would most likely result in endless arguments and self-justification speeches. Because a class full of difficult students will always generate some reflexive debating, why not apply the "rational person" test. If a panel of "rational observers" were to witness the vile prohibited act, would they agree it had occurred? Perhaps you might locate some of these rational-type observers to be judges in your classroom? I personally like the "dictator observer" test, which gives the teacher a bit more control: *"If I see it, hear it, or even if I imagine I did ... then it happened. You are immediately busted. Period ... no appeals."*

4. Select mild behaviors that are a chronic nuisance

As we discussed earlier, the school district already has ZT on sinister felony acts (e.g., hot-wiring the principal's '65 VW bus for a lunchtime joy ride, or sending out fake termination letters to the entire faculty). But you know that this OBM strategy works best when aimed at lesser offenses (e.g., using certain unlaundered reflexive language or even attempting a helpless "I can't" message). Just keep in mind that these are not the hard-core behaviors that result in 45-day suspensions—they are just the irritants that go on (and on) like a rainy day.

5. Select consequences that are fully controlled by the teacher

As we've heard from the venerated sages of the teachers' lounge, *"Don't make threats that you can't deliver."* Ideally, the consequence should be unavoidable, assigned quickly, and be easily accessible by the teacher (e.g., loss of one point from a behavior chart, assigned 1-minute increments of recess delay, confiscation of some ordinary schoolwork item). We've had good luck with response-cost token economies where one "ticket" is the automatic fine for any ZT violation. Basically, keep your penalties simple and personally convenient.

6. Consequences should be mild and repeatable

Because we are suggesting target behaviors with a moderate frequency (e.g., chair squeaking, social etiquette foibles, forgetting key tasks, selected gross acts), it is important to have designated consequences that can be repeated 20 or 200 times a day if needed. They should allow the student to remain engaged in learning and cause little disruption to the classroom routine. A rule of thumb might be that a good consequence (e.g., making a canned statement, gesturing toward the student, marking on a lesson book, placing a tally mark on a chart, pulling one ticket from an envelope) should not require more than 10 seconds of the teacher's time.

Remember, these mild consequences are not intended to cause great pain or isolation from society. Rather, I see them as a "response interruption"—just enough hassle to momentarily stop the behavior, let the student know he was nabbed, convince the teacher that she has influence, and provide an easy "reset button" so he can start over. As you might guess, I have some personal OBM-type favorites.

For example, as a teacher-friendly assigned consequence, I like to require that the ZT policy violator close his eyes and count *"out loud in your head"* to any number above 10. (If he feels particularly penitent, he is invited to mentally count to some higher number that better reflects his sense of remorse.) Assuming no one else in class can hear your student counting in his head, the consequence remains nondisruptive. These crafty mental consequences seem to be less disruptive to the class routine than our old penalty of requiring the violator to stand on his left foot and clap his hands over his head 10 times.

As another mild, immediate, repeatable consequence, we may require the student to close his eyes (or keep them wide open) and imagine having a large, messy, banana cream pie pushed into his face. The repeat offender who doesn't seem to profit from experience might be required to close his eyes and imagine having a smelly bucket of slimy swamp water dumped on him, or perhaps falling suddenly into an ice-water dunk tank, or even some guided imagery of himself getting sick in the cafeteria and vomiting all over his clothes. Here's where Appendix E might be interesting reading. You also have permission to skip ahead to Chapter 14 and browse through our consequences card deck.... Second thought, better stay with us on this one.

The best thing about our mild-mannered consequences is the shock effect, without all that cleanup work. The busted student grins or grimaces, rolls his eyes, puts up with the teacher's inane consequence, and gets reset, back to business. He may even be haunted by that disgusting word picture. Later in life he will recall that the OBM teacher did indeed have the last word. You might also remind the penitent student that he has to *pretend* to *put up with* the mental consequences—to avoid losing any minutes from lunch break.

Getting Started with Your Zero Tolerance Policy

It's basically simple. Once you have your ducks in a row, call a formal class meeting. Some teachers may prefer to enlist a gifted student as the old-English "town crier" to walk around the classroom in period costume ringing a bell and doing the "Hear ye, Hear ye" routine. Personally, I worry about teachers who go that far to call a class meeting. Anyway, explain to the class that an important new policy will soon go into effect regarding your pet-peeve behavior. Be prepared to demonstrate the exact disgusting behavior in question (along with any suggested substitute behavior). Also demonstrate how your swift, unavoidable, but mild consequence will be meted out *for each and every violation*.

Sneaky Trick #1

Introduce the ZT policy as a short-term trial (e.g., for the rest of the day or week) rather than for ever and ever. You can always extend, modify, or terminate the policy at the end of the trial period. Isn't that what they do with temporary taxes, surcharges, and mill levy deals?

Sneaky Trick #2

Because your ZT policy is aimed at some chronic but mild misbehavior, take the liberty of adding "arbitrary and capricious" methods of evaluation that legitimize your lighthearted dictatorial powers. To cut through the whining and chatter, announce that the decision to fine violators will lean to the excessive, strict, and "impossible to please" side.

Sneaky Trick #3

Rather than ending with a pep talk and some pedantic encouragement to avoid the annoying little behavior in question, why not do the opposite? Wear one of those badge-a-minute buttons that grimly states: MAKE MY DAY. Encourage students to "get sloppy" and "take the fall" as early casualty examples of the ZT policy. Predict that there will probably be a good crowd at today's lunch detention gathering. You might even set up a role-play demonstration of how a violation will be handled. Bottom-line wisdom: Keep a gamelike climate as you go after your ZT hit list of mild nuisance behaviors.

Okay, enough abstraction. Following is some sample rhetoric to get you into the concrete. Take a look at our ZT script and the fairly "directive" ZT poster on the following pages.

Zero Tolerance Script

Picture the OBM teacher standing before the class with her standard grim reaper expression. She is prepared to show the ZT notice. The bold information looks something akin to that on an old-west "Wanted" poster—or maybe it's printed in wild fonts on neon green card stock. The award-winning spiel goes something like this:

"Class, I've always believed that language arts is an exciting adventure in learning. It truly deserves our highest respect ... yak, yak, yak ... Therefore, I'm beginning a new policy that will be strictly enforced through next Friday. The next time I introduce our assignment for the day, there will be no groaning, mournful sighs, or cute hissy fits. If I hear any of these rude things—or even if you do anything that remotely suggests to me you're the least bit unhappy—you'll win a helpful reminder. For each violation, you will earn yourself 30 seconds waiting after class so you can meditate on the joy of learning. This is a Zero Tolerance policy, which means no warnings or second chances. [The teacher holds up the colorful poster for all to see and then staples it to the corkboard.]

"Now, just between us, I'm expecting I'll need to monitor at least half a dozen students who will be stuck here after class. These are the kids who will be meditating on alternative behavioral options while everyone else splits for lunch. If you feel lucky, go ahead and plan a good moan when we move into our lesson ... [long pause as the teacher scans the little faces]."

"Well, then, ... Hey, gang, guess what? It's time once again for language arts! That's right. Take out your textbook and your workbook. Turn to Chapter 7 in the textbook, which is on page 104."

The teacher intently and deliberately scans the class for any thinly veiled signs of unhappiness and matter-of-factly "awards" 30-second meditation opportunities where needed. A similar script might be used for announcing a ZT policy for absurd behaviors (i.e., the distraction control strategy). Try inserting such behaviors as yawning, nervous blinking, pencil tapping, or even "whispering out loud in your mind."

Figure 8.1. Zero Tolerance Script

NOTICE

There Will Now Be

ZERO TOLERANCE

for These Behaviors:

with Immediate Consequences for Any Violation

© 2007 by PRO-ED, Inc. 185

Figure 8.2. Notice

Zero Tolerance Policy

Summary of Key Concepts

1. **Choose Your Target Behaviors Wisely:**
   If you are targeting real nuisance behaviors, they should be the mild, chronic, gross type. If you are targeting "distraction" behaviors, they might as well also be the mild, chronic, gross type.

2. **Explain ZT Policy Before Starting:**
   In a new heroic effort to weed out these inane despicable acts, there will now be an immediate penalty assigned whenever a ZT behavior occurs in class. Capricious teacher judgment is final.

3. **Select Teacher-Friendly Consequences:**
   Plan to assign dozens of ZT penalty consequences—and enjoy doing it. These should therefore be low-effort, mild, repeatable, non-disruptive, and fully teacher controlled.

4. **Develop an Irrational Obsession with ZT:**
   If you are using the "distraction" control method, ZT becomes much more than the teacher's program—it's a full-blown neurotic disorder. Stamping out those petty target behaviors in class must (appear to) become the teacher's central life quest. Her eyes become glassy, her voice pitch escalates, and you simply can't reason with her about the ZT behaviors.

Figure 8.3. Zero Tolerance Policy: Summary of Key Concepts

[This note was received in the classroom mail drop.]

Dear Ms. Stewart,

I'm really not sure what's going on around here. You've got some really strange class rules, and it's making me and my friends confused. Like what's the big problem with crumbling up paper when we want to throw it away? And why do we have to breathe through our mouth during worksheet times? I lost three tickets already, and I'm starting to get nervous when I come into your class. Everybody is so worried about all these crazy new rules that there's hardly any fun time to monkey around. I just thought you might want to know about this problem.

(Name withheld)

Figure 8.4. Dear Ms. Stewart

9 Paradoxic Restraint from Positive Changes

Creative Ways To Punish Progress

What happens when you sincerely try to encourage an oppositional student to improve his attitude or behavior? Correct! You get knee-jerk resistance. Okay then, what happens if you just sit down with the oppositional student and try to convince him through logical or moral argument that he needs to get with the program? Correct again. You get more knee-jerk resistance. Well, then, what happens if you fall down on one knee, clasp your hands together, and plead with the student to change his ways? Also correct. You get *both* hysterical laughter *and* knee-jerk resistance. Notice any recurring theme here? These kids are programmed at the factory to resist, obstruct, and dispute. Why do we keep expecting that the old standard warnings and lecture methods will suddenly reach them? It might help a little if we try looking at our oppositional-defiant students as handicapped kids who just don't get it.

Warning of Negative Outcomes

Hopefully, we've learned something here. With these kids, we need to work smarter, not harder (memorize OBM Principle #3 from Chapter 1). Often when I see an oppositional student having a semi-decent day. I use that as an opening for paradoxic restraint. I have a brief visit with the student and try to establish a kind of coach-to-player exchange. While maintaining a rather serious demeanor, I express concern that there may be a downside to any improved behavior at school. In fact, this student might just as well be warned that rapid behavioral improvements can generate a host of negative outcomes. Such an announcement usually gets his attention, and then I follow up with "*... and I'm only telling you this for your own good.*" This kind of wornout phrase is usually helpful for getting his ears perked up and pushing him to find something to resist. For a moment, hearken back to grand old OBM Principle #4: Confusion is almost as good as compliance.

Let's also pause here for just a second and reconsider the psychological profile we have established for this oppositional student. It's like one of those basic laws of Newtonian physics: Any pull in one direction will tend to generate an equal and opposite pull in the other direction. Is this pretty close? Rather than patting him on the back and kindly saying, "*Thanks for selling out to the socially sanctioned authorities and finally embracing the proper goals of education,*" I try to artfully do the opposite. When you apply this paradoxic restraint method, remember that any sign of patronizing condescension or even the slightest smirk on your face will shoot a 12-gauge hole in the bottom of your canoe! But you knew that ...

Problems with Success

Suppose you just won the $10,000,000 that Ed McMahon was promising everyone a few years ago. If we really pushed ourselves, we might actually be able to generate a list of problems that could come with your good fortune (e.g., taxes, con artists, decadence, newfound stupidity, discovery of dubious long-lost relatives, and the magnification of all your moral defects). Stop dreaming. In the same way, it becomes your job to brainstorm plausible problems that could result if your stubborn little student buddy decided to straighten up and fly right.

I have actually used some of the items below with impressionable mid-school bad guys, but the same kind of warnings could be crafted for 3rd graders or high school juniors. Please note that each "problem" paraded before them is actually a hidden benefit—deliberately presented as dreadfully negative. Also, be aware that a good discussion of this list tends to induce a light trance state as the student drifts in and out of his imagination and "tries on" your fantasy predictions. Smooth, very smooth. Now put yourself in Wild Willie's place. Suppose, for some reason, he has just completed two days of fairly decent classroom performance. You have noticed his modest trend toward acceptable behavior and you decide to stage a brief visit to strategically restrain any future progress. We hope you will enjoy the sample OBM miniscripts below:

You Better Watch Out for This "Success" Stuff Because ...

"A lot of your old 'bad news' friends may drift away from you. They may even get into some serious trouble on their own, without you being anywhere around. You may be the last to know what happened when you hear they got busted for something. The police may not even consider you as one of the usual suspects anymore. Hey, that's like being totally forgotten ... what a bummer ..."

"As you improve more and more at school, think of how you're going to handle it when people start to bug you to join their clubs and activities. What about when the coaches and faculty sponsors start to invite you out for sports? Might as well kiss all your free time good-bye."

"Think of your new reputation and all those new friends starting to like you. It can be a real drag. It can also take a lot of energy to just walk down the hall every day and have to say hi back to so many other students. Sometimes you'll wish all those kids didn't like you ... just to get some peace and quiet."

"Some kids just like you who have improved too quickly got really embarrassed when teachers started liking them. You know, waving, saying hi, joking around with you in class. If you're not used to it, that kind of teacher attention can be real difficult."

"I've also known guys like you who insisted on too much school improvement. The next thing they knew, a lot of nice-looking girls started to notice them. One fellow started getting notes in his locker from two

different girls . . . and that led to all kinds of problems. You really have to be aware of the personal stress that can happen if you keep going like this."

"You know, there's probably a few good things out there in your future that you'll have to give up if this behavior improvement stuff continues. You might decide to stay around and graduate from high school . . . not drop out. If you stay in school, you'll miss a lot of good stuff. Think of all those really cool guys who got expelled or dropped out already . . . with all that free time on their hands. All day long they can just sit alone at home . . . kick back and play video games or watch soaps, while hundreds of other kids have to hang out together here at school."

"Think of it. If you quit school early, you could even get a head start on finding some kind of a minimum-wage job . . . and just settle into it for life. Everyone else would have to wait till they graduated or went to college. You could earn maybe several hundred bucks—before all the other kids graduate with their fancy diplomas. You might even save enough to buy some old car, fix it up, and then try to keep it running for the rest of your adult life. Who says you have to graduate to survive? As long as you're happy with fewer things, you don't need to earn as much money as all your friends who graduate. I sure wouldn't cave in to all that success talk from your friends who plan to stay and graduate . . . They're maybe trying to hold you down . . ."

"You've got to stop and think of 'lifestyle quality.' Don't let peer pressure force you to stay in school when you can drop out, walk the streets alone, and really be somebody special. Yes, I can tell you've got a lot to think about before you get all caught up in some kind of new self-improvement and personal success behavior."

"By the way, have you thought what too much improvement (too quickly) could do to your parents at home? All these sudden changes might be too much for your dear old mom to bear. She doesn't have a heart condition or anything, does she? I've heard of parents who had kids improve too quickly . . . They get some kind of nervous spells . . . I think they call them anxiety attacks . . . That's what can happen if parents aren't prepared. You need to go a lot slower. Have you given any kind of warning to your parents? Can you imagine the kind of confusion they might have as they talk about all your new improvements when you're not around? What are they supposed to say to all the neighbors and the other family members who are used to hearing about your problems? What about your little sister? Isn't she used to being the only good student in the family? We have to consider how she might handle all these sudden changes."

Okay, you get the idea. There are dozens of possible warnings about "too much" or "too sudden" success. Keep in mind that you are planting seeds for future pensive thought. You are crafting fantasy daydreams that are ten times more compelling than straight-on pedantic lectures. This is especially true with our early-adolescent oppositional-defiant students. All the while you are embedding these (let's call them what they are) "hypnotic suggestions," you are employing simple everyday language that seems to discourage any positive changes. Hmmm.

How's that stubborn student supposed to resist your ideas? Should he relent? Should he abandon whatever benefits he is approaching? Should he (choke) *agree* with you that he really should go back to something much less appealing? Do you think he will argue that he is not really worthy of all these fantasy benefits you are waving in front of his face?

Talk about pretzel twisting. Is this slick or what? Sometimes our triumphal OBM teachers have to leave the room, find a safe place, and just laugh hysterically for a few minutes.

Who Will Be Most Upset?

Oppositional kids also tend to be very competitive. A slightly different way to induce a light trance state is to make leading inquiries about who will be most upset to learn of his forthcoming improvements. A host of familiar faces will pop into his head, and he'll want to resist the naysayers. As you make inquiries, be aware of how descriptive language can help carry the student farther into your story. Look back over the past section and notice how I used cautionary success inquiries as a means of creating a success daydream.

Ostensibly, we are just making concerned inquiries about the future. At the same time, we are planting seeds of suggestion—and allowing the oppositional student to make observable, measurable improvements in his school life by resisting our concerns. In the immortal words of the A-Team's Colonel Hannibal Smith, "I love it when a plan comes together."

It may be comforting to know that many of the paradoxic restraint inquiries in this handbook have already gone through rigorous testing at our elite OBM Laboratory School for Oppositionally Gifted Students. This unique school has been established as a freestanding entity within the OBM Institute and serves both severe and profoundly defiant kids (K–12) who are bused to our special school everyday by extremely grateful school districts.

Better check out some of these additional sample inquiries:

"What about your math teacher? Isn't he the guy who had you busted last week in the office? He might have been thinking you were some kind of lowlife who would never amount to anything. How's he going to handle it when all these improvements are connected to your name? That poor man might blow a fuse! It's not easy for a faculty member to lose face like that."

"Your cousins are those older guys who do real well in cross country. I'll bet they don't even give you the time of day now that they've earned their letter jackets. Will they be upset to hear about your new reputation here at the mid-school? You know, it just might cause some serious family problems if your parents started bragging about all your new achievements. I sure hope you know what you're doing . . . "

"Maybe your old buddies will be the most upset to see all these improvements. They might be worried that you'll get stuck up and too cool for them. As you get more and more confident, you might even stay in school and graduate. Probably go on to some kind of college and then get one of those good-paying jobs. I bet they'll think you're going to move right out of the old neighborhood. Can you imagine their reaction? I can just see it a couple of years from now. All your buddies . . . unemployed, hanging around the old neighborhood, just killing time, talking trash, and doing nothing . . . And here comes smooth Lewis, the local success story, cruising by in a tricked-out fire red Corvette—tinted windows rolled up, stereo CD playing—and not even looking at them. You can see why some of these guys might get pretty upset with your new style. You'll have to decide if it's really worth all that trouble to keep improving like you are now."

Remember How Self-Conscious You Used To Be?

Keep in mind that adolescents live out each day performing for an imaginary audience—often an audience that is quite critical. In their private world, they are also convinced that they are discovering deep new emotions and profound original ideas—all never before experienced in human history. It's quite normal for an early adolescent to invest a large portion of his waking hours contemplating his newfound emotional life or how he comes across to his peer audience. This is true of even your most oppositional kids. If you understand this gross egocentricity, your OBM interventions can be deeper, focused, and more effective. Okay, let's all say it together: *"Work smarter, not harder."*

More Cheap Hypnotic Tricks

for Storytelling

For your convenience as a classroom practitioner, we're providing a sample list of everyday-language *trance inductions*. These are some of the common expressions you can use to set up a recurring daydream state for your oppositional student. Remember, "natural hypnotism" is really the master storyteller's craft. If you can tell a colorful, engaging story, you are probably trance-spinner material. Look back over the OBM scripts in this chapter and notice all the places where our strong-willed student is invited to drift off into fantasy land. When communicating with resistant listeners, always seek natural ways to mix some of these phrases into your dialogue:

"Remember when ..."

"Can you imagine ..."

"Oh, yes ... I can see it all right now ..."

"I'm just sitting over here wondering if [when, how, etc.] ..."

"You're probably saying to yourself right now ..."

"As you looked around, I'll bet you saw [felt, remembered, etc.] ..."

"Try to picture what happens when ..."

"You can probably hear those same words right now ..."

"I can only guess how you probably felt when ..."

"I'm just wondering what you'll be saying in your mind as you ..."

"It seems that some kids can replay these events in slow motion and even see [hear, remember, etc.] ..."

Figure 9.1. More Cheap Hypnotic Tricks for Storytelling

Paradoxic Restraint from Positive Changes

Summary Points

When you happen to discover your oppositional student complying with a request (or cooperating, acting civil, etc.), always avoid using direct garden-variety praise. Giving him ordinary verbal praise is like pouring a gallon of cold creek water on your campfire. Don't do it. Hard-core, clinically defiant students may actually be sabotaged by syrupy approval. Instead of that warm smiley stuff, try these OBM strategies instead:

1. **Pedantic warnings:**
    "Better watch out for this success stuff because ..."
2. **Fueling progress with imaginary resistance or competition:**
    "Who will be most upset?"
3. **Hypnotic introspection:**
    Enhance your cautionary talk with internal descriptors that arrest the student's attention with visual color, movement sensations, and feeling words. You have been cleared to review our sampler of attention-controlling setup phrases scattered throughout the chapter.

Figure 9.2. Paradoxic Restraint from Positive Changes: Summary Points

Dear OBM Guys:

I warned one of my oppositional mid-schoolers that his friends might be disappointed if he didn't keep up his "crash-and-burn" patterns in my computer skills class. I also pointed out that the students had begun to expect a few laughs each day when he got busted and that they would probably reject him if they didn't get what they expected. His comment was "It's not my job to provide free entertainment for this class!" He remained an uptight, sour guy, but he certainly knew where to draw the line ... and he didn't get a detention for the rest of the semester.

—Keyboarding teacher

Figure 9.3. Dear OBM Guys

10 Divide and Conquer

Strategic Gang-Busting Techniques

Dealing with G. Khan & Associates

It's hard enough dealing with one obstinate student, but sometimes they run in packs. Teachers find that the resistance and cockiness displayed by one lone student can be multiplied when that student is supported by a cheering audience of tough-guy peers. As a rookie counselor in the schools, I recall trying to go directly into the well-defended back corner of classrooms to break up rowdy cliques. Just like you, I've also attempted to move desks, make examples, and preach on the dangers of "hanging around with the wrong crowd."

Any conclusions? We've all learned that whatever social glue holds these kids together is stronger than our feeble efforts with a verbal crowbar. In fact, sometimes my attempt to break up a local power bloc has actually given them a rallying point and helped to strengthen their resolve to stay together (and make my life miserable). I really do believe in working smarter. So now I try to avoid dousing fires with the proverbial bucket of unleaded premium.

Strategy #1: Pull the Plug on the Leader

Old (*made-up*) Indian saying: "Cut off snake's head and rest of body die soon." Sometimes your difficult students hang together only through the daily maintenance and charisma of a self-proclaimed leader. Actually, this is the easiest scenario for "bloc busting." It requires a mild but methodical and step-wise plan for separating the leader from his gangster constituents. For those behavior technologists among us, the proper term for this strategy has always been *successive approximations*. In our case, the first behavior change goal would be a significant reduction in daily contact between Obstinate Al and his feisty followers. Following are a few potent strategies to weave into your daily teaching activities:

1. Adopt-a-Teacher's-Pet:
Gradually let everyone discover that the gang leader is one of your personal favorites in class. Not his ruffian cronies, just him only ... because he's really special.

2. Selective Blindness:
Generally ignore any of Impossible Al's misbehavior. Better yet, just crack up with laughter at his shenanigans ("Isn't that just the cutest thing? ... yak, yak, gush,

yak"). Of course, you will discount any similar efforts at humor by his lowlife associates (e.g., *"That's just low functioning and disgusting ... Why can't you guys be more like my buddy Al?"*).

3. Token gifts and favors

Frequently bring in curiosities for the big fella (e.g., newspaper clippings, special interest articles). Speaking in front of his outcast buddies, ask Al if he would like you to "put in a good word" for him with some of his other teachers ... Suggest that maybe a few good words will counteract any bad press or even those unfortunate disciplinary write-ups.

4. Blame others

Whenever Mr. Wonderful gets into some kind of scrape, always jump to his defense and immediately redirect blame to his nearby hoodlum friends. If this one seems to ring a not-too-distant bell, that's because it's partially recycled material from our favorite verbal jousting responses (Chapter 4, incredibly slick item #10). Try this little script on for size:

"We all know Al can't be the problem here. He would never do anything foul like this if he wasn't covering up for the rest of you thugs. If I find that you boys are taking advantage of my buddy, I'll dream up one of the worst consequences you've ever had! Al, just let me know if any of these lowlife types try to drag you down into trouble ... I really don't understand how you are able to put up with this crowd ... You must be some kind of a saint or something."

5. Keep little secrets

Try to build up a repertoire of "inside jokes" with Al. Ideally, these should be related to funny anecdotes that his buddies did not experience. Find out some interesting or humorous things about Al's personal life (e.g., his brother's custom Harley, that new pit bull puppy at home, a clever remark he made at the Mensa meeting) and then make oblique eye-winking references to them in class.

6. Backhanded compliments

When your buddy Al does some academic task half right, use his worksheet as an example for the class. *"Hey, everybody, check this out. Your paper should look just like Al's perfect job right here."* Tell his sorry friends that they need to follow Al's sterling example and get with the program. From time to time make comments about how you retold Al's last hysterical story or joke in the teacher's lounge and brought down the house. (You don't need to explain that there was just one gravely ill teacher in the lounge, and she was semicomatose.)

Okay, put yourself in the place of Big Al's disciples. How long are you going to pay homage to this favored peer while he enjoys every privilege in the book and you are left out in the cold? Suppose your whole gang is in a prisoner of war camp (always a good word picture for school) and old Lucky Al keeps getting himself invited up to the commandant's private dining room for the evening meal. You are sitting there spooning cold swill, while Comrade Al is learning to use a lobster fork. Sooner or later, this strategy will pull the plug on the leader.

Strategy #2: Polarize the Gang Factions

Here's one we blatantly lifted from a dozen or more *Mission Impossible* TV episodes. After the smoke cleared from his self-destructed tape recorder, Mr. Phelps would often find himself holding mug shots of rival bad guys from some obscure Balkan state. These guys represented internal factions of an evil political party that was considered an annoyance to the West. Mr. Phelps's secret assignment was to split up the power bloc but without any show of force or embarrassing headlines. You may remember the opening music score and the pictures of each IM Force member being flashed onto the screen? In recent OBM workshops I have used a brief video montage from some opening moments of the original *Mission Impossible* series. This stuff seems to bring burned-out teachers back from the donuts and coffee table. Usually, they're smiling. For those returning promptly, I'd reward that behavior by letting them see one of Mr. Phelps's legendary tape recorder burnouts.

Classroom gang busting may seem like an impossible mission to many teachers. Suppose there is no real charismatic leader to go after (as in our first strategy), but the group is still solid and noncompliant in your classroom. Not to worry here, either. As with your work with Big Al, you will need to apply these innocuous strategies on a methodical and daily basis. It's a very worthy OBM challenge ... *should you decide to accept it.*

The basic plan with a very tight subgroup is to find real or imagined differences in the group that can be magnified and exploited. If the differences become stronger than the commonalties, the group will dissolve—and lose its disruptive power in the classroom. As with other OBM strategies, the teacher is not confrontive and seldom uses raw power. This is increasingly true the older the students are, the more they weigh, and especially when you have to look up to speak to them. Somewhere in this paragraph you'd probably expect me to add the "working smarter" phrase. But I won't, since you're probably already thinking about it. Below are a few polarization strategies. Perhaps you will think of even better ones—and be tempted to mail them to the OBM Institute?

1. Divide Through Language Crafting:

Once you've sized up the group and found some representative factions, casually start to refer to multiple groups (never to one entity). *"Looks like the rappers are sharp today. They're gonna catch you skater jocks if you don't stay focused on this assignment."* Notice how we split the gang simply by directing attention to some obvious differences?

Here are a few more innocent "group splitting" comments:

> *"All you competitive athletes over there who had the coach for social studies last year should be two steps ahead of these other boys."* Note the quiet comparison of "competitive athletes" with "other boys." This one is a wedge ... even if it's not true.
>
> *"Why is it you northside guys always sit over there? Don't you trust these downtown boys? Do you have something against the creative way they spray-paint their skateboards?"*
>
> *"Seems like you three guys are the handsome musketeers of this crowd. What happened to these other fellows? A train wreck or something? How come they're not ... like totally cool ... like you?"*
>
> *"So today we have the jocks over here and the cybertechs right behind them ... no wonder you guys have trouble communicating."*

Notice how this last remark split up a tight group through casual labeling (and again, it doesn't matter if it's inaccurate), and then the teacher had the nerve to toss in the unfounded assumption that they can't communicate. More seed planting. Pretty soon this gang won't even be able to agree on who to bully at lunch.

2. Divide through subgroup competition

In order to have competition, you have to have opposing teams. No one should be too upset if the bad-guy clique is divided up for some classroom competition. By the way, once you have created some teams, why not attach some colorful names to each of them? Later, make reference to individual ruffians as star members (or respected alumni) of specific teams. Throughout the following days find reasons to frequently use the team labels and draw various comparisons between the subgroups. Who knows, the labels might stick. *"Looks like the Northside Buccaneers are leading the Raiders again today. These guys will need to slug it out in the last round of our Science Bowl ..."*

(**Life-saving hint:** Never set up a competition that pits the bad guys [as a united group] against the rest of the free world. You knew that, right?)

3. Divide through spontaneous wagers

Sometimes a friendly wager might help to polarize factions of a tight-knit group. Suppose there are two strong personalities in a gang. It might be interesting to challenge your two young bucks to compete in a foot race, arm wrestling, or their knowledge of Hamlet. (One of these items may not fly.) Make some kind of silly bet and egg on the two sides. Let the champions of each faction strut around and boast a little like those cerebral-elite professional wrestlers. Build up the importance of the competition, and you just might polarize the gang into two or more warring camps.

4. Control through mutual suspicion

Remember that stool pigeon in the *Stalag 17* movie? There was one rotten informant planted among the Allied prisoners, and everyone was kept on edge wondering who it was. The same can happen in school settings among certain groups of difficult students. It's funny how nasty rumors can get started, leaked out, and almost drag a slick gang operation to its knees.

You will remember OBM Principle #4: The next best thing to compliance is bewilderment. When a group of noncompliant students are caught up in confusion and mistrust among themselves, they have less energy available for ruining the teacher's day. They might even settle down and learn something!

The OBM teacher who is able to gather information in one location (even unfounded rumors and gossip at the *National Enquirer* level) and artfully let it leak out in another setting can generate the illusion that there is an "ear" within the gang. Spending some private time with several individual group members can help with the cross-check of rumors, ripple the waters of trust within the group, and give rise to even more suspicion.

Another Compelling OBM War Story

I knew of one stealthy mid-school principal who came to the end of his rope with an in-house gang and decided to "go strategic" (i.e., rather than "ballistic"). Following a weekend vandalism incident, he decided to round up the usual suspects for a mandatory interview that was to be hosted in his office. In preparation for the meeting, he sent all the suspects to an empty classroom where they were told to wait until they were called by the secretary. As the story goes, this inept Columbo-style principal had *forgotten* to turn off the intercom system in that vacant classroom. Bumbling and forgetful as he was, he had left the wall speaker in the silent, "receive" mode. Wouldn't you know it, he had also mistakenly turned on an old tape recorder in his own office where the PA panel was located. You'd have sworn he had some kind of old-folks memory problem—or maybe some rehab training with Matlock & Associates.

During the 15 to 20 minutes these local choir boys were waiting for their interview, their principal learned all kinds of things about the nature of crime on his own campus. He learned about old unsolved incidents, recent ones, and nefarious agendas for the future. He heard angry statements like "Hey, Eddy, you and Rob really stepped in it this time. How could you be so stupid to spray-paint your idiot slogan on the gym wall? That was even more stupid than Randy's flat-tire job on all those busses. Now we're all taking heat ... way to go, you moron!" Of course, Eddy responded with something juicy like "Well, at least I'm not going to take the big fall for you and LeRoy ripping off that raffle ticket money. I'll bet that's really why we're being called in right now."

Our resourceful principal was sitting in his office just smiling and chuckling to himself during most of the dialogue. He pictured himself as a good ol' boy southern sheriff who had just bagged a Winnebago full of intoxicated rock musicians. The grins and coffee sipping continued "business-as-usual" until he heard some more talk like "We don't need to worry about that sorry principal ... He's even dumber than he looks. That loser will believe anything we tell him. You should have seen him eat up that last story about Lenny's history book being loaned to a crippled vet. He's such a jerk. All we need to do is stick together and use the same story ..."

After some spirited pledges to secrecy and threats to any traitors, the boys soon learned from the secretary that they were to return to their classes "because the principal had an urgent call" and was now too busy to see students that day. The following day each boy was summoned to the office for an individual interview. Our "dumber than he looks" principal had watched his share of *Rockford Files, Magnum P.I.,* and *Remington Steele* reruns. Without revealing identities or details in our handbook, I can assure you that this entire mid-school gang was skillfully dismantled and brought to various levels of justice. The point to make here is that each gang member somehow (independently of the others) came to the certain conclusion that he had been sold out by his comrades. Whatever happened to trust?

Final Words

When our difficult students band together, their oppositional traits tend to be magnified. However, gangs and other power blocs all have "built in" vulnerabilities that can be strategically exploited to neutralize their threat to humanity. It's also helpful when we discover interesting skeletons in their closet.

Divide and Conquer

Summary Points

There are two basic approaches to crunching a clique or neutralizing a gang: You can either get rid of the leader or split the rank-and-file members. Here's our flyover summary:

Strategy #1: Pull the plug on the leader
1. Adopt the leader as the teacher's pet.
2. Show selective blindness to the leader's misbehavior.
3. Give token gifts and special favors to the leader.
4. Blame others and defend the leader.
5. Keep little secrets and make inside jokes with the leader.
6. Give backhanded compliments to the leader.

Strategy #2: Polarize the gang factions
1. Divide through subtle language crafting.
2. Divide through subgroup competition.
3. Divide through spontaneous classroom wagers.
4. Divide through mutual suspicion.

Figure 10.1. Divide and Conquer: Summary Points

[Another unedited note taken from the classroom mail drop.]

Dear Ms. Shriver:

Some of us guys were wondering why Donovan is the only one in science class who didn't get busted. Every student in our group did something to bug the substitute. So why was he let go from detention? I'd also like to know why you let Donovan use your computer to do his report while the rest of us had to write ours on paper. Most of us guys used to think that Donovan was the coolest kid in class. He was the one who always started things, and now he's stuck up and gets away with murder around here. It's not really fair. Ryan and I would like to have our desks moved away from him, to the other side of the room.

—(Name withheld pending investigation)

Figure 10.2. Dear Ms. Shriver

11 Wacky Coupons and Behavior Permits

Creating a Bureaucratic Paper Chase

It's a foundational tenet of big government—it's almost "the American Way": If people have a need, find a way to make a federal program out of it. At least write a 3-year grant to study the possibilities. Hey, even if a few people show interest in some new diversion, hobby, or fad, find a way to restrict it, license it, and tax it. Next, get the presses rolling and turn out thousands of pages of confusing fine-print regulations. Might also put a few more attorneys on payroll to help with interpretation.

Before we grumble about cumbersome Big Government methods, let's stop and consider the hidden genius of bureaucratic regulation. We never claimed that OBM strategies make any common sense. Rather, we tend to view them as uncommon sense—the ordinary, rational things are what classroom teachers try *before* they consider our interventions. The present chapter suggests that one alternative way to control a behavior is to regulate it to death. Why not target some silly nuisance behavior and strategically squeeze all the joy out of it—until your strong-willed student concludes that it's just not worth the effort?

OBM Example: Another Outrageous Way To Neutralize the Gang Problem

Many of the disturbed high-risk students seen on the school psychology caseload are inordinately impressed with gang culture. These younger wannabes perceive our local gangs as viable family substitutes. They see the rigors and dangers of gang life to be miles ahead of the sad existence they now face. Somewhere inside they know it's a dead end, but they are drawn like the proverbial moth to a flame. So far, nothing new.

In one of our infamous Friday afternoon supervision sessions, my state-licensed *Far Side* staff was discussing the gang problem—and began to stray into some divergent OBM gang-busting strategies. Some say this eventful session may have simply been a side effect of the strawberry

Twizzlers that were served, but there's no real evidence for that accusation. Here's a recently declassified summary of that staff meeting:

Suppose one of our local mid schools was to concede defeat and publicly surrender to the gangs? (Hardly, but stay with me.) Suppose the administration and staff agreed to open the campus to gangs. In fact, any gang at all could be represented on campus *as long as it was done correctly*. Since we already have fairly accurate lists of each gang's membership, a special "by invitation only" assembly would be called for all legitimate ranked-in gang members to announce the details of opening the campus.

As a modest concession to being welcomed on campus, the punk fellowships would be asked to endorse certain policies. I won't go into detail on all of them, but you can use your imagination—that's all we did. Notice how Big Brother is already gearing up the printing presses in the following examples:

1. Each gang would have to complete a comprehensive application packet and compile a roster of active members on campus (sounds like a bowling league).

2. The school would collect a token registration fee and take photographs for the new gang ID cards. These custom cards would, of course, bear the selected gang colors and emblems *alongside the mid-school name and logo*. Next, gang members could pose for group shots displaying their secret hand signs. These glossy photos would be available for purchase (to give to proud family members) and for later use in the annual gang yearbook.

3. Each gang would select a rehabilitated addict or ex-con as a sponsor (from a prepared list of community volunteers). Of course, it's entirely possible that the approved list might include some narcs.

4. Each gang would be given a designated day when colors would be mandatory for all members. All those black T-shirts and colors jackets would have to be clean and pressed on those days. If not, it would be the same as dising the brothers in the hood. And that's not real healthy.

5. The school would recognize only two types of gangs: Easy Gangs and Tough Gangs. To get recognized on campus as an Easy Gang member, only a simple application form, the small fee, and the ID card would be required.

6. To gain recognition as a Tough Gang member (and who would join any other kind?), there would be a lengthy application and qualification process involving rigorous training in physical fitness, self-defense, urban problem solving and memorizing the code, secret handshake, sing-along theme song, and creative expressions (e.g., barrio calligraphy, tattoos, emblems, decals, pierce jewelry).

7. Weekly meetings would be required for each registered gang, and the leader would have to file a brief written report with the campus Gang Coordinator. A copy of the report would be retained by the Gang Secretary (or some other designated member who was able to read). Special meeting rooms and times would be scheduled, and "security badges" (gang IDs with Velcro fasteners) required to be displayed by all attendees.

8. Each month would have a scheduled (fully videotaped, with continuous color commentary) "reality sport" combat day in the gym fashioned after a mix of paintball, *American Gladiators*, and *Junkyard Wars*. A rumor might be leaked that some government "special ops"

representatives might drop in to look for talent. (You might even enlist a mysterious character to show up in army fatigues and dark glasses.) Every gang would pay a small team entrance fee. The suggestion might be that tough gangs can show their stuff while the "others" lose face and probably have weaknesses to hide.

9. Any gang member having an attitude or behavior problem during competition would be labeled a disgrace to his colors and referred to the gang's own disciplinary committee (and I wouldn't even want to know what happens there!).

10. The academic curriculum would remain basically the same, except that names would be changed (e.g., practical math would be Money Talk, PE would be Street Games, social studies would be Barrio Sociology, shop would be something like Low Rider R&D, and American government would have something to do with landmark criminal defense cases).

11. Each month one gang would designate an ad hoc committee responsible for designing and placing fresh graffiti on selected walls and outdoor campus buildings. Individual gangs would have to raise money (legally, say through bake sales or tattoo-a-thons) to purchase their own paints and materials.

12. Each gang would submit one member's name to the Gang Coordinator for the coveted "Gangsta of the Month" recognition. The winner's smiling face would then be published in the monthly newsletter, "*The Rap Sheet.*" This would be a great photo-op with a brief story covering the boy's gangster career and maybe some cordial poses with his proud mother and her smiling boyfriend. The central picture would show the winner in his gang colors receiving a plaque from the glad-all-over assistant principal and uniformed security personnel.

We could go on and on with ways to institutionalize, emasculate, marginalize, co-opt, and overregulate gangs. The simple goal would be gradually to "squeeze the joy" out of counterculture rebellion. Once the local gangs conceded "a few rules" to the establishment (*believe it or not, flower child, that's us these days*), they would be marked for eventual neutralization. Can you imagine barrio gangs turning into Boy Scout troops and sports teams? Can you imagine kids *dropping out* of gangs—as an act of youthful rebellion? Enough already. Let's get into the meat and potatoes of this classic chapter: the dark side of classroom coupons, tickets, passes, and permits.

Using the Paper Chase To Control Behavior

I think we have made a case for the age-old concept *If you can't beat 'em, regulate 'em.* Suppose little first-grade Horacio is obsessed with tattletales. Every day he makes a dozen spy reports on peers who are "playing too rough," "not sharing the ball," and "talking mean." It seems Horacio is intent on controlling the class by designating poor Ms. Farnsworth as his enforcer. Since this fellow is invested in knowing and using "the rules," he is also a candidate for OBM behavior permits.

Ms. Farnsworth, a portly, mild-mannered elementary teacher—is also secretly a fledgling OBM practitioner! She is uniquely effective in certain OBM methods, simply because no one would ever suspect her deeper strategic motives. She has already attempted to redirect, understand, counsel, and reward Horacio toward more prosocial living. All to no avail. Turning to OBM methods, this teacher will now stop trying to extinguish the tattletale compulsion and begin to license, tax, and regulate it. She has prepared a supply of bright-colored Tattletale Coupons with a catchy graphic and fine-print instructions. A partial script of her private visit with little Horacio follows:

"Hello there, Horacio. I want to thank you for caring so deeply about the behavior of all the students in our class. In order to save time, however, you need to start keeping your mind on only the most important behavior problems. Also, because my time is very limited these days, I'm going to need to charge something for helping you control student behavior. [Note: The teacher maintains a straight face as only that crafty Ms. Farnsworth can do.] I have a supply of coupons here that are each good for reporting on one student. If you needed to tell me about two boys who were fighting, of course, you would need to give me how many coupons? [The bewildered child answers correctly.] That's right, and you would also need to save your coupons for reporting only the most important problems. It would be too bad if you used up all your coupons right away and then you saw someone cutting in line. You wouldn't have a Tattletale Coupon, and so I couldn't listen to that important report. You can only get your coupons in the morning before class, and you can only buy five each day. The way you pay for your supply of coupons is by telling me one good student behavior you saw recently in class. That's it. You'll get your five coupons and be off on a new day of helpful behavior watching."

You get the idea. Ms. Farnsworth could reduce the number of daily coupons in the future. She might also offer some incentive for "saving up" coupons (e.g., spending them on some prosocial activity?). One hidden benefit of coupon therapy is that the student becomes sensitized to how often he performs the target behavior. Who knows, he might even start to hoard his "reporting" episodes. Another fringe benefit is that the particular nuisance behavior has now been given a name and is out on the table for some frank teacher-student dialogue during the day.

Here is a sampling of the wacky coupons we have created for our oppositional students:

Out-of-Seat for No Good Reason Coupon: This is one to collect from the habitual classroom wanderer. Isn't it high time he started paying for those little excursions to the pencil sharpener? The coupon is good for only 60 seconds, and you might add an expiration date.

Voluntary Time-Out: Here's one I've seen used for multiple purposes. You can give (or sell) one to the classroom hothead and instruct him to use it *before* he gets in trouble. It might even help this student learn to monitor his anger level. The teacher might use the slogan "Use it before you lose it." Get it? Another use is for the semiconscious student who spends most of the afternoon pushing Zs with his head down. Enforce the no-sleeping-in-class rule and require that he pay one coupon for 10 minutes of "resting" in the time-out booth. If he needs more rest, he'll have to get sharp and purchase more coupons (or stop watching *MTV* until 3 a.m.).

Getting-the-Last-Word Coupon: This one is perfect for the highly verbal but oppositional student. It may be redeemed *"for permission to have the last word while making the usual excuses or insisting you are right."* Imagine the teacher's joy as she ends a minor disciplinary consult with the student by (automatically, with a knowing smile) stretching out her hand for a coupon. That really gets to these kids. Their last-word self-justifications are deeply reflexive. I seem to recall one kid so upset with himself for falling into a "last word" coupon charge that he folded his arms across his chest and gritted his teeth for 5 minutes. The teacher's facial expression said it all—at last she had some control.

Bugging Coupon: Here's a multipurpose permit that pokes some fun at students who do things to annoy their peers. Whenever the problem child is caught in some harassment of a classmate, he is required to atone for his sins by giving the valuable coupon to his victim. Our coupon thing confuses the social roles and distorts the entire dynamic of victim and perpetrator. Maybe this would be a good time to review Chapter 3: "Rent-a-Thug." See how everything starts to fit together?

Bad Attitude Coupon: Do you have a student who gets in a foul, pouty mood and seems bent on maintaining it for the whole day? For those "attitudinally challenged" students, why not require the payment of a coupon? Our old standby has this fine print: *"Present this coupon to your teacher for the right to enjoy 10 minutes of really bad attitude during regular class time."* You can even turn the coupon into a badge or permit. Students who are in the process of enjoying their negative 'tude time might be required to display the coupon somewhere conspicuously on their desk. I've seen the coupon worn over a shirt button as a badge. At the end of the 10-minute period the teacher can announce that it's time to go back to "normal mood" (and some kids will say, "Oh? Okay ...," and change instantly). If the bad mood isn't ready to blow over just yet, no problem; simply ask for a second coupon to be displayed.

Whining, Grumbling, and Complaining Coupon: This one is for a more vocal case of bad attitude. Why let your little malcontent sit there spitting and sputtering for free? Charge him for it and at least you maintain some semblance of leadership. Our coupon carries the instruction: *"Present this coupon for the privilege of being miserable in class for 5 minutes."* Some kids will need to earn a good supply of these, as the 5-minute time slots go by pretty fast.

Goofiness Coupon: Our original graphic showed Mustache Pete the organ grinder with his dancing monkey, Fred. The instructions stated, *"This coupon may be redeemed for permission to act goofy and disgusting for a period of 5 minutes."* Unfortunately, we could not include the original version of the Goofiness Coupon. It seems that Mustache Pete was offended by the graphic we used and threatened to litigate over the defamation of organ grinders and other street musicians. Fred was more flexible in the negotiations, and you will see that his image has been retained in our revised Goofiness Coupon.

Usually, 5 minutes is way too much time to use the material, and the student begins to run out of material. Originally, I designed this one for an elementary teacher who had received one of my difficult special education students into her afternoon class. This kid delighted in outlandish classroom interruptions that drove the teacher bananas and tended to alienate the other students. The teacher loved the coupon idea and enhanced it to the max.

Whenever Rowdy Raymond looked like he was ready to launch into one of his show stoppers, the teacher would quickly collect payment of one Goofiness Coupon and then give him the center spotlight. Her announcement would be something like *"Class, can we have everyone's attention over here. Please stop whatever you're doing for just a moment. Raymond is ready to entertain us with one of his memorable comic routines. Ray, you're on!"* At that point, Rowdy Raymond would just stand there with a sheepish expression. The teacher wouldn't let him sit down for a while because the floor time had cost him a valuable coupon. Believe it or not, that OBM teacher extinguished the class interruptions in about two or three trials. (Go ahead, compare that with a 2-hour FBA meeting, some fancy behavior intervention plan, and a crate full of happy face stickers.)

For your convenience, we're throwing in a bunch of sample coupons. Go ahead and use them right out of the box or develop your own custom red tape for the classroom paper chase.

Figure 11.1. Tattletale Coupon

Figure 11.2. Out-of-Seat for No Good Reason Coupon

Figure 11.3. Voluntary Time-Out

Figure 11.4. Getting-the-Last-Word Coupon

Figure 11.5. Bugging Coupon

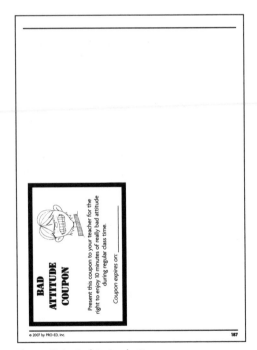

Figure 11.6. Bad Attitude Coupon

Figure 11.7. Whining, Grumbling, and Complaining Coupon

Figure 11.8. Basic Goofiness Coupon

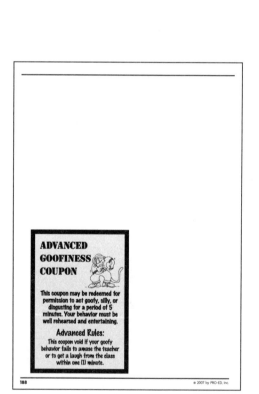

Figure 11.9. Advanced Goofiness Coupon

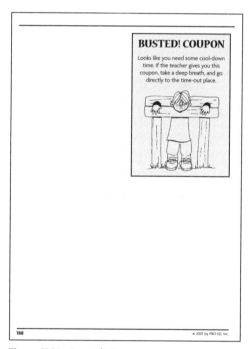

Figure 11.10. Busted! Coupon

Figure 11.11. State of Confusion Coupon

Figure 11.12. Panic Card! Coupon

Wacky Coupons and Behavior Permits

Fine-Print Summary

Basic Idea:
If you can't stop some chronic disgusting behavior, at least you can license it, tax it, and overregulate the joy right out of it. When you run into a student behavior that has resisted the usual attempts at extinction, you might consider using wacky coupons, tickets, passes, and unusual behavior permits. Maybe we have finally learned something valuable from big government bureaucracy!

Time-Saving Hint:
Here's one that could have come from Martha Stewart on a good day. Instead of digging up fancy fonts and clipart graphics to make behavior coupons, why not assign Oppositional Eddy the task of creating his own designer collection? Tell him that if you're not really impressed with his line of coupons, you just won't use them.

Life-Saving Hint:
You might peel-and-stick some fine-print lawyer talk at the bottom of your OBM coupons. Consider these ideas: only one coupon per hour/class/day; all the teacher's decisions are final; offer may be withdrawn at any time; coupons are nontransferable and have no cash value; coupon expiration date; coupon not valid during a time-out, etc.

Note: We could give you a better chapter summary, but we'd have to charge a coupon.

Figure 11.13. Wacky Coupons and Behavior Permits: Fine-Print Summary

Dear OBM Guys:

You will remember me from one of your OBM workshops. I'm the teacher who refused to do the visualization exercise … and then struggled for the rest of the day with an impulse to flap my elbows and cackle like a chicken. (Sorry for those outbursts.)

Anyway, I'm writing to report that I have finally arrived as an OBM practitioner! This week I had a class of 18 mid-schoolers take advantage of my *half-off* coupon for a big homework assignment. Instead of the usual 50% return, I had a full 100% return with the reduced assignment. By the way, I started out by awarding the homework coupon to each student who started a worksheet within 30 seconds. Everyone earned a coupon, the worksheets were all completed, and then everyone cashed in the coupon. I don't know how far this thing can go.

Thanks for the idea, and the unusual workshop experience.

—Ms. Upton

Figure 11.14. Dear OBM Guys

12 Those Voices in Your Head

Using "Canned" Audio Messages

Borrowing Some Needed Clout

Sometimes the classroom teacher has little in the way of direct raw power over the strong-willed student. Anything new? No, but through skillful observation of the difficult student, it may become apparent that there is someone else who *does* hold considerable influence. That someone may have real clout that is rooted beyond your classroom setting. It's always a thing of beauty to see smart-aleck Bernard (smack in the middle of his infantile resistance routine) suddenly mellow out like someone flipped a switch. Here's your hard-core oppositional student going through his usual act, when he happens to glimpse unexpected Major Player #1 entering the classroom. An instant conversion takes place before your eyes. You turn to smile at this awesome influence who has entered the class. (Note: This is also the time when I like to lean over to impossible Bernard and whisper, "Keep it up. You look so normal!")

Most frequently, this Major Player is a tough parent who is frustrated at the reports coming home from the principal's office. By the way, if this influence is the child's controlling parent (i.e., "the Handler"), you can bet your next-year's raise that the other parent on the team—mother or father—is much more permissive and maintains some kind of enabling or protective alliance with the little tyrant. That's just the way it is. Other times, that powerful, influential person is a favorite teacher, a sports coach, or a stabilizing grandparent. Perhaps our Major Player is the Chinese immigrant custodian who teaches martial arts, a charismatic bus driver, a "Joe Friday" probation officer, or maybe it's mysterious Uncle Carmine in a dark, pinstriped suit. Whoever it is—he or she *has got the clout.*

Of course, we can't help but wonder during those brief transformations, "How could we bottle this magical influence and use it later?" So glad you asked. Our top-notch team of researchers at the OBM Institute has labored far into the night, toiling over this very question. After years of study and painstaking field tests, we have developed a simple method of preserving emotional influence for later classroom use.

Canned Voices

If little Attila H. won't listen to you, why not put a convincing voice right in his head? In the noble spirit of cooperation, we have often invited our influential Major Player to a private meeting at which one or more special messages are recorded on cassette. These are then labeled, "Last Ditch Warning" or "Encouragement," and filed away for strategic OBM use. When the classroom power monger gets up to his old tricks again, he soon finds himself slumped in the time-out corner with headphones in place. He is then overwhelmed by a familiar authoritative voice in his head reminding him of what he really wants to be doing.

After years of real-world use and dozens of funny war stories, we still aren't sure which taping methods work best. The following paragraphs describe a few of the procedures that have been used.

Spontaneous Jive

Some parents and "significant other adults" are comfortable and secure in taking a microphone in hand and telling it like it is. They often have a special patter that has been developed over many years of relating to the child. If the OBM teacher simply tells them that a few choice words are needed on respect, back talk, and getting started to work on time, these cooperative folks are off and running with the finest pedantic rhetoric you ever heard.

For example, try to picture how this one works. Young Willie has all the potential in the world. He could be a doctor, lawyer, or even a mid-school teacher. But he's also afflicted with strong oppositional traits. His dear old Cosby-like dad picks up the microphone for a 5-minute back-porch "visit" that comes off smooth and authoritative. This parent has plans for Willie and isn't about to let him smart-mouth his way out of fifth grade. Okay, and how about a well-informed Aunt Phoebe, who is also invested in Willie's education. You can't possibly measure her verbal skills with any known technology. She immediately captures the microphone and gives poor Willie a dose of what-for that builds up like a steam locomotive, rumbles on through the country, and goes the distance like a southern preacher. Yes, it's an art form.

Much of my school psychology practice has been based in the rural communities of the culturally diverse southwestern desert. I recall working there with a squirmy resistant Navajo boy who was a perfect third-grade candidate for some OBM "cooling of his jets." A planning meeting was set up, and a large contingent of extended family members arrived at the school. Similar to other ethnic groups, the Navajo folks have definite leanings toward matriarchal leadership. Sure enough, when the family group was seated, it soon became obvious that the mother and aunts were not the ultimate source of authority. Difficult questions were discussed briefly in English and then carefully translated into Navajo for the boy's grandmother, who was sitting quietly and majestically at the rear of my office. All heads turned in unison to receive her wisdom and final decisions on the boy's fate. I would wait for the interpretation and then proceed with the matters at hand.

Okay, let's see how many rocket scientists we have here today: When it came time to ask that someone make a taped "warning" or "redirection" message for this boy, who do you suppose I asked? Very good! (This OBM stuff must be creating geniuses among us.) I respectfully explained that we could really use a brief message from Grandma to help this kid get his mind back on his work, and on the need for respect toward his frazzled teacher. This grandma stayed behind in my office and spoke sincerely and confidently into the microphone. To this day, I do not know what Grandma actually said on the tape. No doubt I had run into another high-verbal-skills speaker.

The teacher was provided with this classic tape and asked to keep it in a safe place (e.g., near the Civil Defense supplies). Each time there was some problem with defiance, the boy was sent to a bean bag chair and required to listen to his tape. Grandma's message did work some kind of magic on this kid—and all went well until the tape came up missing!

Word on the street has it that the kid was fascinated with his tape and somehow convinced his teacher to allow him to take it home overnight. That's right, an hour bus ride out onto the rez. Oddly enough, the tape disappeared at the boy's home camp, and we could never relocate Grandma, who lived another hundred miles or so off the grid. Everyone concluded that the teacher needed a lot more smart pills. Her penance was to suffer through the remainder of that millennia-long semester without Grandma's help.

Talk Show Interviews

Suppose the parent, grandparent, or last year's coach is willing to help out but not sure how to handle a hot microphone. In this situation, I just invite him/her/them for a private interview "about" the child. We like to put the tape recorder out on the table and simply chat for a while. I will often throw out some lead questions and let my guests refer to the child by name. Classic pump primers include the following:

> *"So, what are the serious concerns that bring you all the way in to school today?"*
>
> *"I understand you got some disturbing news from school that has you pretty upset?"*
>
> *"Do you have something important that you need to say to Rocky?"*
>
> *"I can tell by your clenched fists and gritted teeth that you have something important on your mind."* (Well, maybe not.)

During these interviews we are always mindful that the noncompliant student will someday be listening to our tape as an "overheard" conversation between adults. (For more insight on this dynamic, you will want to listen up when we get to Chapter 13: *"The Strategic Power of Gossip and Hearsay"*). As long as the parent is doing well, I let him or her carry the ball throughout the interview. Somewhere along the way, I will naively ask if the parent *really* expects the child to accept these comments and behavior suggestions. The intent is to have my interview guest make some clear assertions. I want the parent to sense that his or her credibility is on the line. Once we finish our private interview, I like to slide the microphone over to the parent and ask something like, "So, what important message would you like to leave for Junior?" Check out some of these classic exemplars:

> *"Justin, listen son . . . when you hear my voice telling you to chill out and go back to work, it's like I'm right there in the class talking to you. I expect you will do exactly as I'm asking . . ."*

> *"Billy, if you are allowed to hear this message, consider it your last*
> *chance to avoid big trouble at home. Here's what I want you to do as*
> *soon as you finish the tape ..."*

> *"Now that you have listened to my little message, I'm giving you one*
> *chance to follow my instructions, like right away ... or else go back to*
> *class and keep up your old routine. It's your choice, and you know I'll be*
> *told whether you respected my message ..."*

Sometimes the parent speakers will branch off into what Grandma would think, how deceased Uncle Joe would be so proud of improvements, or the fact that the family reputation is at stake. Coaches remind the kid of school pride, eligibility for playing in the next game, and how the guys on the team are counting on him to try hard. Juvenile probation officers are a different breed. They remind the willful student of his contract with the juvenile court that calls for full compliance with school conduct rules. These guys evoke memories of courtrooms, stern judges, and uniformed officers. For some local tough guys, that "empathetic" JPO voice on the tape sounds like Eastwood with an attitude and brings up vivid images of a bleak gray weekend cell at the detention facility. Hey, we'll take whatever clout we can get.

Idiot Cards and Prepared Scripts

This one reminds me of an old TV car commercial that attempted to poke fun at the phony testimonials concocted by some Detroit competitors. We are presented with a gaunt, middle-aged man in a disgusting plaid leisure suit. He is trembling like a goosey Don Knotts, awkwardly posed with one arm along the roof of his car. This unlikely picture of sincerity swallows hard and sweats right into the camera: "In my own words ... This ... is truly ... a fine ... automobile" (forced smile).

Actually, that is about as credible as some of the tapes I have received from clueless parents who are allowed to read a prepared script. It might be better than nothing, but a script always cries out for enhancement. Following is a sample explanatory statement to give the parent (or other speaker) some ideas, and then in Figure 12.1 a sample "canned" statement for him or her to read. It might best be used as an example of some content issues, before working on the *real message*. We will assume the guest speaker is a concerned parent and that the malefactor student is the pride-and-joy little shaver in the family.

Here's a good explanation to warm up today's guest speaker:

> *"You have been asked to record a message to this student because of your influence*
> *in his life and his obvious respect for your guidance. Imagine that your son is on the*
> *verge of getting in trouble at school. Suppose he is worked up about something and*
> *is hurling caution to the wind. Suppose he is about ready to throw a fit in class or*
> *become grossly disrespectful to a teacher. What could you say at this point to redirect*
> *your child? What words could you use to transmit some of your parental influence*
> *from home to a classroom situation? Below are some scripting ideas that will show*
> *what some other parents have used in their messages. These ideas are just to get you*
> *warmed up a bit."*

Note: When you do the final taping, be sure to select a good background musical score to create the right mood. Our team favorites include *Greensleeves, William Tell Overture,* and the theme to *Hawaii Five-O.* We have even experimented with Hugo Montenegro's theme to *The Good, the Bad, and the Ugly,* with mixed results.

Sample Script for Preparing the Speaker

A Parent Message

"Joseph, this is your dear old dad speaking, and I want you to listen very carefully to what I have to say. I want you to pay serious attention just like I was standing right there talking to you. Whatever respect you would give me in person is the same respect I want you to give to my voice message right now.

"If you are listening to this tape, it means that you are probably about to get into some kind of trouble, but you haven't actually done that yet. Maybe you've said something or done something that has your teacher concerned. We all understand that school problems are normal for everybody—the work you have to do, the things other kids do, the rules the teachers have to enforce—all that can get anyone upset from time to time. BUT none of that stuff allows you to act up or disrespect your teachers. Nothing that has happened so far today gives you the right to throw a fit or say anything disrespectful. Kids who do that kind of stuff are telling the world that they can't manage their own behavior, and that they need outside controls.

"No matter how right you are, or how good your ideas are, nothing allows you to act up today. This message is your opportunity to take a few minutes to calm down, think straight, and get yourself under control again. Maybe you should just take a few deep breaths and try to think of the end of school today. Imagine yourself leaving school and coming home with no black cloud over your head . . . and no negative messages coming home to me. All I'll know is that you used the tape successfully, and I'll be proud of you.

"Of course, we all know that some kids who aren't in control need some kind of penalty or consequence at home to help steer them away from misbehavior. It could be what you need today. I'm not sure. Only you can decide to respect my message, and after you finish this tape your behavior will tell me your decision.

"I know you are a smart kid. I believe you can make good decisions . . . even when they are really hard decisions. That's 'cause you're my kid, and I'm betting everything I've got on you being a winner today. Don't let me down. I'll be waiting to learn of your good decision about respectful school behavior."

Figure 12.1. Sample Script for Preparing the Speaker: A Parent Message

---

Try a RAT Card for Feedback

Notice how the last parent speaker seems to expect some kind of feedback about how the tape affected Junior's behavior? Whenever a parent comes in for a planning session (and "private recording session"), we also take time to decide on some kind of system for immediate feedback. It's only right that our speaker receive information on how well the eloquent recorded message controlled his offspring. We feel that these "calm down" messages tend to put the parent on the spot. Everyone is waiting to see whether he or she has any clout. This isn't family therapy or parenting rehab time, and so we like to select only those speakers who already seem to have some transmittable influence.

Why not use our simple prepared card to "rat" on the student? We have cleverly padded the meaning of RAT as an acronym for *Reporting Actions Taken*. This card is a report of little Reginald's decisions following an encounter with that persuasive voice in his head. The RAT Card also bears student and teacher signatures. Call us old-fashioned, but we like to use a carbon-paper sandwich to make two or three identical RAT cards. Of course, it's not that we don't trust our strong-willed student to deliver the *original* card home to Daddy. No, no, no ... It's just our quirky way of keeping track of the program. Besides, we keep hearing of alien abductions and drive-by note grabbings when messages are sent home like that. Here's the deal: We send the bottom copy home *that afternoon* with the student. The original (top) RAT Card is kept for a future parent-teacher meeting; if there is a middle copy, it could show up any day in the mail at home or at the parent's place of business. It's all arranged with the parent at the first meeting, and you'd be surprised at the honesty and mutual trust that's generated. Take a look at the sample RAT Card we've tucked in Appendix G. *Note*: Sometimes it's just okay to rat on kids.

This behavior report card confirms that _____
Student's Name
listened to your private taped message at: **Time:** _____ **Date:** _____
Trigger situation that prompted the need for a taped message:
_____
_____

Response to the message:
☜ Improvement   Deterioration ☞
(+3 +2 +1   0 -1 -2 -3)

Teacher Comments: _____
_____

_____   _____
Teacher   Student

© 2007 by PRO-ED, Inc.   189

Figure 12.2 RAT Card

Other Nagging Details and Considerations

• Encourage your message recorder to use the jargon and native language used in the home.

• Why not produce two or three brief tapes and rotate their use?

• What about oppositional kids who are also ADHD? When that time-release pill isn't cutting it, consider a mobile consequence. Provide a Walkman tape player and have the student walk around the track or playground perimeter while listening.

• Why not have the student produce his own self-control tape? He might whisper corrective messages into the recorder, produce a dynamite tape, and maybe even come away with a stronger sense of conscience? At least, consider having young Adolf write out some scripting for his parent.

- Suggest that surviving parents (who are still communicating with each other) tape a private dialogue *about* the student that ends with a few direct behavioral instructions.
- Why not tape a "secret" group discussion *about* the student (i.e., behind his back)—with several key family members—and end with everyone agreeing on a family message for the kid?

Canned Audio Messages

Summary Points

Ask your student's parent or significant family member to provide a brief support message that will be tape-recorded for future private listening. The taped messages might be a combination of warnings and encouragement. Consider these production methods:

1. **Spontaneous Jive:** Tell the parents what you need and let them crank out a down-home message. You might also let them check out Figure 12.1 so they can see a sample message.
2. **Talk Show Interviews:** To help provide some minimal structure, design a few "short-answer" questions for the parent and tape your discussion for the student. This chapter offers a few examples for your consideration.
3. **Idiot Cards and Prepared Scripts:** When you need to give the tongue-tied parent maximum guidance, write out the exact words and have the parent do several practice readings.

The RAT Card is a hook or gimmick to keep parent investment alive while you are periodically using the tape. Keep sending them home, adding personal notes, and repeating your thank-yous. Always describe the tape-recording as a vehicle of the parent's influence . . . *not* an instrument of the teacher's power.

Figure 12.3. Canned Audio Messages: Summary Points

[This unique letter was shared by an OBM teacher.]

Dear Ms. Dolores:

Thank you so much for using that recorded message on cassette that we sent in. We had little Pugsley's grandfather say a few words from the heart. Hopefully, the brief message will help the little fellow straighten out when he gets a bit feisty. Don't worry too much about that glassy stare and the frozen catatonic features you see while Pugsley listens to the tape. That's just Grandfather's special way of relating to him. You see, Grandfather died over twenty years ago. Once again, thanks for your help.

—Ms. Addams

PS: If Pugsley needs more encouragement, you might remind him that we can always bring Grandfather into the school for a visit.

Figure 12.4. Dear Ms. Dolores

13 The Strategic Power of Gossip and Hearsay

Design and Application of the Overheard Message

And Now, Back to Our Mission Impossible Team

Here we are in Chapter 13 already, and by this point you are starting to see that OBM methods are steeped in benign subterfuge. Things are *never* as they appear ... except sometimes. We like to believe that the original *Mission Impossible* TV series was near the apex of strategic plot development. Probably even beyond the inspiration of *The Man from U.N.C.L.E.* or even *The Wild Wild West.* Sure, all these elaborate ploys and counterploys might never have been pulled off so smoothly, but, hey ... they *could* have. And what a syndicated inspiration to all the following generations of classroom behavior modifiers!

One thing we try to strive for in OBM is utter simplicity ... unless contrived complexity is a facade for simple genius. The more grandiose and cumbersome our management plans, the more chances for surprise we have to live with. It's good not to depend on too many players or too many steps, or attempt to exert management control across too much time. OBM teachers like to craft the smooth turn of a distracting phrase, a haunting word picture, a wide-eyed misinterpretation, or even a confusing request in the face of defiance. All these are the unseen badge of competence.

In this chapter we go back to the glory days of "attitude change" research in the ivory towers of social psychology. You might remember Leon Festinger (or not) as a pioneer name connected to the cognitive dissonance phenomena. You'll probably be pleased to hear that we won't be reviewing all that literature today. However, further off in left field, in an obscure published article in 1962, Festinger and Elaine Walster had the gall to "rediscover" the commonsense notion that overheard verbal communications can be very persuasive in changing attitudes. That is, whereas we might be suspicious of a direct, "in your face" persuasive message, we tend to judge an accidentally overheard message as more believable. Hmmm. So whenever we stumble upon a juicy conversation that was clearly not intended for our ears, and certainly was not meant to persuade or influence us, ahh, that message easily slips through a few more layers of our skepticism.

All the widget salesmen know this one. That's why there's an entire genre of advertising that lets us listen in on private conversations in which the virtues of the new and improved widget are discussed over the backyard fence. Do you suppose we might find some application of this principle with those feisty and very suspicious oppositional-defiant students? *It does present some interesting possibilities.*

Head Work

Suppose you are dealing with Charlie, the class clown who always has a smart comeback to your directives, and who thrives on opposing, arguing, and obstructing. Perhaps he pictures himself as a champion of all the oppressed working students and really believes that the other kids love his defiant antics. This kid may even interpret the occasional detentions he has to serve as his acts of martyrdom for all those disenfranchised little people. He probably wears the usual blinders and can't see that the majority of the class is totally fed up with him. Most kids would just like him to deflate his massive ego, shut up, and get with the program.

Two "Attitude Change" Methods

Our average teacher A decides she'll try to reach Charlie with a heartfelt sit-down talk. She wants to point out that Charlie's "stuff" really isn't funny and isn't accomplishing anything. At some deeper empathetic level, she also wants to connect with her student and let him know that she truly cares about him as a person. She hopes to point out some of his strong qualities. She'd like to give him some tips on repairing his public image and building healthy friendships in the class. Well, that's a tall order. Let's listen in to hear how she might sound on this noble quest:

> *"Thanks for staying behind a few minutes, Charlie. You've been in my class now for how long? ... Yes, about 3 months, and that's given me enough time to see that you have some real strengths in this subject. [The teacher lists a few specifics in a laudable attempt at a sincere compliment.] As I recall, talking out in class was our first problem, but it seems that our main conflict this semester has to do with your 'getting the last word' kind of thing. How many detentions have you had? Maybe four or five so far? I hope there's some way we can get past that ... because I think the other kids in this class might give you a lot more respect if they could just see your other side ... yak, yak, yak."*

Can we all agree that this grand pedagogic effort and a dollar bill will get you a see-through cup of coffee at McDonalds? Somehow we all know that Charlie is driven by deeper, more ingrained beliefs and habits than can be touched by this syrupy monologue. Otherwise, he's not really a card-carrying oppositional kid.

Now let's listen in on our above-average teacher B, who uses an OBM format with a very similar message. This time Charlie is called out to some generic school office that is adjacent to a conference room. Our secret operative school secretary has been dying to play the role of sanguine, gum-chewing Lily Tomlin. She leads Charlie into the office with these overrehearsed words: *"I guess your meeting is gonna be in just a few minutes, sweetie. You can wait here until they call for you."* As Charlie takes his seat in the office, teacher B and a well-coached confederate teacher are cued to start their therapeutic skit. Suppose for a moment that you are poor oppositional Charlie, slouched in the next room—with the door only slightly ajar. You just might "overhear" something like this:

> *"... I see four write-ups here ... with four detentions ... mostly insubordination stuff."*

"Okay, yes, he's the next student ... It's Charlie."

"Wow, did you see these test scores? He should be one of your better students ... What's the problem? ... drug addiction? ... head injury? ... lives under the bridge in a cardboard box?"

"No, sorta average home situation. It's just that Charlie is extremely insecure. He's driven to prove everything ... real scrappy little guy. We all think he's probably a Type III ..."

"Let me guess, Type III. He's got the knee-jerk defense style: reflexively argues, does a song and dance about everything, disrupts your class, can't tolerate being corrected ... the other kids think he's a jerk, but he thinks he's some kind of hero ... and probably with a personality style as rigid as a board—am I close?"

"Whoa there ... You must have been sitting in on my class. That's Charlie, all right. Wait till you meet him—you'll see."

"Well, if he's really a Type III, it also means that he just can't shut his mouth ... has to talk out all the time even if it's just nonsense ... and the other kids probably avoid him ..."

"You're right again. You wouldn't believe the number of students who have come to me privately and complained that poor old Charlie is driving them crazy ... One kid even wanted me to move Charlie to the back of the class."

"But if he's truly a Type III, he can't really see how he comes across ... you know, totally blind to himself. Probably keeps a silly grin on his face and won't quit his routine ... Well, actually, 'can't' quit his routine—isn't that what they say?"

"Oh, I don't think it has to be that bad for Charlie. Even though he appears to be a Type III, he's still not calcified beyond hope ... I mean if someone could show him that his life would be better if he could slow down ..." [Other teacher interrupts]

"Yeah, like he could maybe be your top student ... a leader ... popular ... all of that ..."

"... Instead of being our unappreciated class clown ... and gradually falling further behind his potential each year ..."

"So what's this Charlie character like as a person?"

"Well, he's actually got a witty and attractive style if it wasn't for the Type III entanglement. Mostly it's his mouth that sinks his ship ... Otherwise, I actually like the kid ... and some of his papers are the best to read. Too bad ... just wish we could help him."

"Type IIIs usually have to change on their own ... sorry. It would be simple to just tell him to use less than 50 words in any class period. That would skyrocket his popularity in one week ... Of course, he'd never really "get it"—just a waste of time, I'd say. But he's your student, it's your call."

"Come on, we'll be calling him out of class in just a minute. Let's do this review thing and see if he's open to any ideas. There's always hope."

"Okay, I'll buzz the secretary and ask her to call him out ... and let's see ... about how many more students are on the list for today? ... yak, yak, yak ..."

We could go on with the slick overheard-discussion charade, but let's go back to all-ears Charlie sitting in the next office. Unlike the traditional admonitions of our well-meaning teacher A, this overheard dialogue came to him as a crashing avalanche of genuine, unedited opinions. Our rigid-as-a-board student was set up to hear two educators who seem to know quite a lot about "Type IIIs" (whatever they are) and still seem to care about poor Charlie. This strategy is good for blinder busting and denial crunching with your most change-resistant oppositional students. Our *Gossip and Hearsay* strategy is worth dozens of insight therapy sessions and social skill training classes. This intervention comes packaged conveniently in a clean, easy-to-open, 5-minute dialogue module. It really ought to be in a book somewhere.

Variations on a Theme

The trick is to capture the attention of your oppositional student for a few minutes of credible listening. It doesn't have to be in a formal conference room setup. Consider some of these alternatives:

1. Staffings and IEP meetings happen all the time. What if your hard-core student missed his meeting and some unknown operative slipped him a privately recorded cassette tape of some (contrived) post-meeting dialogue? Perhaps it's only 2 minutes of "genuine" exchange while everyone is gathering up papers and chatting by the door. This might come off something like our example script. Hmmm … might be interesting listening, especially if the tape wasn't intended for release. It might be even more spicy if the tape were stolen and certain people were really upset about it?

2. Overheard telephone conversations might be staged with some unidentified authority person. Such ploys are easy to set up if you can tolerate the mind-numbing dial tone in your ear. (Advanced OBM operatives are trained to unplug the phone.) Posing with a phone is an art form. Try it sometime in a busy teachers' lounge. Actually, I'm convinced that a lot of important-looking people are really just standing around having pretend conversations on their cell phones. Some of these phone posers can get fairly animated as they're tying up million-dollar deals in Hong Kong, shouting instructions to their defense attorney, or even calling out for imaginary pizza. Anyway, whether you're a mild-mannered ground-line person or some kind of wireless jockey with unlimited airtime minutes, you can design a convincing phone monologue. This stratagem is particularly designed for the overly suspicious student whose paranoia has been properly piqued.

When your back is toward the open door and you're being "overheard on the phone" by some unrepentant graffiti artist or even a harmless back-talk and excuse specialist, make a few strategic comments and then pretend to interrupt the other party and say, *"No, no, the last name is spelled this way"* and then, of course, slowly spell out the student's last name. You might also like to thank the pretend party on the other end of the phone for his or her willingness to conduct a "formal investigation" if needed. It's a good idea to scribble down a few things and use up some spacer time after hanging up and before turning around to "discover" your hapless student waiting at the door. I don't know why, but it seems these students are always just a bit more cooperative when they arrive a minute early. (Actual results may vary.)

3. Hallway gossip is everywhere and can be somewhat useful. Because of the confusion between classes, it's harder to orchestrate a "con-

fidential" conversation. Sometimes you might get a little mileage simply by shouting an innocent question down the hall or making a simple comment to someone about your target student. Of course, the student must be in the vicinity, within earshot (but out of your company). When the hallway "stage" is set just right, you might throw out something like the following:

> "Hey there! Pass the word. I don't want to hear any more complaints about Miguel. He's really trying these days."

> "... And remember, guys, poor Louie really can't help his mouth. It's an arrested developmental stage ... so give him some slack today."

> "Are you tough guys in my third-hour class still trying to put up with Bill? Patience, guys, patience ... and, please, no senseless acts of violence today."

4. Foggy recollections are another small way to use unknown but possibly credible sources of persuasion. Teachers seem to be naturals with foggy recollections. If you can't remember the source of a comment, there's suddenly a climate of mystery. Who knows, you might actually be recalling a colorful comment from one of those voices in your head. Here's a handy place for applying paired-associate learning with a social facilitation twist.

First, casually introduce your desired key topic to the student in question. This can be anything of concern: the classroom soap opera scene, indicators of blossoming high achievement, or even some elements of sociopathic development. Start out with something neutral, like, *"Did you hear what was on the news last night?"* Make some logical transition into the important content point you want to plant in memory. For example, you might say, *"Yeah, some guy got busted for being a nuisance in an apartment complex, and he had a whole load of lame excuses."* Then, change your physical posture slightly or take a breath and look away for just a second. Finally, turn back to the student and remark, *"Oh ... and I heard your name mentioned somewhere just the other day."*

Of course, with your foggy memory, who knows exactly where you heard that name uttered. And you never indicated that the student's name was in any way connected to the first part of your rambling chatter. It doesn't really matter, because you have just forged a paired association between the student and some important concept (e.g., being a nuisance, or maybe having a load of lame excuses). It will be a haunting connection. The added glue for the association was that magical hearsay component. Way to go, Rufus ... and see how easy that was?

The Condensed Concept

When it comes to changing the rigid worldview of your oppositional-defiant student, the "overheard" message tends to have more impact than a direct lecture or an emotional appeal. After all, rational people visiting in private have no reason to influence or coerce. Their private opinions are more likely to be blunt, honest, and believable. As a nearly full-fledged OBM practitioner, you should consider writing, directing, and starring in one of your own teacher productions. The strategic use of gossip and hearsay is just that simple—*at least, that's the way I heard it.*

Gossip and Hearsay

Summary of Steps

1. **Select a Target Student:**
   The best candidate is an oppositional kid who has some major blind spots that fuel his defiant behavior.

2. **Script a Private Dialogue:**
   Briefly sketch out a candid discussion between yourself and another knowledgeable staff person. The behavior or attitude topic should be cleverly introduced and discussed.

3. **Train Your Confederate:**
   Review your script with a credible accomplice and ask for a stellar performance.

4. **Set the Stage:**
   Find a setting or situation where the target student can be placed to "accidentally" overhear the dialogue.

5. **Run the Treatment:**
   Have your candid discussion about the problem. Why not have your helper make the prediction that the student is not really capable of discovering his blind spot?

6. **Enjoy the Fallout:**
   Watch for classroom situations in which a knowing look or excessive empathy might nudge the student toward insight.

Figure 13.1. Gossip and Hearsay: Summary of Steps

Dear OBM Guys:

Your "Gossip & Hearsay" thing really caught my attention. After reading Chapter 13, I decided to set up a full stage production for one of my "blame and denial" students. The problem is that my "confederate" teacher kept cracking up and laughing hysterically while I was trying to do the private discussion. We learned later that our "socially sensitive" target student bought the whole thing anyway, cleared up some major blind spots, and became more sober about responsibility. However, because of all the laughter and some offhanded compliments thrown in by my helper, the student was convinced that he has undiscovered entertainment potential. The blame-and-denial problem turned into an obsession with being our classroom comedian. Now he pesters me to tell his corny standup jokes to the class! I guess we're moving in a better direction, but I'm looking into Chapter 11 for another solution.

—Ms. Vermillion, 7th-grade English teacher

Figure 13.2. Dear OBM Guys

14 Luck of the Draw

The Alternative Consequences Card Deck

Working Smarter

Sometimes you're faced with a whole menagerie of wiseacres in one tasteless dose. Perhaps your last-hour class was hand chosen by dark forces who gave you two kinds of trouble: (1) oppositional-defiant students with learning problems ... and (2) oppositional-defiant students with ADHD. Ah, but you've been dabbling in this OBM stuff, and you're convinced there might be a chance to gain some control of the daily civil unrest.

You've been strategically visiting with the principal, Mr. Mealimouth, and intermittently telling him how much the staff admires his dependable disciplinary support. You've convinced him through colorful anecdotes of how many of the disciplinary problems you are routinely handling on your own. That's your PR prep work for the time when you will need his rarely seen backup. You've made it clear that you're no whiner, but when you do send them down, you "just know" the administrative support will be there. How refreshing. Okay, you're set up for, say, at least three quick-action disciplinary backups (which in your school is usually tied to those dreaded lunch detention write-ups ... and that's just fine with you).

Remembering some of the OBM principles from Chapter 1, you decide that your wiseacre class is not the place for red-faced lectures about respectful behavior and the value of education. Realistically, you don't have the social mix or time of day that would allow you to create (or demand) that big 100% group effort. Given the disorderly end-of-day classroom climate, you have decided to "work smarter" by crafting a gamelike playfulness with your inmates rather than using one of our more feisty zero tolerance plans. A very wise decision ... you will be rewarded.

Tell You What I'm Gonna Do ...

In your own disarming manner, you introduce the new classroom management plan with an unrehearsed standup monologue that goes something like this:

"As you all know, it sometimes gets pretty loud and rowdy during this class ... And I don't like to always get stuck with all the disciplinary stuff. Even though it's getting close to the end of the day, we still need to get some work done in here. Someone has suggested that maybe the entire class should be given one lunch detention for every time the noise gets out of hand. I've been talking with Mr. Mealimouth, and he's willing to set up a mass lunch detention if it's needed. But you know me ... old softy that I am ... I've been thinking of some way to get tough and raise the standards here but still give everybody a chance to avoid lunch detention. The plan I will be using is called Luck of the Draw. It's quite simple, actually. If you get busted for behavior problems in here (well, any-thing less than a criminal misdemeanor), you will be offered the option of serving your one lunch detention ... or drawing a consequence card from this deck. [Our riverboat gambler–OBM teacher proudly fans the stack of pasteboards.] If you choose to go for a consequence card, you must follow the printed instructions exactly as they are stated, or you automatically get your one lunch detention. It's just kind of a reduced-sentence plea bargain thing, and it should save my voice and energy. Okay, so everyone understands the deal: If you get busted, it's either one simple clean lunch detention, or you can go for the Luck of the Draw ... and please no whining if you get something really gross."

Just a quick survey—how many of our readers out there can guess what the first ques-tions will be? Yes, we all can see that our smiling OBM teacher has the entire class dangling on her curiosity hook and is ready to start reeling in the big ones.

Your Fate Is in the Cards

Take a look at some of the suggested consequence cards on the following pages. I'd say that none of these is as bad as doing a real lunch detention. But that's just the point. This is OBM, where the *appearance* of having control is nearly as important as *actually* having control. Some of you oppositional readers who skipped earlier chapters may not be with me, so let's think this through together. The target behaviors in this class are generally mild but high frequency ... and, of course, there's the risk of escalation. Remember, all that Ritalin is wearing off at the end of the day, and the herd is getting a bit restless in your corral.

Our shrewd OBM teacher was shopping for a management strategy that

- produced a gamelike challenge (not an open battle of wills);
- was only mildly aversive (even as simple as a brief "response interruption");
- could be repeated multiple times during a class period;
- protected the teacher's credibility and authority;
- was easy to administer without (much) class disruption;
- preserved the student's good will;
- provided for an automatic escalation of consequences if needed; and
- actually contained the rowdy behaviors (well, sort of).

Frankly, I'd be just a bit disappointed if any of our graduate-level OBM trainees out there were to slap the requisite pages on a copy machine, load in some colorful card stock, and simply burn off a stack of consequence cards. Your boundless creativity has hardly been tapped, and who knows what cool ideas are waiting to spill out of your head. Why not just read through our cards, maybe spend a few more minutes communing with an old *Far Side* calendar; and then go forth boldly and customize your own card deck? Make each item fit your special style. Add some local school color that only your gang will understand. Most important, adjust those alternative consequences to mesh with the bleak realities of life in your own classroom. Okay, maybe it's just easier to visit the copy machine …

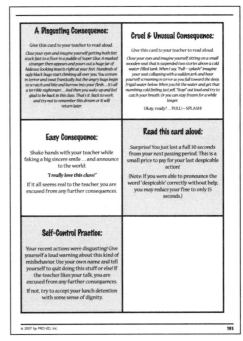

Your Only Chance to Escape:

You must stand up. Count out loud backwards beginning with your grade (number of years) and ending at your grade (number). Do it right the first time. If you do it correctly, you may sit down quickly and pretend you are working. If you mess up, you can think about it during your lunch detention.

Simple Survival Action:

You must shake hands with one (1) person in this class and give them one (1) sincere-sounding compliment or word of encouragement.

If the teacher likes it, you may quickly sit down and your bad luck may be over … or not.

Accurate Reporting Practice:

Fully describe your disgusting offense to the teacher—with all the nitty gritty details—and tell exactly why it was wrong.

Do this well and you will be pardoned from other consequences. If your details are not good enough, find a comfortable seat in lunch detention.

Time-Delay Consequence:

Way to go! You lose 30 seconds from your next passing period. When the bell rings, start watching the clock. If you mess up, you get one (1) detention. This is a small price to pay for your last display of immature behavior!

It Could Be Much Worse:

You will be the *last* student to exit this classroom at the end of the period. Accept your fate with dignity … and live with the inner pain.

If you forget and exit ahead of anyone, you may reflect on your sins during lunch detention. Have a nice day.

Temporary Paralysis:

You must write with your subdominant hand for the next three (3) minutes. Your work will be graded as usual. If you try to switch over before your time is up, your dominant hand may begin to wither, lose all strength, and grow warts. That would be nobody's fault but your own … and you can think about it in lunch detention.

190   © 2007 by PRO-ED, Inc.

Figure 14.1. Alternative Consequences Card Deck

Avoid Serving One Detention:

Give the teacher two (2) sincere-sounding 'thank yous' about the joy of learning in this wonderful class—within the next 45 seconds. (The clock is ticking right now.)

Social Degradation Experience:

You have to stand by your desk and witness a classroom vote on your offensive behavior. If over half of your peers vote to condemn your actions, you must stay in your desk for 60 seconds after class is dismissed. If you get a good vote from your peers, you are released from any consequences … except those imposed by your critical inner self.

You have 120 seconds to print these exact words on a full sheet of paper:

I always do my best in this class. I'm one of those kids you can count on for 100% effort.

(Sign your name & give it to the teacher for future reference.)

Luck of the Draw!

You are hereby dismissed from your consequence. Shake hands with your teacher and have a nice day.

Your Fair Choice:

For your last nuisance misbehavior you have earned one (1) detention consequence. You may choose to trade detention for the loss of your chair for four (4) minutes. During this time you must stand and continue your assigned work … and no crybaby stuff.

Imaginary Consequence:

Give this card to your teacher. Teacher reads:

Someday you will find yourself eating with your friends in the cafeteria. Suddenly, the food you just ate will start to swell up in your stomach … and you will feel it pushing way up into your throat. Others at the table will look at your sick expression. You will suddenly feel out of control and try to stand up. As you do, your stomach will explode out of your mouth and scratch and bite out of your mouth and feel your clothes, your hands, and the table. It will be a gross smelling mess, and you will hear others screaming and moving away. The whole cafeteria will be looking at you in disgust as you try to clean yourself. Okay, your consequence is over and don't think about it.

Your Choice:

Right now you owe one (1) lunch detention for your consequence. To escape your detention: Stand on your left foot and blink your eyes 10 times without losing balance. If you mess up, suffer through the detention and don't make it worse with your infantile crying.

© 2007 by PRO-ED, Inc.   191

Figure 14.1. Continued

Imaginary Consequence:

Give this card to your teacher. Teacher reads:

Close your eyes and imagine that you are alone, sitting at your desk. Without any sound at all, someone sneaks up behind you with a jar of about 1,000 live cockroaches. This person carefully pulls back your shirt collar and then dumps the whole jar of bugs down your back! You scream out in terror and the bugs start running all over inside your shirt while they are nipping and scratching you. You pass out screaming. And then you wake up, glad it was just a dream. That's your consequence, but you may find it hard to get out of your mind. Return to your work and stop the wimpy shivering.

A Really Dark Consequence:

You have just lost all good luck for the next 24 hours. You will be hassled by stupid mistakes, forgetfulness, hiccups, banana peels underfoot, and black cats in your path. If you return to this class with a good attitude, the bad luck may go away … or not.

No whining or your bad luck may get you one (1) lunch detention.

Double-or-Nothing Chance:

You can escape detention in two ways:

A. Flip a coin with the teacher—

Heads - You win *two* lunch detentions.
Tails - You get NO detention.

B. Draw another card and live with the consequence.

(Hint: Your luck hasn't been all that good today.)

Busted Again!

For your last miserable disruptive behavior, you should receive one (1) detention consequence. However, you may choose instead to be the last student to exit the classroom at the end of this period. If you forget to be the very last student out, you will serve your assigned detention time … and stop with the whimpering already.

Social Skills Consequence:

For your consequence, you must wave at one person in this classroom and then give them a sincere-sounding compliment about something they have done well in recent days. If the teacher likes it, you may sit down and no further penance is needed; otherwise, you can think about it in lunch detention.

Sentence Completion:

You have exactly 30 seconds to complete this simple sentence:

'I really love this place, and it's mostly because _____.'

If the teacher buys your answer, you're off the hook for now.

192   © 2007 by PRO-ED, Inc.

Figure 14.1. Continued

A Disgusting Consequence:

Give this card to your teacher to read aloud.

Close your eyes and imagine yourself getting both feet stuck fast to a floor in a puddle of Super Glue. A masked stranger then appears and pours out a huge jar of hideous-looking insects right at your feet. Hundreds of ugly black bugs start climbing all over you. You scream in terror and sweat frantically, but the angry bugs begin to scratch and bite and burrow into your flesh … It's all a terrible nightmare … And then you wake up and feel glad to be back in this class. That's it. Back to work, and try not to remember this dream or it will return later.

Cruel & Unusual Consequence:

Give this card to your teacher to read aloud.

Close your eyes and imagine yourself sitting on a small wooden seat that is suspended two stories above a cold water-filled tank. When I say, 'Pull—splash!' imagine your seat collapsing with a sudden jerk and hear yourself screaming in terror as you fall toward the deep, frigid water below. When you hit the water and get that numbing cold feeling, just yell, 'Stop!' out loud and try to catch your breath. Or you can stay frozen for a while longer.

Okay, ready? … PULL!—SPLASH!

Easy Consequence:

Shake hands with your teacher while faking a big sincere smile … and announce to the world:

'I really love this class!'

If it all seems real to the teacher, you are excused from any further consequences.

Read this card aloud:

Surprise! You just lost a full 30 seconds from your next passing period. This is a small price to pay for your last despicable action!

(Note: If you were able to pronounce the word 'despicable' correctly without help, you may reduce your fine to only 15 seconds.)

Self-Control Practice:

Your recent actions were disgusting! Give yourself a loud warning about this kind of misbehavior. Use your own name and tell yourself to quit doing this stuff or else! If the teacher likes your talk, you are excused from any further consequences.

If not, try to accept your lunch detention with some sense of dignity.

© 2007 by PRO-ED, Inc.   193

Figure 14.1. Continued

Optional Card Deck Modifications

1. Slim to none: Adjust the number of "escape" cards in the deck to fit your current mood. If the joy is wearing thin, remove all the escape cards but one. Stare down your most challenging off-task student and draw a line in the streets of Dodge City: *"There's only one escape card left in the deck ... and you don't look like the kind of student who would find it."* Maintain your intense gaze for just a second more, shuffle the deck confidently, and back off a few paces. Next, just stand there cracking your knuckles while the student decides whether to draw a consequence or plead for mercy. (Just a thought.)

2. Allow the student violator to draw two cards and pick which one will be his consequence. Use a 10-second time limit for him to make up his mind or the choice defaults to—you guessed it: one regular lunch detention.

3. Add cards that require classroom housekeeping and community service tasks. These should be token jobs that have to be done at the end of the class period ... or on the student's own time. Don't use any that would take up teacher time for monitoring their completion. (You knew that already ...)

4. One of our printed examples presents a "Double or Nothing" challenge. Think of some way to add a bit of spice by upping the ante on a consequence. Make 'em sweat a little. Out here in the frontier wilderness, we try to get the deed to the ranch, rights to the mining claim, or just the title to a Chevy pickup. Your classroom wagers may vary.

5. The codependent teacher may wish to distance herself one step from the negative consequences. To do this, allow a "designated peer" to draw a card and read the disgusting consequence. That way, when some unsavory ordeal is selected, the teacher can sympathize with the poor student ... and remind him that it was *his* buddy who drew the rotten card: *"... So why do you hang out with unlucky guys like him?"*

6. We're still trying to keep that gamelike atmosphere, right? To do that, consider more ways to include predictions and friendly wagers. For example, approach your Oppositional Eddy and make a public wager. Bet him that he will definitely get himself busted sometime during the class period (and have to draw a consequence card, as per the game rules). However, if he avoids getting busted, *you will draw a consequence card* from the deck and live with whatever it states. I doubt if Eddy could resist the deal, and who knows, he might mellow out this period and get started on his term project. *Personal note:* If you do the wager thing, I recommend that you prepare a special card for the top of the deck that says: "Collect $10 from each player."

7. If the Luck of the Draw plan catches on, why not allow students to purchase or bid on the privilege to add new (reasonable) consequences to the deck. It would be ironic if an oppositional student later ended up drawing his own consequence. Such things do happen ...

8. Make my day: As you start the new card deck program, make the public prediction that there will probably be two or more students who will just have to test the deal on the very first day. If you're feeling really psychic, you might also predict that the knee-jerk program testing will happen within the first 15 minutes of class. This is a great setup for your

"knowing look" and some "I told you so" comments. While you're still hot with the predictions also mention that some students might start to reflexively argue or whine or resist a card consequence … and will find themselves waking up in lunch detention just the way the program is supposed to operate.

In all my travels across this great land, I've found that lunch detention is nearly a universal "corrective consequence." If your school doesn't have some generic penalty like that—that is mild, verifiable, and repeatable—then it may be time to start lobbying for a bit more common sense added to the water supply. For everyone else who might try the card deck thing, we close with this venerated slogan that may be suitable for your bulletin board:

Don't do the crime,
If you can't do the time.

Luck of the Draw

Summary Points

Basic Idea: When a student gets busted for who-knows-what, he may be offered an opportunity to draw a random card from your "alternative consequences" card deck. Instead of the usual punishment (e.g., lunch detention), the card deck offers humorous, less painful consequences that create a gamelike climate—and ensure that the teacher has the last word.

Here are some points to remember with this OBM strategy:

1. Make certain there is some standard schoolwide disciplinary consequence already in place. Appeal to that onerous default consequence if the student messes up with the card deck thing.

2. Prepare your cards ahead of time. Use our examples or be insanely creative.

3. Practice your introductory spiel in a mirror and then do your standup routine. This strategy probably does not require a power-point presentation.

4. Check out all our suggested modifications. If you plan to run this "special offer" all semester, it will be important to add some fresh cards or new procedures from time to time. It's always a great idea to sell (or auction off) the opportunity for students to add a new card to the deck. If you find a gem, please send it to us at the OBM Institute.

Figure 14.2. Luck of the Draw: Summary Points

Dear OBM Guys:

Here's my two cents. When I did my consequences card deck, I added about five copies of this item:
"Your alternative consequence is to be encouraging and friendly to the teacher for the rest of the class period. In order to avoid your lunch detention, you must say one pleasant happy-face thing or give one sincere compliment to the teacher before leaving the room."

—Basic math teacher

Figure 14.3. Dear OBM Guys

15 Creative Solutions Sweepstakes

Fabulous Prizes for Thinking Outside the Box

Taking It to the Streets

We all know that crowds are fickle and the teaming masses can turn on you in an instant. As with other OBM strategies, there are times to use this intervention and times to keep turning the handbook pages. When the auditorium is electric with "Bravos" and thunderous applause at your stellar performance ... it's a great time to ask for anyone's "honest opinion" of how well you did. On the other hand, when you're peering out into the night through the bars of your cell and all you can hear below are the chants of an angry mob with ropes, torches, and sharpened agricultural implements ... well, that's probably not the best time to survey opinions or request solutions.

On a day when your difficult classroom crowd is somewhat manageable, it could be a good time to experiment with the OBM Solutions Sweepstakes. You have in mind a mild classroom problem that just won't go away. It could be the gossip mill, backpacks in the aisles, or slow starts on term projects. Maybe it's just the usual wailing and lamenting about your onerous homework assignments. Whatever the irritation, here's a way to turn it into an upbeat problem-solving exercise for the entire class. And when your non-OBM colleagues hear about what you did, they'll probably conclude that you're a borderline genius—or maybe that you recently stayed at a Holiday Inn Express.

Here's how we set up the contest:

> **1. Define the problem:**
> *"Hey, everybody, I need a good solution to this vexing problem ..."*
> **2. Explain the contest deal:**
> Invite all your students to brainstorm creative solutions to the problem. Have them write out their ideas in a basic step-by-step format. To qualify for the contest, the ideas must be submitted to you by a certain day or time (like maybe the end of the period). For your convenience, you might just use our Sweepstakes Official Entry Form, which, oddly enough, is included in Appendix G.
> **3. Include the usual lawyer-talk details and restrictions:**
> All entries must be signed and become property of the teacher. Administrators, staff members, and teacher's pets are not eligible to enter. The teacher's official selection will be final ... or the teacher has the option to nominate the top three ideas and

call for a class vote. You might require that all entries be submitted on the official entry form—and have proper spelling? The winning idea must be practical, ethical, and workable within the classroom setting. Runner-up ideas might be held for later use. If an entry is selected for secondary use, a smaller prize could be awarded to the beautiful mind who submitted it. The winner agrees to have a signed copy of his or her brilliant idea submitted to the OBM Institute, where it could be exhibited in our B-Mod drive-through Hall of Fame (optional).

4. The sweepstakes award ceremony:

Consider a multimodal grand prize package that includes both symbolic and tangible components. For example, your sweepstakes winner might receive a fancy computer-generated certificate of appreciation, generous classroom applause, handshakes, and photo ops with the smiling building administrators. On a good day, your prize might also include one of those large dollar-size chocolate bars, some level of preferential seating in the classroom, and about four of your coveted "No Homework" coupons. By the way, have you noticed how much money was spent on this fabulous incentive package? Way to go! We always favor brains over bucks.

Certain creative solutions might be worth more than others. What if some undiscovered genius in the third row came up with a foolproof remedy for "bad attitudes" or "lost homework"? That would be a special situation where a dream vacation package might be in order. You proudly announce your sweepstakes winner to the class and then wave good-bye to young MacGyver as he departs on a fantasy vacation trip. Start out with a giant full-color travel poster of the Virgin Islands, Grand Cayman, or Fiji. No, you don't just hand the kid a rolled-up poster. Your winner is allowed to display the beautiful trance-inducing poster near a special desk location where he can imagine walking on the beach and splashing in the warm water. To carry the theme, you let him borrow a pair of sunglasses, and you provide a couple of Mounds or Almond Joy bars (for the coconut theme) and maybe even a can of tropical punch soda. By the way, since it's an imaginary vacation, you might include a check for $10,000 in imaginary spending money … so your big winner can bring back some decent travel gifts for the class. Remember, your sweepstakes prize should be more of a feeling than substance.

5. Implement the winning solution:

Once all the fanfare and camera flashes have receded, it's time to explain to the class how the solution plan will be tried out. Discuss all the details and have the class vote on when to start with the idea. At this point, the savvy OBM teacher will remind everyone that if the plan is anywhere near successful, there just might be reason to schedule some minutes of free time for the entire class.

6. Keep the door open:

This cute little gimmick is voluntary. Not every student needs to submit a contest entry for each time a sweepstakes is offered. Make the prizes fairly attractive, keep it fun, and be generous with your compliments toward nonwinning ideas. Let the students know that there will always be other problems that need a creative solution. Sometimes they're urgent and other times they're just little headaches. At any rate, emphasize that possibility thinking is always valued in your class even when there's no official contest going on. You might even use a successful contest as a springboard for weekly brainstorming sessions on other matters.

If you find yourself with a lot of extra time on your hands, you might check out Chapter 17, "Narcs-R-Us" for a foul-ball spinoff of the contest idea. This kind of extra study and conspicuous diligence could earn you some bonus points.

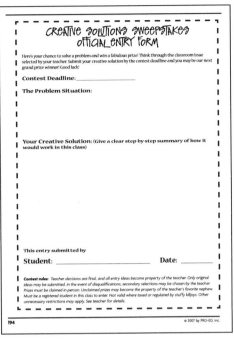

Figure 15.1. Creative Solutions Sweepstakes: Official Entry Form

---

Creative Solutions Sweepstakes

Key Summary Points

1. Meditate on OBM Principle #5 (Transform "problems" into educational projects). It's actually good for the class to experience the birth pains of workable solutions.

2. You shouldn't carry the personal burden of troubleshooting every glitch that turns up in your classroom. Share the load. It's tough enough just to teach the content material.

3. Students who help solve unique classroom problems tend to accept more "ownership" of the class. That can't be bad.

4. Advertising, public relations work, and an expansive imagination are a big part of the sweepstakes idea. If you're not feeling much like a game-show host today, just postpone the contest until your manic cycle kicks in.

5. Prizes and rewards are mostly an abstract social thing; however, always include some tangible anchor items. These help connect the warm feelings with reality.

Figure 15.2. Creative Solutions Sweepstakes: Key Summary Points

Dear OBM Guys:

Seems like the gang at the institute is sniffing way too much White-out these days! I tried your Solutions Sweepstakes idea for finding a good plan to handle classroom bullies. I nearly got fired in the process! Call me naïve, but I had no idea of the wild, bizzare solutions that my kids might concoct. After cringing, I selected one of the fairly tame solutions to try out—but somebody got a look at the whole stack of headbanger suggestions. One thing led to another, and I found myself scheduling meetings with concerned parents and getting calls from *The O'Reilly Factor*. It all seemed so innocent. What happened? You guys really need to underline the disclaimers in your book!

—Mr. Wilson, 10th-grade resource classroom

Figure 15.3. Dear OBM Guys

16

The Teacher Hot Seat

Real and Imagined Customer Satisfaction Surveys

How Much Heat Can You Take?

What we're talking about here is the brutal honesty of an OBM-style "customer satisfaction survey." That's right, just like they do in the real world, and even on that *eBay* Web site. The Hot Seat is just our humble way of asking students to provide feedback on the teacher's instructional style, behavior management skills, and other classroom matters. Of course, you might expect that the OBM version of this common business tool would be ... well, just a bit different. Very good. In fact, there are actually two survey tracks to choose from: the honest vanilla feedback questions, and our strategically "juiced" questions. We're going to assume that there may be a few non-OBM–minded readers still with us at this late point in the book. To be fair to everyone, we're going to start with our basic survey, which comes in only the one mild flavor. After that, the remainder of survey ideas are pure OBM ... and you're on your own (or you might call the OBM national hotline).

A Genuine Customer Satisfaction Survey

Your students are your customers, and we hope that many of them will "buy" the learning you serve each day. From time to time, it's just good practice to conduct a survey of customer satisfaction in each of your classes. It is surprising how many "blind spots" we can develop that might be easily corrected. As the semesters of our teaching career start to stack up like an IHOP special, we fall into convenient ruts and quirky nervous habits that can downright bug our students. Of course, we can't see them ... and that's probably why they call them *blind spots*.

We all know of "other" teachers who reflexively trigger student problems (over and over). Those teachers are selectively blind to their foibles and repeatedly get burned with each new crop of students. Deeply entrenched teaching habits seem to die hard, and witnessing these self-defeating patterns can be much like charting a thousand trials with Homer Simpson reflexively reaching for the donut on a electrified shock grid. *("Donut! ... hmmm ... Ouch! ... Donut! ... hmmm ... Ouch! ...")* A workaday lab rat would probably adapt much quicker when a behavior is not effective.

If you are secure enough to use an anonymous survey, there will be plenty of helpful students standing by ready to provide tactless and painfully blunt reality checks. This student service could be especially helpful with managing oppositional students. It's also free for the asking, so why not make use of it?

Our Basic "No Frills" Survey Procedure

1. Select a few items from the approved list that follows or just make up your own.
2. Write them on our convenient blank Teacher Evaluation Survey and then crank out copies for the class.
3. Boldly ask for anonymous responses (no names). Assure your paranoid kids that you are totally incapable of identifying any students simply by their handwriting ... even though you have corrected hundreds of their handwritten papers all semester.
4. Take a deep breath and study your survey results. Privately create your own professional development plan.
5. Thank your students. Let them know that the survey was not an empty exercise ... and that you will actually use the results to improve the class. Try to sound sincere.
6. Remove and shred all surveys that contain bizarre incriminating accusations or any other material of possible interest to a grand jury. Store the remaining balanced and reasonable comments for future reference.

A Few Sample Items for Essay Assignments, a Poetry Contest, or a Questionnaire

- How well do I present and explain new material?
- How well do my homework assignments build your skills?
- How well do my tests fairly measure your learning of the class material?
- How well do I protect student dignity and self-esteem during class discussions?
- How safe do students feel in asking me questions?
- How clear are the rules and expectations in my class?
- How well do I enforce the class rules?
- How fair am I in running the class?
- How physically safe do you feel in my class?
- How easily can you get my attention when you need help?

Along with our generic "fill in the items" survey form, we are also providing a rather transparent *Customer Satisfaction Survey*. This instrument places your students in the role of educational "consumers" and asks for marketing feedback. There are six general items, which seem to cover the waterfront fairly well. Ordinary kids will really

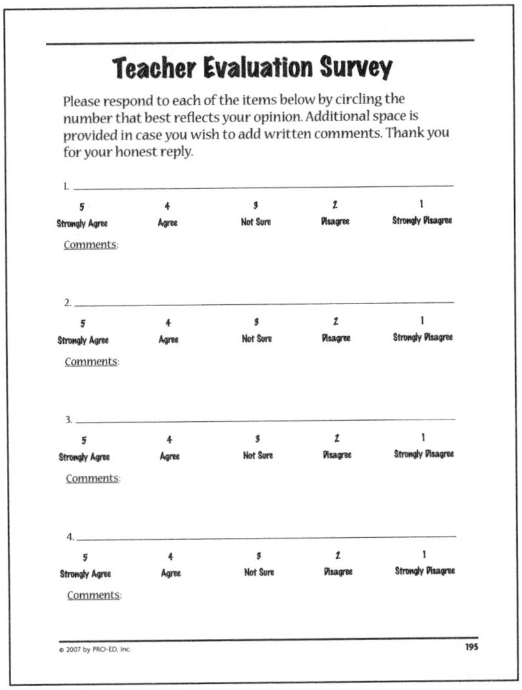

Teacher Evaluation Survey

Please respond to each of the items below by circling the number that best reflects your opinion. Additional space is provided in case you wish to add written comments. Thank you for your honest reply.

1. ______________________________

5	4	3	2	1
Strongly Agree	Agree	Not Sure	Disagree	Strongly Disagree

Comments:

2. ______________________________

5	4	3	2	1
Strongly Agree	Agree	Not Sure	Disagree	Strongly Disagree

Comments:

3. ______________________________

5	4	3	2	1
Strongly Agree	Agree	Not Sure	Disagree	Strongly Disagree

Comments:

4. ______________________________

5	4	3	2	1
Strongly Agree	Agree	Not Sure	Disagree	Strongly Disagree

Comments:

© 2007 by PRO-ED, Inc. 195

Figure 16.1 Teacher Evaluation Survey

like it. The more sophisticated oppositional students will go along with the survey and give so-so ratings on everything. It's possible you might even get some indication of a particular pet peeve. Generally, your oppositionals will be coolly suspicious of all those honest inquiries and will try to avoid showing their hand. That's okay, we'll be brewing up something special for them.

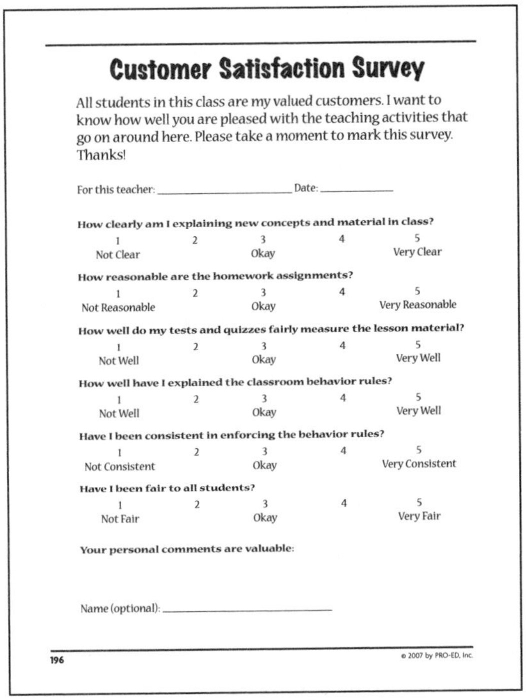

Customer Satisfaction Survey

All students in this class are my valued customers. I want to know how well you are pleased with the teaching activities that go on around here. Please take a moment to mark this survey. Thanks!

For this teacher: ____________ Date: ________

How clearly am I explaining new concepts and material in class?

1	2	3	4	5
Not Clear		Okay		Very Clear

How reasonable are the homework assignments?

1	2	3	4	5
Not Reasonable		Okay		Very Reasonable

How well do my tests and quizzes fairly measure the lesson material?

1	2	3	4	5
Not Well		Okay		Very Well

How well have I explained the classroom behavior rules?

1	2	3	4	5
Not Well		Okay		Very Well

Have I been consistent in enforcing the behavior rules?

1	2	3	4	5
Not Consistent		Okay		Very Consistent

Have I been fair to all students?

1	2	3	4	5
Not Fair		Okay		Very Fair

Your personal comments are valuable:

Name (optional): ____________

196 © 2007 by PRO-ED, Inc.

Figure 16.2 Customer Satisfaction Survey

OBM Spin Doctor Modifications

There are ways of doing surveys … and there are ways of doing surveys. More than a straightforward information-gathering device, a customer satisfaction survey can also be used as a clever behavior change "intervention." It's true. In this chapter, we'd like to suggest a couple of strategic twists to the venerated "needs assessment" and teacher evaluation ideas. These twists have to do with manipulating the survey response format and subtly manipulating the meaning of the survey.

Human beings (and even oppositional students) have a remarkable tendency to seek consistency between their publicly embraced values and their actual behavior. Beyond the expected tension of talk versus walk, there's some inner human drive to balance out all the truckload of things we believe about life, so that everything sort of fits together as a seamless worldview. There's also a lot of mental gymnastics going on inside to continually keep knowledge, beliefs, and values in a more or less balanced state with our actual behavior. All this is the focus of cognitive consonance theory, and the general idea seems to hold true even for hard-core classroom tough guys.

Before I ventured into the public school setting, I practiced shrink craft in much safer environments such as mental hospitals and outpatient clinics. I've worked with brilliant paranoid schizophrenics who invested Herculean efforts in the twisting and turning of their crazy delusional systems so that all the bizarre details would have some logical fit. Mental consistency seems to be a primary drive, even if you're insane. Oppositional kids don't get a free pass here, either. Whether they understand it or not, these characters are also driven to maintain a consistent worldview that justifies all their rigid defiant shenanigans.

Have you noticed that your oppositional-defiant students always have some good reason for disrupting, arguing, or throwing those little hissy fits? To them, it's all perfectly rational and consistent with the extreme demands of classroom life. And so we hear such gems as these:

> "Whenever I don't scream and cuss, no one around here will listen to my answers … some kids are just soooo jealous."
>
> "Yes! I always have to argue with the teacher because she's dead wrong and no one else in this sorry class is willing to straighten her out."
>
> "That last little screaming fit was actually forced upon me by those idiot classmates you put me with."
>
> "Sure I'm always late to this class, but there's nothing happening here, so I'm not missing anything … right?"

At other times, the mental logic is even more insidious:

> "I get into fights easy … but it's because I have all this fiery red hair."
>
> "I can't wait in line like those other kids cuz I've got my grandpa's stubbornness."
>
> "Mom says I'm turning out just like my real dad … That's what got him sent up."

Four Slick Applications of Consonance Theory

Brilliant Idea #1:

Design a customer satisfaction survey to deliberately squeeze out some positive responses.

Open-ended items, multiple-choice questions, and rating scales are supposed to provide a continuum of possible responses from one extreme to the other. Average intensity responses are generally smack-dab in the middle with the two opposite poles at either end, right? Well, not even—this is OBM. Remind yourself that we're not here to conduct objective research; we're just colluding to shape a few attitudes. Go ahead and help your sour student to endorse something positive, and it will come back to haunt him later. One way to spin a survey is to manipulate the response options or the characteristics of the rating scale. Take the survey item *"Our teacher is fair with the rules."* When untamed Jungle James looks down at his response options, the poor fellow finds only these choices:

5	4	3	2	1
Always true	Very true	Often true	Most often true	True enough

Imagine the contorted facial expressions as your oppositional student ponders the available choices. Also note that we have provided some sense of a fair response scale from much to less. However, even if Jimmy-me-boy marks the most negative response (*True enough*), we can all applaud his approximation of a positive attitude toward the teacher's management efforts. Consider a later debriefing interview with James and the teacher commenting, "Well, I'm really pleased to see you marked 'True enough' when we're talking about fairness with the rules. I guess that means we all have some agreement on the basics, and that's just great!"

Rigging a Positive Spin

Okay, so there's that automatic human attraction thing toward mental consistency. Oppositional kids do defiant things because they nurture skewed beliefs about how things fit together. If our humble survey can ask the questions so they have a particular slant, our feisty little character will find himself marking in a *slightly* more positive direction (and hence, viewing the world that way). With oppositional types, even a tiny-wee-small positive movement on a rating scale is like a major therapeutic breakthrough (and much more likely to occur). If we can get little Ernesto to affirm something that's even just a teeny bit more in some positive direction, there will always be an unseen force tugging at him to conform to what he just declared (especially if some smiling face reminds him of it).

Some Delightful Formats for Your Classroom Survey

Your customer satisfaction surveys can come in at least three formats: (1) bold open-ended questions (most dangerous), (2) multiple-choice questions, and (3) bipolar rating-scale items. Properly prepared, any of these may help squeeze out a positive affirmation or two. Try on some of these positively slanted items:

Open-Ended Questions—with Implicit Expectations

- Even in this class, there are two good things I always look forward to doing:
- The very best time of day for me to get some serious work done is:
- Our teacher helps me the most with:
- If you want to fully concentrate on your work, the best place to sit in our class is:
- The number-one top rule in our class that helps me most is:

Multiple-Choice (Limited Option) Questions

Our teacher is really good at: (*check one or more*)
____ Explaining the work so we understand what to do.
____ Enforcing the class rules in a fair way.
____ Helping us figure out how to solve work problems.
____ Helping students stay out of trouble.

The class rules that help me most are: (*check one or more*)
____ The ones about getting work done.
____ The ones about respect for others.
____ The ones about safety in the hallway.
____ The ones about controlling my behavior.

I can usually count on having a good day when: (*check one or more*)
____ I get started on time.
____ I understand the work.
____ I have said something positive to at least two friends.
____ I have stayed in my own work area.

Contrived Rating-Scale Items

Our class rules help me stay on task and out of trouble.

Always true	Very true	Often true	Most often true	True enough
☐	☐	☐	☐	☐

I don't mind receiving school discipline when I really deserve it.

Always true	Very true	Often true	Most often true	True enough
☐	☐	☐	☐	☐

My classroom conduct is helpful because it shows the other students how to behave.

Always true	Very true	Often true	Most often true	True enough
☐	☐	☐	☐	☐

My teacher can count on me for a good attitude on a gloomy day.

Always true	Very true	Often true	Most often true	True enough
☐	☐	☐	☐	☐

Why Not Stir In Some Filler or Distractor Items?

Don't even try to imagine a class survey without filler items. These are like the added fiber in a bland low-carb diet. Distractors provide the illusion of substance and content breadth for your assessment of student satisfaction. A little comic relief might also put the oppositional kids in a more open mind-set. The items below will allow your oppositional student to reply honestly with an affirming positive response. (And that's a switch.) Here's some items that can be worked in to either multiple-choice or rating-scale inquiries:

No matter how well things go, I am willing to leave school at the end of the day.

Always true	Very true	Often true	Most often true	True enough
☐	☐	☐	☐	☐

Our school day is plenty long enough and does not need to be extended.

Always true	Very true	Often true	Most often true	True enough
☐	☐	☐	☐	☐

We have free drinking water for everyone at our school fountains.

Always true	Very true	Often true	Most often true	True enough
☐	☐	☐	☐	☐

Our teacher lets everyone in the class breathe deeply whenever they wish.

Always true	Very true	Often true	Most often true	True enough
☐	☐	☐	☐	☐

I believe that our school should continue to have a lunch break.

Always true	Very true	Often true	Most often true	True enough
☐	☐	☐	☐	☐

Brilliant Idea #2:

Assign an innocent "as if" response set to capture your difficult student.
Okay, enough tinkering with the survey format. Let's wade out a bit deeper into the OBM pool. You can artificially *stretch the range* of student responses ... and thereby get some attitude flexibility. Begin by asking the oppositional student to respond to your original survey items (the basic straight ones) *as if he were a negative, angry kid who* argues and makes endless excuses. (Hey, that shouldn't be too hard.) Next, give him a fresh survey sheet and ask him to relax, do some breathing, switch off the pretend angry

thinking, ... and now just respond to each item as a "regular" mild-mannered kid, *much like himself* on a really good day.

So what have you done here? You have now forced the little tyrant to conjure up an extreme angry "negative self" ... and show with the survey responses that it's actually quite different from his "real self." Yes, it appears that his real self is actually a more or less satisfied customer in your class. Who knows how far you can push that compelling reputation?

By skillfully guiding the oppositional kid to consider even more extremely negative behavioral styles, you may open some discussion of the fair-play limits he voluntarily places on himself. Here's an example of some syrupy possibility talk: *"Well, you may do a few bad things during the school day ... but never as bad as that imaginary 'much worse' kid from the survey. I'm just wondering how it is that day after day you're able to be so much better than that kind of kid? What special things are you saying to yourself in your head, or doing at school to avoid those really bad behaviors? What's the big secret of your success? ... Don't hold out on me—I'm the teacher."*

Now the grinning OBM teacher has the rest of the semester to pester the student who has been cast as "holding out on the teacher" or "hiding" the wonderful secrets of his success. It's often fun and stress relieving to bug oppositional students. Actually, if it wasn't for those stone-faced guys down in the OBM Legal Department, we'd be tempted to slip in some favorite excerpts from our "Gags & Practical Jokes Guide" for use with oppositional types. I guess the occasional "bugging" will just have to suffice.

Brilliant Idea #3:

Threaten to penalize yourself severely if you don't get some affirming feedback from the survey.

Become a whiny codependent victim and maybe extort a little sympathy. While maintaining a featureless blunted affect and a blank stare at the back wall, use your monotone voice to inform the class that you have volunteered yourself to be severely penalized (*not!*) if any personal flaws or shortcomings are revealed on the survey. These self-inflicted consequences might include immediate resignation from the school and reckless abandonment of a 20-year educational career. If the survey results are even more sour than expected, it could force you to enter a mental hospital, join a convent in Madagascar, sign on with a Liberian steamship crew, donate your new puppy to cosmetics research, or even skip lunch on Wednesday. Instead of a direct power confrontation, your customer satisfaction survey can have wonderful emotional strings. As a labile, possibly suicidal teacher, you ask for honest critical feedback (*wink, wink*) but simultaneously pass out tickets for a major guilt trip if anyone dares speak any evil. *"... And I wouldn't want anyone in here to feel it's their fault ... it's just something that's been building up for quite sometime ... especially when this class is so rowdy and I can't seem to control it ..."*

This disgusting paradoxic ploy will probably work with sensitive, bright-eyed little huggables ... but it could miss the hard-wired classroom tyrant who is just sitting there with a Freddie K. smile and waiting to get at your silly survey. Of course, if things don't look good, you can always throw up your hands and announce, *"Well, I guess it won't help to penalize myself just yet, maybe we can dream up some other ideas ..."*

Brilliant Idea #4:

Request a professional development plan (for yourself) from your most challenging student.

"Honestly now, ... am I being tough enough around here?" Ask the targeted student if your management efforts are tough enough to keep those really difficult students in

line. Insist that he boldly point out your wimpy or weak areas of discipline. Start out by asking him to complete a special private survey. You can use one of ours or make up your own. Treat his completed work as a highly regarded document that will merit much of your time for close study and reflection. Next, introduce "part two" of the contrived teacher evaluation project. Hand your slightly bewildered student a blank PDP form. Ask him to suggest a year-long development plan that will beef up your style to absolute maximum power. Be sure to mention the Hershey Bar reward you always give out when a kid helps with a PDP. Everyone's so busy these days, why not just use our no-frills quick-'n'-easy form?

Professional Development Plan
(CONFIDENTIAL)

Prepared for this teacher: ____________ **Semester:** __________

Our classroom can sometimes get too loud and rowdy, and then nobody gets any work done. Here are my helpful suggestions for how the teacher can practice really strong behavior management skills in our classroom.

1. In order to manage us students better, **our teacher should start** (doing what?):

2. In order to manage us students better, **our teacher should stop** (doing what?):

3. In order to manage us students best, our teacher **should keep using** some methods that already work pretty well (like what?):

I sure hope this helps out:

Student signature

 197

Figure 16.3 Professional Development Plan

The Teacher Hot Seat

Summary Points

This chapter is about how to request honest, down-and-dirty "constructive criticism" from your students. As usual, there are two basic approaches—the ordinary way and the OBM way:

1. A Genuine Customer Satisfaction Survey: This is our basic "no frills" student feedback questionnaire, which might cover any number of classroom factors. Check it out or use the blank Teacher Evaluation Survey to directly target your own "issues."
2. OBM student feedback surveys: Design a survey with spin-doctor modifications just for your oppositional types.

Brilliant Idea #1

Design a customer satisfaction survey to deliberately squeeze out some positive responses. Check out the OBM magic of contrived choices, open-ended questions with implicit demand features, multiple-choice items without much choice, and our own skewed version of attitude rating scales.

Brilliant Idea #2

Assign an innocent "as if" survey-taking response set to capture and confuse your difficult students. It does seem that wearing a different hat can radically alter a defiant style. Check it out.

Brilliant Idea #3

Threaten to penalize yourself severely if you don't get some affirming feedback from the survey.

Brilliant Idea #4

Request a professional development plan (for yourself) from your most challenging student.

Figure 16.4. The Teacher Hot Seat: Summary Points

Dear OBM Guys:

I'm not sure what went wrong! I used your basic survey form and got crucified. Look, I've been teaching the same subject the same way for twenty years, and nobody ever complained. Now I send out your idiot survey, and half my students tell me I'm boring, dull, and whatever. Is it possible they have me confused with another teacher?

(Name withheld for obvious reasons)

Figure 16.5. Dear OBM Guys

17 Narcs-R-Us: The Classroom Mail Drop

Comments, Suggestions, and Crime-Stopper Tips

All About Narcs

For those of you who have been on a missionary assignment in Papua, New Guinea, for the past 30 years, the term *narc* may not carry much significance. Let's just do a quick review for everyone—yes, even for those of you smug readers who were hard-core *Miami Vice* groupies a couple of decades ago.

The root phrase here is *narcotics officer*, which is the kind of undercover cop who busts the drug pushers. Down in the tough barrios and housing projects, there was a little drift in the term, and it was extended to cover the local informants who supplied information to the cops. Somehow with the mix of confusing values on the street, the informants (i.e., the narcs) were cast in a negative light, as if they were evil agents in the neighborhood. Hence the birth of the expression "Don't narc on your friends," which now means about the same as "Don't rat on your friends." In earlier, less hip times, the term was equivalent to *rat fink, stoolie, tipster,* and so forth. Just for the record, some of us still see *narc* as equivalent to "courageous local hero" ... but we are also savvy enough to know the popular low-end meaning of the term.

Lots of Mileage from a Cheap Sneaker Box

Think of all the unsolved mysteries floating around in the average school. Maybe last week the wrong kid got busted for vandalism, and maybe those phony bomb threats each Wednesday afternoon are actually being called in from the old gymnasium office. In an unrelated incident, maybe the school lost a full trunk load of computer stuff ... yep ... just vanished into thin air.

Now, let's stop a second and think this through together. In most schools there's a quiet marginal kid moving along in the hallway crowd who knows an incredible amount about almost everything that's going down in the school. He's not really part of the criminal circle, but he knows the bad guys and what they're up to. He doesn't always approve of those unholy activities, but he's a survivalist and doesn't want any reprisals. This kind of kid knows how the Ferris Bueller message got spray-painted on the water tower, and he even knows the exact garage where all that Macintosh stuff is piled up in a corner. It's just a fear thing that keeps concerned citizens, like him from stepping forward. Now you're seeing at least one of the purposes for the classroom mail drop.

And it has other purposes or uses. Many times the teacher could profit from constructive comments about the burdensome weekend homework, or maybe even some feedback on the class rules or those inhuman pop quizzes. How about a heartfelt thank you for that excellent science unit on snakes? Sure, it's always good when our students put their cards on the table. But some kids can be timid or even downright afraid to communicate with the teacher . . . and that goes triple if they have some sensitive information to share.

While we're at it, where does your typical student go when he or she has a brilliant idea for improving the class? What about that incredible no-cost solution to some irritating daily problem? Of course, our grumbling oppositional-defiant types also need a sounding board to express their difficult opinions. For these guys, the mere act of writing out a note and working within "the system" could be seen as major milestones in socialization. So what to do, what to do?

Ideas, Gripes, and Hot Tips

Solutions and information are often free. All you need to do is ask. Our OBM team is suggesting that you somehow decorate or transform a PayLess shoebox into your own personal mail drop. Find a protected but accessible location to place your box. Inform your students that this is a secure place where any written messages for the teacher may be deposited. The little notes may be signed or unsigned, and only the teacher will have access to them. Let your darlin's know that you will be checking your mail a couple of times every day. Nothing will sit in the box and get ancient. You might stress the confidentiality thing but note that only signed messages can ever dream of getting a personal response. Also point out that there may be unseen reasons a certain wonderful idea or concern cannot be handled in just the way the student might wish. Even though you may occasionally get a juicy tip regarding evil deeds, it's better to aim your mailbox request for comments, suggestions, and classroom improvement ideas. By the way, it's probably not a smart idea to label your box "Narcs-R-Us."

Strategic OBM Adaptations

Sure, it's easy to request the regular mundane feedback. A comment on the unit exam or even some creative plastic surgery suggestions for the teacher might be useful. But what about deeper strategic applications? Somehow the R&D staff here at the OBM Institute . . . well, they just couldn't leave that "secret" and "confidential" stuff alone. The question posed to our experts was "How can a suggestion and tips box be used for managing oppositional-defiant students?"

At this point in your OBM education, you're aware that our think-tank groups at the institute can get pretty intense with creativity. The Narcs-R-Us lock-in session was like that. By the time the last slice of pizza was lifted and the Cokes were all warm, our gifted *Far Side* crew had generated a dozen special ideas for using the mail drop. Only four of those strategies have been released from committee . . . and those are fully disclosed for you in the following pages.

Contrived Peer Pressure

We all know that kids tend to live out their bleak daily routine in kind of a *Truman Show* performance for a critical imaginary audience. So why not get some positive use out of this form of early-adolescent angst? The teacher's special mail drop can be used to generate tremendous amounts of peer pressure. It all depends on what you happen to pull out of the box and how accurately you read it.

Imagine our mild-mannered OBM teacher, casually leaning against her desk by the open box . . . and just randomly pulling out those folded notes. Everyone (especially our oppositional student) is interested in that stack of anonymous comments from who-knows-who. The teacher's chatter may go something like this:

> *"Hmmm, well, here's the third one in today's mail . . . Seems there's another person out there who doesn't appreciate the recent displays of developmental immaturity around here . . . [teacher reads silently for a moment] . . . Hmmm, I guess I can read this part . . . 'Several of us were hanging out at my house last week, and everyone was telling how much they really want to barf when a certain student gets into the whining and crying and arguing stuff. We've got a lot of work to get done around here, and the cry baby routine gets old, especially in this grade. Some people just don't get it . . . they think like we're all impressed or something, but my friends are just getting sick of it . . .' [The teacher pauses and scans further down the note.] Well, I guess this writer is pretty close to all the others. There are some creative suggestions here, too, but I'm afraid the school wouldn't let us do some of these things . . . Well, Let's look at maybe one or two more notes from the box . . . "*

Just let your newly developed OBM imagination run for a while with this one. Our teacher looks warm and humane as she "does her best" to filter out some intense material and protect all identities. Students are reminded from time to time that all submitted material becomes the teacher's confidential property, so that none of the mailbox contributors will be embarrassed or identified. She also lets everyone know that many of the written details have to be deleted from her public readings. This allows those fertile imaginations to work overtime in supplying probable content. She compliments all the participants but never reveals just how many of the students have actually dropped a message in the box. Of course, there's no real need to point out that the teacher also claims the right to stuff an unlimited number of anonymous comments in the box.

Classroom Crime-Stoppers Program

Why not offer a "No Homework" pass, or even 15 bonus points for information leading to the identification and timely adjudication of person or persons who disassembled the teacher's orange Yugo and moved it to the auditorium? Of course, it's not that you'll always get "real" tips in the box. The power comes from having certain students *think* you're getting lots and lots of real tips . . . and that those tips are being given gleefully from all strata of the classroom society. Also, if the tipster can remain anonymous and still collect some unknown reward, and the particular type of reward isn't revealed publicly, well, who's to know whether there's been a payoff yet, or even several payoffs, for all that helpful information? The teacher can sincerely than all those who have submitted information? The teacher can sincerely thank all those who have submitted information (and earned those private rewards). Your imaginary groundswell of cooperation from the faceless throngs just might prompt some real informants to get in on the rush.

It's time for a well-placed reminder about our target population for the OBM manual: It's still the hard-core oppositional-defiant students. Remember, those students have a rigid character style. They are stubborn, suspicious, intrusive, and in conflict with any authority structures. However, they are not to be confused with other problem groups like gang bangers, those with severe conduct disorders, or juvenile criminal offenders. Our beloved oppositional-defiant types are more smooth and abstract in their resistance. They whine and argue and resist but seldom commit felony acts. We're all straight on that, right?

The great news is that your Narcs-R-Us mail drop intervention can work for multiple types of classroom challengers. Nearly every student wonders what the rest of the group is privately thinking. In fact, the target student's response (or lack thereof) to peer feedback can also be diagnostically significant. When you identify a problem kid who is totally insulated and oblivious to his peer group, you may have a player in need of more serious interventions.

Assumed Knowledge from the Street

Let's stay with the element of our helpful but unidentified peer audience. While juvenile offender types have a fear of discovery and prosecution, oppositional kids are more worried about revealing their psychological cards, losing power, and perhaps being humiliated. Again, the mail drop offers something for everybody.

Take, for example, the young aspiring criminal type. He may want publicity for his street prowess, but he sure doesn't want to get nabbed for a series of petty crimes. We've all seen these guys sitting on their hands and riding away in the back of a patrol car. They usually try to muster an unconvincing grin for the crowd, but it's just not a good photo op. Despite the bravado, "information leading to arrest" is a slap-down they would like to avoid.

Anonymous information from the faceless crowd can be a useful threat to use with these kids. Imagine the following semiprivate comments from our smiling and concerned teacher:

> *"You really wouldn't believe the serious stuff some kids send me in my mail drop box. From time to time your name comes up ... and I hope not all the stuff is true. Actually, with all these people saying things, I'm surprised you haven't gotten busted yet. I'm also surprised that you let so many of your 'friends' know all the details about your night life. I thought you were more of a private kind of guy. You must be a really trusting person ... or something else. Maybe you should warn all your buddies to clam up and stop the leaks. These notes have been coming in for some time. Sooner or later we're going to have to do something with them."*

Notice that the teacher hasn't said one thing that's truly specific, only broad, general chatter. Of course, our target student does have some things to hide, and he's probably filling in the blanks and sweating a little. Right now, his thoughts are probably swirling in "who" and "what" kind of questions. Our teacher is protected by the advertised "Crime Stoppers" promise that all suggestions, comments, and information received is to be without names so no identities can possibly be leaked. This use of the mail drop helps deflate the local tough guy and make him defensive, suspicious, and perhaps just a bit more manageable.

Now let's look at the use of your mail drop with the in-your-face oppositional student. He doesn't have a juvenile probation officer snooping for dirt, but he does have that vulnerable soft underbelly of social angst and suspicions. It's sometimes hard to believe he has any fears at all, given the way he tries to run the class. Like his criminal counterpart, your oppositional kid claims that he could not care less about bad press—but all the while he's keenly intent on what's being pulled out of your secure mailbox.

Picture our OBM teacher doing one of her daily mail checks. She's impressed with the several responses received in just one day. Her chatter is reminiscent of a talk show host and goes something like this:

> "Hey, everyone, it's time to go to the mailbox. Let's check out the anonymous comments and information . . . at least the ones we can read aloud. This is a G-rated class, you know . . . Hmmm. 'Dear Ms. Smith, I'm writing for myself and two friends. Could you tell us if there is some kind of counseling or therapy help available for totally obnoxious students? We are concerned that a certain student may need help with good manners and learning not to run everyone's life. Any help you can give us will be appreciated.' Signed, Three Girls."

The teacher is silent for a moment, holds a concerned expression, and appears to be scanning through some other notes. Then:

> "Well, to the Three Girls, it seems there are some other folks concerned about the same problem: 'Dear Ms. Smith, I need some help. I have a friend in this class who tries to control me, all my other friends, and the world. Do we have any help for pushy people around here? I'm writing for myself and some friends'. Signed the Lunch Bunch. . . . Looks like there are several more notes in here with the same concern. What is this, the Dr. Laura show or ask Dr. Phil or something? Why don't all you concerned people out there gather a little courage. Name names. Talk facts, and send me some straight mail with more suggestions than questions!"

Let your OBM-sharpened imagination carry this scenario as far as it needs to go. Remember, oppositional kids have been pushy and intrusive since way back when they were watching Miss Piggy and the Power Rangers. Somewhere along the line, someone has already accused them of being nosy or pushy, or threw out something quite similar to your (possibly edited or creatively fabricated) mailbox notes. The point is that even many deeply ingrained character traits can be squelched a bit or nominally suppressed with good old peer pressure. That even goes a bit for some kids who just don't get it and carry a totally distorted idea of how they come across in public. For those hard-case students, just keep working your mailbox magic as an educational tool to gradually shape some insight. We've decided not to give any more scripting examples for this particular intervention. Everyone in the OBM think tank agreed that people who should be using the narc box will already know how to run this stratagem.

Bogus Suggestions Blamed on the Unwashed Masses

Sometimes it may be useful to have everyone think that the entire class is clamoring for higher standards and more rigorous academic work. You can prime the proverbial pump with a simple blackboard notice: *Today's Mailbox Question: How's the work in this class?* Next, prepare your own "model student" responses on separate pieces of color coded paper and boldly stuff the box. Later, when it's mail-call time, pull out your own crafted responses for shaping student opinion:

> *"Class, it's time to check out the old mailbox here and see how well everyone is satisfied with the geometry class. I'm just going to randomly draw a few notes and read them aloud. If you don't hear yours, don't worry. I'll look at all of the responses later and let you know if I see any trends worth following.*
>
> *"Dear Teacher: How are we supposed to learn anything around here if we don't get enough homework? When we get enough good homework assignments, I feel like I'm okay with the class.*
>
> *"Dear Ms. Abernathy: We really need more practice time in class ... and more of those helpful daily quizzes. I know if I get an A on the quizzes, I'll probably get an A on the test.*
>
> *"Dear Ms. A: I think this geometry class is really watered down. My brother said when he was in here, you hit the material a lot harder. Is that true? Most of us plan to go to State, and if this stuff is weak, then we'll all be hurting ... Please don't dumb-down the hard chapters for us ...*
>
> *"Dear Teacher: This is my favorite class and the homework is more fun than any video game. You'd be my favorite teacher if you'd just expect a lot more from all of us. Please show us your love for geometry!"*

After flipping through a few more of the folded pieces of paper, the teacher mumbles something about reviewing her syllabus. She then concludes with, *"This is truly an amazing class. I sense a real expectation for learning and high achievement. If that is everyone's wish, I promise to keep up my end of the deal ... straight teaching modules, meaningful homework, fair quizzes ... and I'll push you as far as possible in one intense semester of learning. Is everyone with me on this? Well, okay, stay sharp, and let's get back to those wonderful triangles."*

Coping with Critical Feedback Notes

What if the nerdlich teacher puts out a mailbox and finds that even his "supposedly" bright and capable students begin to send unreasonable complaint notes? And what if they all seem to be excessively critical of his well-polished stories and those personal but interesting illustrations? The recovering-geek instructor might even find undue criticism of his witty lecture comments that brought sustained laughter at the Integrated Circuit Board Conference. What to do? It's obvious that these students need a little prompting to appreciate the humorous material that's added to the calculus lecture.

Here are some typical unreasonable notes found in the secondary instructor's mailbox:

> "Get real or get moving, I've heard that corny joke since I was in day care."
>
> "Wipe that ketchup off your tie or quit wearing it every day."

"Fire your writers and get some new material ... better yet, drag them into the street so we can get a clear shot at 'em."

"Somebody wake me up when this semester's over."

"If I pass this class, does it mean I may become like you when I'm older?"

With just a little creative spin doctoring, that overly critical and unwarranted feedback can be totally rehabilitated. Below are some "transformed" notes (*preloaded in the box*) that may be safely drawn from the recent mail stack and read aloud for the eager class:

"Mr. Wilson, we sure love to hear about how you dressed up like Spock and solved that Romulan equation at the Star Trek convention. Please tell us one more time (especially during trig class)."

"Your jokes are sure witty, Mr. Wilson. They have given me a new love for science. Right now, I'm feeling smart as that wheelchair physics guy on The Simpsons."

"Thanks, Mr. Wilson! You're a real nifty fellow. I always wondered why chickens cross the road ... but now I see the deeper connection with artificial integers."

"That's a swell-looking new pocket protector you got yourself, Mr. Wilson. And it matches the old ink stains on both of your school shirts."

You've Got Mail

Every classroom could learn something valuable from a humble shoebox. Whether you are intent on gathering real tips and suggestions or carefully fabricating your own helpful responses, you can be assured of an attentive student audience whenever you review the mail. Our best wishes go with you as you gently influence your challenging students with peer feedback and creative suggestions.

Chapter Summary Points

Setting Up Your Classroom Mail Drop

1. Dress in your customary trench coat and dark glasses. Drive to a nearby town and find a PayLess shoe store.

2. Wait in the parking lot until they close for the night.

3. Go around behind the building and quietly lift the dumpster lid. Remove a shoebox that hasn't been crushed by an overzealous sales associate.

4. Quickly return to your car and drive home—without raising any suspicion.

5. In the privacy of your home kitchen, select a large, razor-sharp butcher knife and wantonly plunge it into the box lid. Saw out a gaping slot in the lid and secure the lid to the box with masking tape.

6. Next day, place the box near your desk and introduce the idea of receiving private mail from students. (Review the chapter scripts.)

Figure 17.1. Chapter Summary Points: Setting Up Your Classroom Mail Drop

Dear OBM Guys:

Our teacher put out a private mailbox for any notes that the kids want to send her. Some of us think that's an evasion [*sic*] of privacy. My friend's dad has a lot of personal experience with the police, bail bonds, and parole officers. He knows some really smart lawyers, too. Anyway, he says that our teacher can't really bust anyone with the notes in that narc mailbox. Is that true? We need to get this thing straightened out pretty quick before there's any trouble. Our mid-school is turning into some kind of prison camp. Anything you do around here can end up in that mailbox. It's like there's secret cameras everywhere! All that's safe for me and my friends to do around here is go to class and eat lunch. Either the mailbox goes, or I do!

—Dominic B., grade 8

Figure 17.2. Dear OBM Guys

18 The Gotcha! Game

When Students Monitor the Teacher's Enforcement

When a rational educator first hears of a Gotcha! Game in the classroom, what expectations come to mind? Basically, you might expect that the teacher would plan to stay alert to target behavior violations among the students. Whenever one was observed (as with the ZT policy, Chapter 8), the teacher would approach the student, announce "Gotcha!" and give some reasonable consequence. This was basically what you expected, right? Well, not even ...

This is *Outrageous B-Mod,* so we can always expect some delightful twist to the standard methods. The *Gotcha! Game* is a *reverse* strategy that places the *students* in charge of monitoring the *teacher's* compliance. This one is like a zero tolerance deal in reverse. Remember in our ZT contingency, where the teacher promised to be diligent in scanning the class and responding to every possible rule violation?

Well, it all came together at one of those legendary R&D think-tank sessions. A dozen creative professionals were gathered in a conference room far down the busy corridors of the OBM Institute. Another planning session was winding down. The popular ZT intervention had been thoroughly wrung out, and the team was about to move on. A brief pause hung in the air, and then a timid but very clear voice at the end of the table spoke up: "So, uh, who evaluates the teacher?"

This was one of those moments well framed in our collective memory. The following events unfolded in a slowed *Matrix*-like reality. Coffee mugs remained suspended in front of waiting mouths. All heads turned slowly in mechanical unison. The group focus moved to a thin, be-spectacled young man in a white lab coat. "Well ... uh, all I asked was who monitors the ... you know ... the teacher." Moments passed, and then the pregnant silence was broken all around the room with exclamations of "Brilliant" and "Inspired!" Some of our distinguished scientists rose to their feet, and applause broke out around the room. It was clear to all present that another OBM intervention had been birthed.

We call it the *Gotcha! Game.* It helps tighten up any classroom program by *assigning to the students the task of monitoring teacher compliance with a behavior program.* Picture if you will an entire class of oppositional students who have been charged with assigning humility-building penalties to the teacher if she gets soft-hearted, a little sloppy with the rules, or just goes simple. True, the students must still comply with the existing behavior policies, but now there is parity because the teacher is also put on the spot. There's no slack time and no free rides. She is required to consistently bust each and every program violator—or get nabbed herself.

Whenever the teacher blatantly overlooks some mild target behavior in the rear of the classroom, some feisty volunteer student (probably chief violator Oppositional Eddy himself) is authorized to point a bony *ET* finger at her and boldly announce, "Gotcha!" When caught in the act of slacking off, the teacher agrees to accept some token penalty or required act of contrition. Imagine this one being used in one of those self-contained SPED programs where the offending teacher is required to stand on a chair and sing a song requested by a vigilant (grinning) oppositional student. The *Gotcha! Game* is intended to keep everybody sharp. No wonder it's usually set up with all kinds of fine print.

Potential Penalties for the Teacher

You'll remember gag penalties like celebrities getting their head shaved or the university president kissing a pig. We've even heard some old-timers promise to eat their hat. What could a teacher offer as a self-penalty for missing an obvious rule violation? In order to protect our family of OBM teacher colleagues, we have not mentioned these types of consequences on the sample Rules Poster (at the end of the chapter). For conscience's sake, you should consider some self-penalties anyway. While it might be more fun to survey the class for ideas or turn the whole question into an essay assignment, we have taken the liberty of suggesting just a few penalties for the teacher:

- Do a 30-second impromptu impression of that uptight teacher across the hall "having a bad hair day." (Why not have that same uptight teacher step into the class to judge the performance?)

- Offer the class a 20-second demonstration of how she herself might have looked in this grade—doing the same target behavior 60 years ago.

- Award a high-value Goofiness Coupon (check out Chapter 11) or a credit coupon to the student who first gave the Gotcha! signal. (See the sample rules poster and credit coupon at the end of this chapter.)

- Agree to wear Groucho glasses for the remainder of the class period ... or until the next class rule violation, whichever comes first. (Who knows, your savvy students might drag out the spell of good behavior for quite a long time.)

- Give a Bonus Point voucher slip that may be attached to either a homework paper or the next unit examination. Pleasant rewards like this one may work all right, but keep in mind that factory-wired oppositional-defiant students will probably respond best to the symbolic power that comes from prescribing a negative consequence to the local authority figure. (That's you.)

- Sometimes the class participation may be overwhelming. Not to worry. Just jot down the initials of each properly responding student, place them all in a jar, and hold a daily lottery drawing for your offbeat reward.

- In times of austerity and budget constraints, be creative with social reinforcement. Have your first responding Gotcha! student stand by his desk and receive an affirming cheer and a rousing hand of applause from the in-house audience. You might even play a tape recording of the *Pomp and Circumstance* musical score as a backdrop for the thunderous ovation.

Okay, but Don't Run It into the Ground

Try to picture yourself actually playing that violent arcade game where you hold a bright yellow nerf bat and must clobber elf noggins as they randomly pop up out of the floor and surprise you. You stand in position and hammer one . . . and another pops up. You quickly nail it . . . and then there's another, and on and on it goes until your quarter is spent. In a similar manner, we have found that it takes about 2 weeks of ZT consequences to stamp out one chronic nuisance behavior. Once that particular behavior fails to rear its ugly head anymore, you can always just drop the ZT policy. We've found that it's usually smart to get rid of a program before it turns mundane and boring. If you just can't let it go, try substituting another annoying behavior and changing some of the consequences. No matter how things go down, it's probably still a good idea to keep your yellow nerf club handy in the bottom desk drawer.

Check out the following pages for some sample forms and support materials. These may not be as wonderful as the gems your own classroom committee produces.

Postscript: We are often asked whatever became of the young OBM technician who suggested the concept of the *Gotcha! Game*. It's true that he is no longer with the institute. I understand that he became a freelance inventor and developed a machine for shrinking kids. It was based on his own peculiar idea for making student problems seem smaller. Someone told me they made a couple of movies about the guy.

Optional Response Card

Display this card conveniently near the *Gotcha! Game* rules poster. In the unlikely event that a student observes the teacher letting a genuine rule violation slip by, all he has to do is grab the *Gotcha! Card* and officially present it to the teacher with a clear description of the observed infraction. This is offered as a painless alternative for stuffy teachers who can't handle being "pointed at" by critical students.

Figure 18.1. Gotcha!

Figure 18.2. Gotcha! Game: Bonus Points

Bonus Points Bonanza

Here's a sample credit card that might be used to reward a vigilant student. It's a humane alternative to one of those other demeaning teacher consequences. These coupons are for uptight, anal-retentive classroom instructors who could never actually stand on a chair and sing some golden oldie for their fourth-hour algebra class. A veteran OBM practitioner would probably consider *both* a wild required ordeal for the forgetful teacher *and* some bonus points or even a coveted homework exemption coupon for that fine, deserving student.

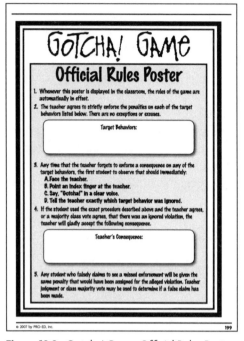

Figure 18.3. Gotcha! Game: Official Rules Poster

The Gotcha! Game

Summary Points

Oppositional-defiant kids love to have some control over the authority figures in their stressed-out lives. The Gotcha! Game gives them such an opportunity while also drawing them into the classroom behavioral expectations. Below are a few points to remember:

1. This is a slick, reverse ZT strategy, which appears to put the teacher on the spot while actually demanding more vigilance and participation from the students.

2. Juice the game a little by including novelty penalties for the teacher as well as prestigious earned benefits for participating students. You might even check out Chapters 11, 14, and 15, along with Appendix D, for practical guidelines on rewards (e.g., teacher-controlled, minimally disrupting, repeatable).

3. Use of the rules poster and game cards just might provide a tangible anchor for the game ... or not.

4. The savvy OBM practitioner will occasionally develop strategic blindness and forgetful spells ... just to trigger a Gotcha! response from a sleepy class.

Figure 18.4. The Gotcha! Game: Summary Points

Dear OBM Guys:

You need to remind your readers that the Gotcha! Game can get way out of control. At least, it did in my classroom. I set up a ZT policy for "whining and grumbling" and then got stupid and added the Gotcha! deal. You never realize how much whining and grumbling goes on in an average day until you have 20 fifth graders closely monitoring every second of audible dialogue. By first recess on day one I had diligently busted four students (using recess minute fines) and been Gotcha'd twice. My consequence was to sing the "Ring Around the Rosies" nursery rhyme through a paper megaphone—for each of my missed enforcements. I hate that song. For the first few days I ran myself ragged trying to stay sharp. To be sure, the epidemic of reflex whining did go way down.

Tell your OBM operatives to try my survival idea: "escalating penalties." It will put more pressure on the students and give the teacher a break. Use some kind of points, credits, or minutes economy and simply inflate the fine for each violator by one additional unit during the day or class period. Of course, tell everyone to keep the teacher's Gotcha! penalty at a safe and sane 1-to-1 ratio. Another smart move is to just experiment with the idea for one day.

—Ms. Simpson, grade 5

Figure 18.5. Dear OBM Guys

19 Outrageous B-Mod

A Few Parting Shots

Salute to the Pioneers

This handbook has introduced only a few of the OBM strategies that have been developed for managing your favorite you-know-which type of students. We need to keep in mind, however, that nearly every form of classroom behavior management owes some recognition to those bearded early learning theorists. We're pausing here for a moment of silent respect as someone reads the honor roll of names such as J. B. Watson, E. R. Guthrie, E. L. Thorndike, E. C. Tolman, and even the late, great B. F. Skinner himself. As you might guess, those deep cerebral theory builders would turn over in their graves if they could see some of the spin in the past chapters. Our grinning apologies to the ivory tower. We freely concede that OBM methods are largely built upon the classical principles of human learning—*but served up with a spicy attitude*. Even the strategic ploys and deeper hypnotic techniques lean heavily on conditioned responses, successive approximation, and schedules of reinforcement. This stuff oozes out everywhere, so we'll just have to live in peace with our learning theory roots.

My own academic history includes fortunate encounters with some noteworthy contemporary psychologists who have made contributions in their chosen areas of study. I learned of the above theory builders from my first graduate advisor, Dr. Steve Davis, a frontline learning theorist, author, and unabashed rat runner. He's been teaching and mentoring at Emporia State University in Kansas, in case you want to send your kids to an undergraduate program where there's more studying and probably less Frisbee throwing. (I was forced to say that.) Although I'll always remember Dr. Davis as perpetually 35 years old, it's likely he may have ripened on the academic vine and has cleaned out his office desk for a low-key retired life—without the rat lab cages.

When it comes to learning principle *applications* in the classroom (i.e., hard-core applied behavior analysis), I learned more from Dr. Jim Koller than any other single source. Professor Koller has been active in lecturing, consulting, and training doctoral-level school psychologists at the University of Missouri–Columbia. He was busy teaching functional behavior analysis decades before it became a three-letter acronym (FBA) or a popular IEP buzzword. I mentioned these two favorite mentors in the first *OBM Handbook* and am pleased to report that there have *still* been no genuine attempts to rescind my graduate degrees.

Ground-Floor Research Opportunities

Following the initial publication of the *OBM Handbook*, there were many attempts to torch my broom-closet psychology office. There were also some tacky demands that the early OBM staff immediately "cease and desist" from their important groundwork with these new interventions. It seems that a few of those stuffy "points-and-charts" guys were quick to collude with the insight-and-empathy counseling people. The two groups agreed that the world did not need any new wacky approach to managing difficult students. I guess that was because there were already plenty of wacky *ineffective* approaches to go around. Anyway, as you can see, the cat's out of the bag now, and OBM methods are moving into the marketplace of ideas.

During those early days, a few timid voices (bless them) began to ask sincerely, "Where did these OBM ideas come from?" Graduate students in special education have inquired about potential master's thesis projects. Sincere child therapist types have even asked for a bibliography of written work on this cryptic subject. We have tried to help everyone find their way.

OBM technology does seem to represent a departure from existing behavioral interventions. We like to remind people that scholarly fields evolve in predictable ways. First there are the ideas, then the various foundational studies, and then the latecomers get into subtheories and spin off ideas. We have already presented many of the basic ideas, and now it's time for some brave souls to start the early demonstration testing. While OBM is not presented as a general classroom management method (e.g., like a token economy classroom), it does show promise for niche "situation management" or "disgusting quirk management" specifically for oppositional students. We like to describe OBM as a collection of face-to-face "micromanagement" strategies. It's time for some daring classroom teachers or graduate students to put these methods to objective testing.

First things first. In order to set up a research project, some bright SPED graduate student would need to select (or develop) a method for easily screening a sample of hardcore oppositional-defiant subjects. The difficult part would then be to keep this illustrious group out of manifestation determination meetings and expulsion hearings while the study was in progress.

Suppose you already have your jar of live wiggly subjects. It's then high time to select one or more mini-interventions from this handbook. As an early demonstration study, it would be fair enough just to test the basic efficacy of OBM. That means just to show that the methods can objectively change certain disgusting behaviors among a targeted group of oppositional students. It would not be rocket science at first, just a clean demonstration project with good record keeping. After that level of study, we might move on to the more joyful task of actually comparing the relative effectiveness of OBM strategies with some of those Brand X interventions.

When the wannabe researchers inquire at my door, here's the basic handout they are given:

OBM Early Research Protocol

1. Trap some live subjects: Screen a very strong sample of oppositional-defiant subjects. There's no shortage out there, but get the most rigid and stubborn ones. You might use a "teacher nomination procedure" to get a roster of extreme characters. Try not to place too many of them together in one room—there may be some danger of reaching a "critical mass" of obstinacy.

2. Choose your OBM treatment: Select a simple, clean OBM intervention. Don't take on the vague Sigmund Freud monologues, our gang-busting ploys, or the gossip-and-hearsay thing. Those are cool strategies, but they depend heavily on the teacher's presentation skill and artful packaging. Rather, start with some powerful basics like maybe the Pretend Jerk project, wacky behavior permits, or even some good ole practice tantrum sessions. You'll also need to "review the literature" on your chosen OBM treatment and be able to explain briefly why the method should work as it does. Cite this handbook along with some writings of the classic psychotherapists discussed later in this chapter. Even at this late date, there's not much else in print.

3. Choose Brand X: When you are ready to compare the effectiveness of OBM, you'll need to select one of those Brand X classroom interventions. At this point it's wise to choose a well-known "packaged" program to run in the next lane. Let's face it, hard-core oppositional kids have a knee-jerk resistance to almost any structured management efforts. Perhaps even more amusing would be a Brand X intervention that has oppositional-defiant students sit in a circle to share their feelings. By the way, if you use a well-known classroom program or technique for your comparison intervention, you will probably have a ready-made bibliography to use in your literature review.

4. Choose your research staff: Find a skilled team of adventurous educators to run the parallel classroom interventions. Try to enlist experienced educators with lots of letters after their name. However, you might define OBM "competence" as anyone who's completed one of our workshops, or at least read the handbook and maybe clipped a few *Far Side* cartoons. At this point you just flat-out need to read up on experimental and quasi-experimental research designs. A lot of smart folks have thought through the best ways to logically balance out the presentation of experimental treatments. You might end up using matched side-by-side classrooms. What about balancing the use of your hard-working research staff? Maybe you'll decide on the often used "intrasubject replication design," in which each subject gets observed during an alternation of treatment and no-treatment conditions. You might get brave with this one and look at behavior changes in the same students with alternations between OBM, Brand X, and baseline conditions. Some of us love this design-and-inference game with all the balancing maneuvers and statistical number crunching. Others simply put up with it in order to get a thesis completed.

5. Credible measurements: For the dependent variable, you will need to select some widely accepted measure of classroom behavior (e.g., BASC or Conner's subscales, green tea leaves, or even your own home-made behavior frequency chart). Find something squeaky clean that offers good reliability and will allow you to easily record aspects of your target behavior. *A word to the wise*: Keep your study focused on one (or a few) clearly defined target behaviors. Don't attempt to use OBM to affect global adjustment measures or broad personality traits. You knew that, right?

6. Brief treatment program: Once all your ducks are in the proverbial row, decide on a time-limited behavior change program with those feisty oppositional kids. We can do some well-earned grinning here, since it's clear that strategic methods work quickly to bring behavior changes in defiant students. Most of the Brand X programs will get bogged down explaining the rules and token values, or the need to be honest with our feelings—while the strategic OBM interventions are already yielding early fruit. To be fair, do some spaced follow-up measures to establish long-term behavior changes. This is where our emphasis on subtle transformations may be "worth its weight."

7. Report your findings to someone who cares: Crunch your numbers and graph the results. Draft the most bare-bones, parsimonious write-up that is possible. Always start your report small because these creatures eventually take on a life of their own and grow into monster productions. With each revision they are capable of swelling in unexpected directions. If you get this far, why not write to the research staff at the OBM Institute and request a free, objective consultation?

Psychotherapist Beginnings

Until very recently, the terms *common sense* and *psychotherapy* were seldom used in the same breath. The same goes for *simple, brief,* and *cheap* (one of these terms is still in question). We'd like you to know that OBM ideas come out of some good places where you will hear those unlikely terms. There are some colorful pioneer writers—primarily psychotherapists—who should bear some of the theoretical blame for the emergence of OBM classroom methods.

Foremost among these is Milton Erickson, a maverick psychiatrist-hypnotist who probably seldom scrutinized any ids or egos. I'll bet he was also quite indifferent to the academic learning theories of his day. In his own unorthodox way, Erickson told delightful metaphoric stories that invited his patients to slip into productive daydream trances. During a period when most "therapy" was bound up in lengthy analysis, he also master-minded hundreds of elegant homework assignments that disrupted "symptoms" without dubious analysis and insight and freed up his patients to make wise choices.

Beyond Ericksonian hypnosis there's a busload of contemporary practitioners who write, lecture, and do training demonstrations—primarily for social workers and family therapists. These folks all do similar work but describe their own particular brands of therapy with such labels as "Brief," "Solution Focused," "Systems," and "Strategic." In case you have been enticed to read more in this fascinating field, some of the heavyweight names include Jay Haley, Cloé Madanes, Bill O'Hanlon, Steve de Shazer, Michelle Weiner-Davis, and one of my favorite iconoclasts, Dr. Joel Bergman. There's also a pair of irreverent therapists who go by the names Bandler & Grinder. These guys worked for years trying to systematize a raft of really slick hypnotherapy tricks. When you consider that their first book bore the title *Frogs into Princes,* you'll probably understand why their "outrageous" work is welcome here. They even came up with a credible-sounding name for their craft: neuro linguistic programming (NLP) . . . sure.

This *handbook* includes some glimpses of what goes on in the live OBM workshops. While captive trainees do receive an extensive notebook of our "classic" OBM materials, the core strategies remain basically the same as those before you. On the other hand, it might be mentioned that our dedicated R&D staff has now cataloged over 60 separate OBM interventions. That's way too many chapters, even if you took your Ritalin. Besides, many of those offbeat classroom strategies have not yet been packaged for civilian use. We may have to visit again on this matter.

Some Words on Ethical Practice

Because at times we may seem a bit overzealous with this OBM stuff (*understatement*), here's the part where we try to put the outrageous methods into some perspective. First, as therapists, consultants, and evaluators, we do a full spectrum of clinical work. During an average day in the schools or at my clinical office, I do many other interventions beside OBM. The whole idea of developing these techniques was to broaden the range of methods available to the classroom teacher (certainly not to limit them). Teachers with multiple skills are more confident than "single tool" educators. Use what works. Get rid of what doesn't. And we'd be downright proud if you'd just keep a few of our OBM strategies in mind as an option.

Some readers (not you, of course) may also need to be reminded that OBM methods are intended for intense interpersonal situations where the teacher must deal personally with extremely oppositional-defiant students. These fancy ploys and gimmicks are not meant to replace good planning, district-wide behavior policies, and a general classroom management program. They're also not intended for ordinary even-tempered students who are just having a bad day. Save OBM to help the oppositional-defiant kids who are really wired to resist.

Also, for the record, we never use or recommend OBM techniques for abused or seriously emotionally disturbed students. A little ED may be okay in our clients, but we take care of our genuine hurting and disturbed kids in other supportive ways. Besides, that leaves plenty of authentic hard-core oppositional students to work on. Those are the kids who we believe can really profit from these fast-acting and witty stratagems of OBM.

Famous Last Words

A good universal maxim to use in selecting a particular OBM method would be the Golden Rule from the Master Teacher. We've read through the transcripts from his open-air seminars, and you've probably already heard of his famous *"Do unto others"* principle. Here's our reframed application: Suppose you were an impossible student who was bent on ruining your school career. (I know this is hard to imagine, but stay with me.) If one of your past teachers knew of a painless but effective gimmick to redirect your self-defeating energy, would you fault that teacher for applying an OBM intervention? If your answer is "No problem, go for it!" and if you really do care about effectively guiding your resistance-impaired students—then welcome to the fascinating world of strategic management.

Your OBM Potential:
A Self-Assessment Exercise

How well do your personality style and life experience match the classic OBM model? Answer these cryptic inquiries "honestly" and score yourself below.

1. When you arrived home from school, did your mother often find **"Kick Me"** stickers attached to your sweater?

   _____ No   _____ Yes, but elementary grades only   _____ Yes, through college

2. When you used to read the **Calvin and Hobbes** comic strip, were you:

   _____ Entertained by Calvin's struggles with authority   _____ Flooded with ideas for tougher discipline   _____ Prompted to lecture this kid on obedience

3. When you are approached by **"hustlers"** on the street, do you frequently:

   _____ Hit *them* up for spare change   _____ Ask if they accept Visa/MC   _____ Let them select any bill from your wallet

4. When you first saw **The Sting** (with Redford and Newman), were you:

   _____ Captivated by the plot   _____ Mildly amused   _____ Asking if you missed something

5. When you watched Lt. **Columbo** interview a crook, did you think:

   _____ "Genius at work"   _____ "This guy should have retired in 1978"   _____ "Are there any sitcoms on somewhere else?"

6. When you learned that Gary Larson was quitting the **Far Side**, did you:

   _____ Struggle through a *"dark night of the soul"*   _____ Seek help with bereavement issues   _____ This is the first I've heard about it.

(continues)

7. Do you find syndicated detective shows like **The Rockford Files, Simon & Simon, Remington Steele, and Magnum, P.I.** to be:

_____ Intriguing plots and setups   _____ Good for a few laughs   _____ Disgusting escapism

8. Do you feel lost and frustrated in taking this self-assessment?

_____ No, and I just thought of some more items!   _____ I see where it's going   _____ Yes, it's moronic and degrading

9. Over the years, have you frequently heard the comment **"You just don't get it."**

_____ No   _____ Only from supervisors   _____ Frequently, and it still makes no sense to me

SCORING: Give yourself 100 big points for each response scored on the left-hand side, 5 points for each response in the center position, and no more than zero points for all others.

Your OBM Total: _____

<u>Interpretation</u>:
700 and above: Definite OBM career potential! (*Get liability insurance*)
30 to 699: With guidance and flexible thinking, you'll enjoy OBM
zero to 29: Please review the *OBM Handbook* "Disclaimer"

Some Questions To Ask About Problem Behavior (before you "go strategic")

1. How chronic (i.e., long lasting or habitual) and severe is it? Could I live with it if I slightly reduced my expectations? How different is this particular behavior from the class mean?
2. Does this particular behavior defy my authority as the classroom teacher? Does it impede my opportunity to teach? . . . or the learning opportunities of other students?
3. Have I stated in clear specific terms just which behaviors are required in my classroom? Have I communicated exactly what I want from this student?
4. Have I discovered what it is that really bugs me about this student's behavior? Just what is my emotional reaction to this student as a person? Does he or she "remind" me of someone? Is there a clash between our temperament styles?
5. Am I struggling with stressors in my personal life that reduce my ability to tolerate certain misbehaviors? Am I taking care of myself, and do I feel good about my chosen profession?
6. All behavior is caused by something. Have I determined what motivates this student's problem behavior? Here are just a few possibilities to consider:

   a. **a blatant quest for power or control**
   b. **an excessive need for attention**
   c. **a displacement of anger toward a parent**
   d. **"modeling" of a sick behavior from home**
   e. **a manipulation strategy spawned out of street survival needs**
   f. **a hidden revenge motive**

7. Is this student's misbehavior a result of repeated failure and frustration with the standard curriculum? If so, have I reasonably tried to adapt or modify the curriculum?
8. Have I determined whether this problem behavior is **"premeditated,"** a **"reflexive habit,"** or an issue of **"developmental immaturity"**? My intervention planning will vary accordingly.

Behavioral interventions are not "one size fits all." OBM is appropriate for some of the students described above but not others. Stay sharp and keep each of these questions in mind as you shop for strategies in the OBM Handbook.

OBM Guide to Subtle Transformations

Throughout the *OBM Handbook* we have illustrated dozens of unorthodox techniques for taking control of disruptive and oppositional behavior. You may notice that many of our elaborate OBM strategies include one or more of the "Subtle Transformations" in the list included here. In most of our strategies, it is essential that our daring and resourceful OBM teacher request some early minor variations in the problem behavior. This brings to mind that nearly formulaic point in every *Columbo* mystery episode when he's being thrown out (or frozen out) of the prime suspect's Beverly Hills mansion. Our favorite sleuth never just exits. There's always that pregnant pause at the door (you've seen it), where he hesitates a moment and then turns back with "just one more question." Of course, we all know that this particular question was probably the central reason for the house call. But it had to be skillfully presented as an afterthought. Okay, does everyone have the illustration? It's time for the bus to be moving along now.

After explaining how the oppositional student is to continue pretending, practicing, helping out, or performing that disgusting behavior for some contrived reason, the fully functional OBM teacher will pause for a moment and add something like:

> ***"Oh, and by the way, could I ask that you do***
> ***that pretend behavior just a***
> ***bit differently ..."?***

As insignificant as it may seem, requiring even the slightest alteration in the "raw" misbehavior will put the teacher on the road to blissful control. Some old familiar terms like *shaping* and *successive approximation* may come to mind right now. Following are some of the basic types of change that the OBM teacher might request from the classroom tyrant as he is doing his routine:

1. Change the *frequency* of that annoying behavior.
   Examples:

   *"That pencil tapping habit is still only fairly disruptive. I mean probably most kids in the class are bothered by it ... but not all. If I'm going to learn how to handle really disruptive behaviors, you're going to have to tap **a lot more each class period maybe twice as much**, even when you don't feel like it."*

   *"What you're doing is okay so far as it goes, but for effective development of a whiny-sounding voice, we're going to need **at least ten more practice trials** each morning."*

   *"Sometimes you resist things and argue with me—just as we planned—but other times I see you just going along with the rest of the class and doing really good work. If our secret program is going to work, I'll need to see **a lot more strong-looking resistance** behaviors each day."*

*"I need to have you come up to my desk **at least three times** each class period and urgently request to see the nurse."*

2. Change the *intensity* of that contemptible conduct.
   Examples:

*"Could you remember to resist my instructions **more strongly and openly** toward the beginning of math class? And then you are welcome to just relax and participate normally, or surprise me and practice some more resisting later on."*

*"Let's try this … in art or literature class—you choose one—I'd like you to pretend to be **even more slow—very, very slow**—in starting your work. Look around and make sure you're the last to start."*

*"When you're doing one of those practice tantrums, **try kicking your feet a lot harder, like you really mean it …"***

3. Change the *duration* of that obnoxious routine.
   Examples:

*"I thought you had your getting-the-last-word performance down pretty well until yesterday. It seems you're slipping a little. Remember the deal. You're supposed to keep up the arguing and whining **during the entire time** I'm passing out the worksheets. Somehow, your complaining over the last couple of days hasn't lasted long enough for me to really practice my management skills."*

*"That angry voice sounds pretty sincere, but you need to **hold the mean-looking face just a bit longer**. Try holding it until at least two other students seem to believe that you're really upset."*

4. Change the *time of day* that the heinous act is committed in class.
   Examples:

*"In order to have you give it your best shot, let's have you start the foot tapping and wiggling-in-your-seat practice trials **a lot earlier in class**."*

*"Your grumbling noises have sounded very real during third hour science, and they have been very helpful to me. However, I need to ask for another favor. Would you be able to **shift your grumbling noises to second-hour** social studies and make them sound just as real there?"*

*"**Instead of waiting till afternoon** for your sleepy spells, I need you to pretend to go to sleep at the end of second hour."*

5. Change the *location* where this loathsome charade is performed.
   Examples:

*"Could you **just move over to this desk** here when it's time to do your special practice behaviors?"*

*"This pouting skill is important enough that I need to have you pick a better area ... say **in the back of the class** ... to practice without interruption."*

*"Could we change your pretend behaviors just a little for today? I'd like you to keep raising your hand and asking me impossible questions, but this time **only if your desk is turned a little sideways** ... so you look more confused."*

6. Change the student's *physical posture* while acting out the vile sequence.
   Examples:

*"Next time you do your pretend arguing behaviors for me, could you **stick your chin out**, like this, just to remind me to stay sharp?"*

*"Let's have a secret signal. Whenever you are doing your I-hate-this-class routine, could you remember to **keep one hand clenched in a tight fist**? That will remind me that you're trying to do your best job right at that time."*

*"How about **leaning forward in your desk just a little** whenever you're pretending to have one of those headaches? That will be my signal to ask if you're having one of your near-death experiences."*

7. Change the *sequence* of steps in that habitual disruption.
   Examples:

*"Next time could you remember to do the hissy fit for about 1 minute **just before** I pass out the worksheets?"*

*"Could you write your pretend apology statement to little Reginald **in the morning** —for the things you might say to him during the day? It will probably save some of your recess time in the afternoon."*

*"Next, your assignment is to go to time-out for **5 minutes before first recess** ... and pretend to calm down for something bad that might happen later when you go out on the playground."*

*"Please come to my desk **in the middle of the work period** and give me two pretend excuses for why your homework might not be complete tomorrow."*

8. *Add or subtract* one element from the offensive pattern.
   Examples:

*"Whenever you do your practice 'work avoidance' routine, **always hold an extra yellow pencil in your left hand** so I'll know you're on duty."*

*"Each time, **just before** you do one of the pretend excuses, just take your hand and **snap your fingers quietly** like this. It will help with our communication on this secret assignment."*

*"When you do your morning tattletales, make your report to me **without using your regular voice**."*

Subtle Transformations
Steamed and Summarized on the Half Shell

Here's the system, boiled down to the basics. If you would like to serve up one of our savory paradoxic requests as a way to get started in the OBM business, do this:

1. Encourage the problem behavior,
   for some good educational reason.

2. Take early control of the behavior
   by requesting a small token change.

3. Gradually and methodically erode (or "transform") the behavior
   through a series of small requested shifts in the pattern.

4. Absolutely no smirks or chuckling
   until you reach the safety of your teachers' lounge.

An OBM Look at Reinforcement

Sympathy for Skinner

As you must have gathered by now, we are not real hot on the use of primary tangible reinforcers in our management strategies. From a practical perspective, it's not the classroom teacher's job to constantly dispense toys and goodies. Besides that, it's just not practical to attempt major personality overhauls while also trying to achieve dozens of academic goals. (Yes, I hear the applause.) On the other hand, some of us have paid our academic dues in the school of applied behavior analysis, and we want to give a balanced picture. I was one of those rat-runners and M&M pushers, and so I'm not here to bad-mouth the grand old school of behaviorism. We do need those good folks who are willing to spend a career in the basement lab with rats and pigeons cataloging response patterns, developing learning theories, and cleaning out the cages. Hopefully, from time to time they'll come up with something we can use in the real classroom.

When you hear that someone's oppositional behavior style is "deeply ingrained" in their personality, you can also be certain that the busy public school classroom will not be a good operant-shaping laboratory for successfully fixing that problem. It's just not reasonable for a teacher to invest the 300,000+ operant trials that might be needed to gradually shape Oppositional Eddy into a pleasant, compliant learner—with charming social deportment. Besides, we just don't have that kind of time before retirement.

There's no question that hard-core behavior modification can be effective, but often the required environmental conditions are quite demanding. Our concern regards not effectiveness, but efficiency—especially with this notorious hard-case group. We have found that OBM methods can achieve measurable behavior change in 1 or 2 weeks and often in only a couple of days. Making the same objective changes in student behavior through traditional operant methods (e.g., points and charts) might take months of diligent contingency management and probably a hefty line-item expenditure all for those attractive tangible rewards. Not so with strategic methods. By tactfully requesting and "reinforcing" a complex pattern of *pretend* classroom disruptions, I can quickly extinguish a list of disgusting responses that might have required several rolls of happy stickers and weeks (months?) of intense teacher effort. Yes, the OBM team may stoop to pushing a few M&Ms (or wagering for those heavenly chocolate-covered raisins), but we are not using them for true operant shaping—just as support props in a more sophisticated stratagem.

Secondary Reinforcers Can Still Carry Clout

Rather than trying to achieve primary drive reduction through concrete traditional rewards, we get a kick out of some very slick social reinforcers. As a tacked-on little incentive to ensure compliance with our outrageous assignments, we like to grant our students unusual benefits, contrived freedoms, bizarre privileges, outlandish social recognition, and clearly excessive demonstrative praise. These rewards are highly valued by the student and usually free to the teacher. We like to think you can substitute creativity for big bucks. Hopefully, the list will bring some grins but also serve to hyperstimulate your right brain so that you will be discovering reward items and activities everywhere you look. Brace yourself. <u>This</u> is reinforcement!

Criteria for OBM Reinforcers

1. **<u>Free</u>** or dirt cheap for the teacher.
2. Manageable within the school environment (minimal setup/cleanup).
3. Easily dispensed—especially through coupons, tickets, permits, passes, etc.
4. Supply fully controlled by the teacher.
5. Ethical, legal, and . . . fairly safe.
6. Permitted in your building.
7. Minimal disruption to the educational process.
8. Novel, creative, and possibly fad-inducing.

Student Reinforcement Inventory: A Possibility Menu To Stimulate Your OBM Creativity

1. Chewing gum "permit" good for special permission to chew gum for 1 hour on Friday. Of course, the student shouldn't expect the teacher to also supply the gum. He should bring his own ("If you got 'em, chew 'em") or earn the gum separately. The permit bears an authorization signature and must be worn or displayed during the chewing time. If it works for gum, what about hard candies? How about those novelty candies at the checkout racks? What about some new special wild flavor? It's the thought that counts.
2. Sell "time shares" to the reading corner. These are confirmed reservations for special preferred-usage time blocks. As with the real time-share market, you may attach some fine print such as a modest fee for any trading of time blocks.
3. Early dismissal to lunch. Hey, even a 30-second headstart could mean the difference between indigestion and food tolerance.
4. Early dismissal from class or from school. If the local "hit man" bully is after you, a 1-minute headstart can be quite motivating. Survival incentives come before love for learning.
5. Permission to work quietly on an assignment from another class. Of course, this would exclude such things as the term project for Taxidermy Science 101.

6. A free admission ticket to the next home game. What about permission to sit up with the local radio guy? or an invitation to give some color commentary? If the student isn't really into sports, he might scalp the ticket for quick cash. Maybe he could put it up for auction on Ebay?

7. Free time to listen to music on a cassette or CD player (with headphones). The student must bring his own tapes or listen to the teacher's collection of Lawrence Welk favorites.

8. Two "free" items on the next spelling or math test. Allow the student to circle the two items to be skipped, attach the coupon to the paper, and get full credit for those items.

9. Permission to do only alternate items (odd or even numbers) on the homework assignment. The completed half is graded as if it were the entire assignment. *Here's an embedded OBM strategy:* We have found that students who ordinarily resist *any* homework will complete the truncated assignment—because they don't want to waste the coupon. It's kind of like buying a case of cat food that's half-off, and then going out to adopt a pet.

10. Permission to serve as an aide to the teacher, coach, janitor, or with the school's bomb squad.

11. Preferred seating in the classroom: The student uses a coupon as prepaid rent on a favorite desk position in the room. This rental may be for 1 day, 1 week, or until there is a disturbance.

12. Extra Consultation Coupons: These prepaid coupons are redeemable for special guidance on one difficult work item. Our high-self-esteem teachers print up a limited supply of these coupons resembling a $100 bill and displaying their own staff photo instead of Ben Franklin. The implicit message to the student is that the teacher's consultation time "don't come cheap" and should be valued accordingly.

13. The privilege of "reserving" a cafeteria table for a select group of friends. Why not block off the table with some of that fancy velvet rope from a movie theater? Maybe find a tablecloth and even require a clip-on, black bow tie for each member of the dinner party.

14. While we're at it, how 'bout earning a special reserved seat on the school bus? Better yet, why not earn a prestigious "box seat" at the next school basketball game, drama event, or assembly? Use bright-colored crepe paper to designate the VIP seating.

15. Award a "Panic Card" that can be used for urgent care at the guidance counselor's office. This card also serves double as a hall pass. Let the student know that the Panic Card should be used *before* any crisis gets out of hand (and cannot be used to escape any classroom criminal charges).

16. Permission to use the computer to type out responses to the weekly spelling test. (*Note*: Be sure the program doesn't have a "spell-check" function. You understand the importance of this, right?)

17. Opportunity to make an activities announcement over the school's PA system. This announcement may be prerecorded so the narcissistic student can listen to his own compelling and authoritative voice (and avoid anxiety!).

18. Appointment to serve on a classroom "kangaroo court" to deliberate appropriate consequences for peer conduct violations arising over the past week.

19. Permission to take part in a very special end-of-year water fight (with buckets, hoses, balloons, or squirt bottles provided). Extra points (roughly six billion) may require the teacher to participate. On the other hand, a teacher armed with a fully charged Super Soaker may find some personal joy facing down the classroom tough guy ("Do you feel lucky today?").

20. The earning of "Auction Bucks," which can be used to bid on a menu of classroom privileges. This auction technique is a good (and safe) way to measure the relative value of various wacky benefits in the classroom. Don't worry about losing control of a neat privilege. If it's really hot, the bidding will go wild and one crazed obsessive student will sink his entire point stash into it.

21. Award "Caught Being Good" tickets for behavioral and academic achievements. These tickets are then signed by the student and proudly deposited in a fish bowl in the main office, where a broadcasted weekly drawing determines special winners.

22. Experiment with the policy of keeping one or more front seats vacant. Whenever a brilliant or near-genius answer is given in class, the teacher activates a celebrity music sound track and theatrically announces to the student, "Come on down!" or "Advance to the head of the class!" The selected student then occupies a coveted front seat for the remainder of the class period.

23. Witty OBM teachers with unlimited energy might arrange to have "Special Achievement" certificates delivered to students in the form of a singing telegram. Better yet, enlist the principal to be the messenger, dressed in a gorilla outfit or belly dancer costume. (Hey, you won't know until you ask.)

24. Begin each classroom day by reading a "Morning Report" patterned after a radio newscast. This should review some noteworthy student achievements from the preceding day (e.g., "Yesterday five students were found to have perfect papers, all students completed the worksheets, and the teacher smiled three times ..."). These reports can get pretty wild, and they sound even better if prerecorded and played back "on the air."

25. Earned permission *not* to have lunch with the teacher on Thursday.

Incentives Are Everywhere

In training workshops I have often suggested this outrageous procedure: When you get out of your car in the parking lot, look around on the pavement for any small piece of worthless scrap you might find (pull tab, squashed pen cap, odd-looking pebble, etc.). Bring the junk item into class and tell wild, extravagant stories about it all through the day. Make extreme claims that include references to aliens, spies, Elvis sightings, and rare minerals. During the last few minutes of school, test the value now ascribed to that piece of junk by giving it a wild name and putting it up for class auction. Compare the number of points or credits bid on it with the value paid for earlier "real" rewards. Sometimes this exercise generates another "pet rock" craze—and, of course, another millionaire teacher.

Mild Negative Consequences in the Classroom

1. A simple 30-second "detention" at the end of class.
2. Immediate, standing (sincere-sounding) apology to the entire class.
3. One hour of "voluntary" community service in the cafeteria (e.g., cleaning tables, mopping, washing windows, or entertaining the staff).
4. One-day restricted lunch period (eat in a boring, isolated area).
5. One-hour after-school detention (with required work on a topical learning packet).
6. In-school suspension for 1, 2, 3, or more days (with required work on an in-depth learning packet that addresses the student's particular conduct violation).
7. One-week suspension from sports team practice (or ineligibility to play in the next official game).
8. Formal written apology to the teacher, entire class, or specific victim(s). Must be clear about the misbehavior and approved by the teacher or victims.
9. Problem Behavior Debriefing Form (signed and kept on file for future reference).
10. Loss of desk for one period (work with a seat only). Why not add the loss of a left shoe?
11. Must be the absolute last student to exit the classroom at passing time.
12. Mandatory time-out for 10 minutes (with a verbal request to be readmitted to class).
13. Specially designed restitution project to help the victim or class (TBA).
14. Essay project: 200 words on respect or other positive character traits (responsibility, diligence, perseverance, loyalty, honor, etc.). This might include required hand-drawn illustrations.
15. Fifty "pretend" push-ups, pull-ups, or sit-ups closely monitored by a class peer.
16. Submit to a Peer Review Panel with anonymous feedback through the teacher.
17. Community service assignment at home (1, 2, 3 hours) with verification by a parent.
18. Informal "educational" interview with the juvenile probation officer.
19. Loss of work-study job hours (daily, weekly, etc.).
20. Home-school contract: A parent is required to attend school and escort the student through the entire day.
21. Required "educational" orientation visit to a juvenile offender boot camp, plus a written report on the experience.
22. One weekend of total (parent-certified) in-home grounding: no peers, no electronic media, no fun—total joyless boredom. (Wager that the parent can't pull it off.)

23. Reconvene the IEP committee to consider a "more supportive" (i.e., more restrictive) program.
24. Loss of an assigned private locker (replaced by the teacher's cardboard box).
25. Banishment of all self-confident and pleasant thoughts for one class period. (Ouch! that one really hurts.)

For those of you who are still trying to figure out what's going on, here's our quick summary of strategic interventions for managing hard-core oppositional-defiant students. We gathered these nifty tricks from the old Jedi masters with a promise that they would be used only for good. You will find one or more of them represented in every chapter of the *OBM Handbook*.

1. **Reframes:** Find ways to creatively misinterpret a problem behavior as something quite valuable, educationally relevant, or actually intended for good. Follow the reframe with a syrupy dose of praise and recognition.

2. **Distraction:** Strategically ignore a problem behavior and instead get all concerned about some other petty unrelated matter. Become overly assertive and even a bit emotional and then launch into advice giving and directives about the boring unrelated matter.

3. **Planned Bewilderment:** In the face of stubborn defiance, make a crazy out-of-the-blue statement or ask an unexpected, bizarre question that generates mental confusion. (With oppositional students, the next best thing to compliance is often an energy-draining dose of bewilderment.)

4. **Paradoxical Requests:** Ask for the exact opposite of what is usually expected. Most often this includes a requested performance of the problem behavior ... for some good, logical reason. Always include a "subtle transformation" that slightly alters the requested problem behavior from its original form.

5. **Double-Bind Alternatives:** For students who resist any directives, offer the illusion of there being only two possible choices—both of which eventually lead to the same goal. This might be stated to the student as "If you trod the easy path, the goal is reached. If you refuse and trod the difficult path, the goal is still reached. It's your choice, and thank you." Consult the text, and have mental health paramedics standing by.

6. **Passive Suggestion:** The teacher practices "thinking out loud" around the oppositional student. She occasionally drops some low-key predictions or a mumbled guess about future improvements, unavoidable growth and maturity, imminent progress, etc. Later, any approximation of success can be reinforced with a nod, a smile, or the teacher's knowing look.

7. **Trance-Inducing Metaphoric Stories:** Instead of directly confronting some rigid self-defeating behavior, make up a colorful fable about a roughly similar (but not too similar) situation ... that occurs with animal characters, or in a galaxy far, far away. Have your main character struggle, gain insight, and find a solution. Later, in a golden learning moment, simply make a passive reference to the name of the

main character—and the whole metaphor will immediately download into your student's head.

8. **Psychobabble Diagnoses & Prescriptions:** Oppositional students hate to be figured out, understood, or, worse yet, "diagnosed" with some esoteric label. Some students will refuse to perform their typical immature acts just to prove that the teacher's diagnosis is faulty. Consult Chapter 6 for help with for impossible prescriptions—which set up smother-love sympathy-giving for all that developmental angst.

APPENDIX G

Reproducible Materials

SECRET ASSIGNMENT
Credit Card

Student Assistant: _____

Contracting Teacher: _____

Practice Week # ☐

Workday   **Credit Tallies**

Monday: _____

Tuesday: _____

Wednesday: _____

Thursday: _____

Friday: _____

Total Earnings: _____

Teacher Initials: _____

NOTE: This card is confidential! It should be held secretly by the teacher so that earned credits can be recorded.

CONTRACT FOR PRETEND BEHAVIORS
(A Secret Deal)

In order to help my teacher develop good classroom management skills, I agree to act out the exact pretend behaviors listed in this contract. I understand that this is a training program and my teacher will be practicing discipline and motivation methods during the contract period.

Student Pretend Behaviors:

A. _____   B. _____

_____   _____

Scheduled Practice Sessions:

_____

_____

Payment Agreement:

It will be my teacher's responsibility to keep a written record of my pretend behavior practice sessions. For each scheduled practice session, I will earn _____ points for <u>each</u> of the above pretend behaviors—as long as they look real to my teacher. I understand that my total earned points may be used to purchase one or more rewards at the end of each practice week.

Endorsement Signatures:

We agree to the terms of this contract. Any future changes must be made in writing.

Student Assistant: _____   Date: _____

Contracting Teacher: _____   Date: _____

50 BONUS POINTS
Tough Act To Beat!

Fantastic performance!

Your pretend behaviors looked so real.

And your act was *very* helpful.

SURPRISE!

That was a genuine
"Pretend Behavior"

So … how did I do?

And how many points did I earn?

INSULT COLLECTION CARD

Credits Earned By: _____

Student Helpers: _____

_____

_____

These Helpers have agreed to provide teasing and name calling during the regular school day.

Insult Credits Earned Today

   Monday: _____

   Tuesday: _____

Wednesday: _____

   Thursday: _____

    Friday: _____

Total Insult Credits Earned: _____

Teacher Initials: _____

Save this card to earn fabulous Prizes!!!

INSULT COLLECTION CARD

Credits Earned By: _____

Student Helpers: _____

_____

_____

These Helpers have agreed to provide teasing and name calling during the regular school day.

Insult Credits Earned Today

   Monday: _____

   Tuesday: _____

Wednesday: _____

   Thursday: _____

    Friday: _____

Total Insult Credits Earned: _____

Teacher Initials: _____

Save this card to earn fabulous Prizes!!!

INSULT COLLECTION CARD

Credits Earned By: _____

Student Helpers: _____

_____

_____

These Helpers have agreed to provide teasing and name calling during the regular school day.

Insult Credits Earned Today

   Monday: _____

   Tuesday: _____

Wednesday: _____

   Thursday: _____

    Friday: _____

Total Insult Credits Earned: _____

Teacher Initials: _____

Save this card to earn fabulous Prizes!!!

INSULT COLLECTION CARD

Credits Earned By: _____

Student Helpers: _____

_____

_____

These Helpers have agreed to provide teasing and name calling during the regular school day.

Insult Credits Earned Today

   Monday: _____

   Tuesday: _____

Wednesday: _____

   Thursday: _____

    Friday: _____

Total Insult Credits Earned: _____

Teacher Initials: _____

Save this card to earn fabulous Prizes!!!

Some Lifelong Benefits of Quitting This Stupid School

Your assignment is to create a list of personal benefits to you for taking the bold step of becoming a school dropout. Use your knowledge of older dropouts—from last year—to help you think of all the real benefits.

Student:_____

Class: _____

Monday:

1._____

2._____

3._____

Tuesday:

1._____

2._____

3._____

Wednesday:

1._____

2._____

3._____

Thursday:

1._____

2._____

3._____

Friday:

1._____

2._____

3._____

Some Honest Reasons
Homework Might Not Get Done

Your assignment is to create a list of really good excuses for incomplete homework. Use your own observations and painful experiences in this difficult class to help you think of answers.

Student:_____

Class: _____

Monday:

1. _____

2. _____

3. _____

Tuesday:

1. _____

2. _____

3. _____

Wednesday:

1. _____

2. _____

3. _____

Thursday:

1. _____

2. _____

3. _____

Friday:

1. _____

2. _____

3. _____

How I Would Change the Unfair Rules in This Sorry Class

Your assignment is to create a list of immediate changes you would make in the rules for this dark, oppressive classroom. Use your own bad experiences here to help you think of as many humane changes as possible.

Student:_____

Class: _____

Monday:

1._____
2._____
3._____

Tuesday:

1._____
2._____
3._____

Wednesday:

1._____
2._____
3._____

Thursday:

1._____
2._____
3._____

Friday:

1._____
2._____
3._____

Rude Behaviors I Have Endured from Geeks, Nerds, and Punks

Your assignment is to create a list of the most "crude and disgusting" behaviors you have witnessed in the cultural wasteland of this classroom. Try to recall your very worst social encounters and your most humiliating memories to record below.

Student:_____

Class: _____

Monday:

1._____

2._____

3._____

Tuesday:

1._____

2._____

3._____

Wednesday:

1._____

2._____

3._____

Thursday:

1._____

2._____

3._____

Friday:

1._____

2._____

3._____

A Few of the Reasons
I Always Get Blamed for Things!

Your assignment is to create a list of believable reasons for the unfair accusations thrown at you in this oppressive classroom. Use your own miserable life experiences here to help you think of as many false charges as possible.

Student:_____

Class: _____

Monday:

1. _____

2. _____

3. _____

Tuesday:

1. _____

2. _____

3. _____

Wednesday:

1. _____

2. _____

3. _____

Thursday:

1. _____

2. _____

3. _____

Friday:

1. _____

2. _____

3. _____

More Examples of Why Life Isn't Jolly in This Miserable Class

Your assignment is to create a list of the inhumane conditions endured by students in this class. Use your own rotten experiences here to help you think of as many answers as possible.

Student:_____

Class: _____

Monday:

1._____

2._____

3._____

Tuesday:

1._____

2._____

3._____

Wednesday:

1._____

2._____

3._____

Thursday:

1._____

2._____

3._____

Friday:

1._____

2._____

3._____

POLYMORPHOUS Adolescent Development Test

Adapted from the work of international scholars in polymorphous development
Barry T. Christian, PhD (1997, rev. 2007)

Name: _____ **Exact age at time of testing:** ____Yrs. ____Mos.

Instructions: This exercise is unlike other school tests you may have taken. The items below have no right or wrong answers. This test is also "polymorphous" because it measures many parts or forms of normal and abnormal character development. Try to give the first or second response that comes to your mind. Total honesty is not as important as completing each item.

1. Place a <u>circle</u> around the two symbols that make you feel the most safe/secure/relaxed.

2. My earliest childhood memories seem to be stored as:

   Answer: Glossy color photos   Colorless photos   Video without sound   Any other

3. I can clearly recall a time when I squeezed as many as six quarters together between my thumb and forefinger.

   Circle one only: True   False   Can't remember

4. I have privately written poetry or songs without understanding their true meaning.

   Circle one only: True   False   Can't remember

5. I am quite certain that I have had some unusual dreams in the past year.

   Circle one only: True   False   Can't remember

6. Place a <u>triangle</u> around any symbols that seem very chilling or cold.

7. Old familiar smells, odors, and aromas can easily cause me to daydream.

   Circle one only: True   False   Can't remember

8. During a single day I have noticed the same number appearing at different times or places.

   Circle one only: True   False   Can't remember

9. I have sometimes privately wondered if I am real.

   Circle one only: True   False   Can't remember

10. Cross off <u>any</u> symbols that (for any personal reason) are disturbing to you.

11. While sitting at a particular desk, I recall having a sudden unexplained spell of emotion.

    Circle one only: True   False   Can't remember

12. While walking in hallways, I have noticed students with no real expression on their face.

    Circle one only: True   False   Can't remember

13. <u>Cross off</u> the two symbols that *least* reflect your desired personality style, and <u>circle</u> the two that *most* reflect your desired personality style.

Return this test for proper scoring.   **Please do not attempt to interpret any items on your own.**

POLYMORPHOUS ADOLESCENT DEVELOPMENT TEST

Student Profile Sheet
(EXTREMELY CONFIDENTIAL)

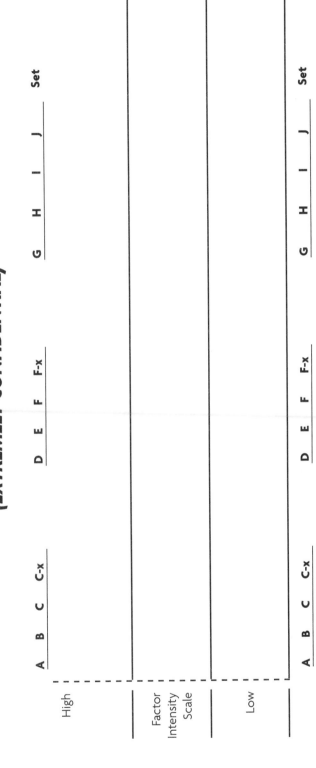

| A | B | C | C-x | D | E | F | F-x | G | H | I | J | Set |

High

Factor
Intensity
Scale

Low

| A | B | C | C-x | D | E | F | F-x | G | H | I | J | Set |

This profile summary sheet may be used for graphic display of the ten primary orthogonal factors comprising the full known range of hyper-accelerated and mulitvariate complex polymorphous development. Both reconstituted introjects and abstract factors have been applied to the raw scores. <u>Note:</u> This scale should not be used for plotting beyond 19 years of age.

Student: _____   **Age at testing:** _____

Norms applied: _____ Male _____ Female

PRACTICE TANTRUMS!

Student: _____   Start date: _____

Practice times: _____   _____

Behaviors	Monday	Tuesday	Wednesday	Thursday	Friday
1.					
2.					
3.					
4.					
5.					
Totals:	_____	_____	_____	_____	_____

Daily Rating Codes:

S = 10 points: Satisfactory (looks & sounds real!)

S− = 5 points: Wimpy job, but acceptable

U = 0 points: Unsatisfactory (not believable)

Teacher Comments:

NOTICE

There Will Now Be

ZERO TOLERANCE

for These Behaviors:

with Immediate Consequences for Any Violation

TATTLETALE COUPON

Present this coupon for the right to report the evil deeds of one other student.

Coupon expires on: _____

OUT-OF-SEAT FOR NO GOOD REASON COUPON

Present this coupon for permission to be out of your seat and do some unnecessary task for one (1) minute.

Voluntary Time-Out Coupon

Present this coupon to receive ten (10) minutes of quiet time at the time-out place.

Coupon expires:

_____

GETTING-THE-LAST-WORD COUPON

This coupon may be redeemed for permission to have the last word while making the usual excuses or insisting you are right.

Bugging Coupon

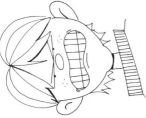

This coupon may be redeemed for permission to BUG others and make a general nuisance of yourself for five (5) minutes.

Special Rules:

- You may not use your normal voice while using this coupon.
- Left eye must remain closed.
- No criminal behaviors allowed.

BAD ATTITUDE COUPON

Present this coupon to your teacher for the right to enjoy 10 minutes of really bad attitude during regular class time.

Coupon expires on: _____

WHINING, GRUMBLING, AND COMPLAINING COUPON

Present this coupon for the privilege of being miserable in class for **5 minutes.**

Coupon expires: _____

BASIC GOOFINESS COUPON

THIS COUPON MAY BE REDEEMED FOR PERMISSION TO ACT GOOFY, SILLY, OR DISGUSTING FOR A PERIOD OF 5 MINUTES.

Special Rules:
This coupon void if no one smiles within 1 minute of seeing your goofiness.

BUSTED! COUPON

Looks like you need some cool-down time. If the teacher gives you this coupon, take a deep breath, and go directly to the time-out place.

ADVANCED GOOFINESS COUPON

This coupon may be redeemed for permission to act goofy, silly, or disgusting for a period of 5 minutes. Your behavior must be well rehearsed and entertaining.

Advanced Rules:
This coupon void if your goofy behavior fails to amuse the teacher or to get a laugh from the class within one (1) minute.

STATE OF CONFUSION COUPON

Feeling totally confused today?

Present this coupon for some extra help in understanding that impossible class work.

PANIC CARD!
COUPON

When life gets tense, use this card for urgent care at the school counselor's office.

(Not good for getting out of trouble!)

This behavior report card confirms that _____

Student's Name

listened to your private taped message at: **Time:** _____ **Date:** _____

Trigger situation that prompted the need for a taped message:

_____

_____

Response to the message:

☜ Improvement   Deterioration ☞

(+3   +2   +1   0   –1   –2   –3)

Teacher Comments: _____

_____

_____   _____

Teacher   **Student**

Your Only Chance to Escape:

You must stand up. Count out loud backwards beginning with your age *(number of years)* and ending at your grade *(number)*. Do it right the first time. If you do it correctly, you may sit down quickly and pretend you are working. If you mess up, you can think about it during your lunch detention.

Simple Survival Action:

You must shake hands with one (1) person in this class and give them one (1) sincere-sounding compliment or word of encouragement.

If the teacher likes it, you may quickly sit down and your bad luck may be over … or not.

Accurate Reporting Practice:

Fully describe your disgusting offense to the teacher—with all the nitty-gritty details—and tell exactly why it was wrong.

Do this well and you will be pardoned from other consequences. If your details are not good enough, find a comfortable seat in lunch detention.

Time-Delay Consequence:

Way to go! You lose 30 seconds from your next passing period. When the bell rings, start watching the clock. If you mess up, you get one (1) detention. This is a small price to pay for your last display of immature behavior!

It Could Be Much Worse:

You will be the *last* student to exit this classroom at the end of the period. Accept your fate with dignity … and live with the inner pain.

If you forget and exit ahead of anyone, you may reflect on your sins during lunch detention. Have a nice day.

Temporary Paralysis:

You must write with your subdominant hand for the next three (3) minutes. Your work will be graded as usual. If you try to switch over before your time is up, your dominant hand may begin to wither, lose all strength, and grow warts. That would be nobody's fault but your own … and you can think about it in lunch detention.

Avoid Serving One Detention:

Give the teacher two (2) sincere-sounding "thank yous" about the joy of learning in this wonderful class—within the next 45 seconds. (The clock is ticking right now.)

Social Degradation Experience:

You have to stand by your desk and witness a classroom vote on your offensive behavior. If over half of your peers vote to condemn your actions, you must stay in your desk for 60 seconds after class is dismissed. If you get a good vote from your peers, you are released from any consequences ... except those imposed by your critical inner self.

You have 120 seconds to <u>print</u> these exact words on a full sheet of paper:

I always do my best in this class. I'm one of those kids you can count on for 100% effort.

(Sign your name & give it to the teacher for future reference.)

Luck of the Draw!

You are hereby dismissed from your consequence. Shake hands with your teacher and have a nice day.

Your Fair Choice:

For your last nuisance misbehavior you have earned one (1) detention consequence. You may choose to trade detention for the loss of your chair for four (4) minutes. During this time you must stand and continue your assigned work ... and no crybaby stuff.

Imaginary Consequence:

Give this card to your teacher. Teacher reads:

Someday you will find yourself eating with your friends in the cafeteria. Suddenly, the food you just ate will start to swell up in your stomach ... and you will feel it pushing way up into your throat. Others at the table will look at your sick expression. You will suddenly feel out of control and try to stand up. As you do, your stomach will explode out of your mouth and your lunch will splatter all over your tray, your clothes, your hands, and the table. It will be a gross-smelling mess, and you will hear others screaming and moving away. The whole cafeteria will be looking at you in disgust as you try to clean yourself. Okay, your consequence is over and don't think about it.

Your Choice:

Right now you owe one (1) lunch detention for your consequence. To escape your detention: Stand on your left foot and blink your eyes 10 times without losing balance. If you mess up, suffer through the detention and don't make it worse with your infantile crying.

Imaginary Consequence:

Give this card to your teacher. Teacher reads:

Close your eyes and imagine that you are alone, sitting at your desk. Without any sound at all, someone sneaks up behind you with a jar of about 1,000 live cockroaches. This person carefully pulls back your shirt collar and then dumps the whole jar of bugs down your back! You scream out in terror, and the bugs start running all over inside your shirt while they are nipping and scratching you. You pass out screaming. And then you wake up, glad it was just a dream. That's your consequence, but you may find it hard to get out of your mind. Return to your work and stop the wimpy shivering.

A Really Dark Consequence:

You have just lost all good luck for the next 24 hours. You will be hassled by stupid mistakes, forgetfulness, hiccups, banana peels underfoot, and black cats in your path. If you return to this class with a good attitude, the bad luck may go away … or not.

No whining or your bad luck may get you one (1) lunch detention.

Double-or-Nothing Chance:

You can escape detention in two ways:

A. Flip a coin with the teacher—

Heads = You win <u>two</u> lunch detentions.
Tails = You get NO detention.

B. Draw another card and live with the consequence.

(Hint: Your luck hasn't been all that good today.)

Busted Again!

For your last miserable disruptive behavior, you should receive one (1) detention consequence. However, you may choose instead to be the last student to exit the classroom at the end of this period. If you forget to be the very last student out, you will serve your assigned detention time … *and stop with the whimpering already.*

Social Skills Consequence:

For your consequence, you must wave at one person in this classroom and then give them a sincere-sounding compliment about something they have done well in recent days. If the teacher likes it, you may sit down and no further penance is needed; otherwise, you can think about it in lunch detention.

Sentence Completion:

You have exactly 30 seconds to complete this simple sentence:

"I really love this place, and it's mostly because _____."

If the teacher buys your answer, you're off the hook for now.

A Disgusting Consequence:

Give this card to your teacher to read aloud.

Close your eyes and imagine yourself getting both feet stuck fast to a floor in a puddle of Super Glue. A masked stranger then appears and pours out a huge jar of hideous-looking insects right at your feet. Hundreds of ugly black bugs start climbing all over you. You scream in terror and swat frantically, but the angry bugs begin to scratch and bite and burrow into your flesh ... It's all a terrible nightmare ... And then you wake up and feel glad to be back in this class. That's it. Back to work, and try not to remember this dream or it will return later.

Cruel & Unusual Consequence:

Give this card to your teacher to read aloud.

Close your eyes and imagine yourself sitting on a small wooden seat that is suspended two stories above a cold water-filled tank. When I say, "Pull—splash!" imagine your seat collapsing with a sudden jerk and hear yourself screaming in terror as you fall toward the deep, frigid water below. When you hit the water and get that numbing cold feeling, just yell, "Stop!" out loud and try to catch your breath. Or you can stay frozen for a while longer.

Okay, ready? ... PULL!—SPLASH!

Easy Consequence:

Shake hands with your teacher while faking a big sincere smile ... and announce to the world:

"I really love this class!"

If it all seems real to the teacher, you are excused from any further consequences.

Read this card aloud:

Surprise! You just lost a full 30 seconds from your next passing period. This is a small price to pay for your last despicable action!

(Note: If you were able to pronounce the word "despicable" correctly without help, you may reduce your fine to only 15 seconds.)

Self-Control Practice:

Your recent actions were disgusting! Give yourself a loud warning about this kind of misbehavior. Use your own name and tell yourself to quit doing this stuff or else! If the teacher likes your talk, you are excused from any further consequences.

If not, try to accept your lunch detention with some sense of dignity.

CREATIVE SOLUTIONS SWEEPSTAKES
OFFICIAL ENTRY FORM

Here's your chance to solve a problem and win a fabulous prize! Think through the classroom issue selected by your teacher. Submit your creative solution by the contest deadline and you may be our next grand prize winner! Good luck!

Contest Deadline: _____

The Problem Situation:

Your Creative Solution: (Give a clear step-by-step summary of how it would work in this class)

This entry submitted by

Student: _____   Date: _____

Teacher Evaluation Survey

Please respond to each of the items below by circling the number that best reflects your opinion. Additional space is provided in case you wish to add written comments. Thank you for your honest reply.

1. _____

5	4	3	2	1
Strongly Agree	Agree	Not Sure	Disagree	Strongly Disagree

Comments:

2. _____

5	4	3	2	1
Strongly Agree	Agree	Not Sure	Disagree	Strongly Disagree

Comments:

3. _____

5	4	3	2	1
Strongly Agree	Agree	Not Sure	Disagree	Strongly Disagree

Comments:

4. _____

5	4	3	2	1
Strongly Agree	Agree	Not Sure	Disagree	Strongly Disagree

Comments:

Customer Satisfaction Survey

All students in this class are my valued customers. I want to know how well you are pleased with the teaching activities that go on around here. Please take a moment to mark this survey. Thanks!

For this teacher: _____ Date: _____

How clearly am I explaining new concepts and material in class?

1	2	3	4	5
Not Clear		Okay		Very Clear

How reasonable are the homework assignments?

1	2	3	4	5
Not Reasonable		Okay		Very Reasonable

How well do my tests and quizzes fairly measure the lesson material?

1	2	3	4	5
Not Well		Okay		Very Well

How well have I explained the classroom behavior rules?

1	2	3	4	5
Not Well		Okay		Very Well

Have I been consistent in enforcing the behavior rules?

1	2	3	4	5
Not Consistent		Okay		Very Consistent

Have I been fair to all students?

1	2	3	4	5
Not Fair		Okay		Very Fair

Your personal comments are valuable:

Name (optional): _____

Professional Development Plan
(CONFIDENTIAL)

Prepared for this teacher: _____   **Semester:** _____

Our classroom can sometimes get too loud and rowdy, and then nobody gets any work done. Here are my helpful suggestions for how the teacher can practice really strong behavior management skills in our classroom.

1. In order to manage us students better, **our teacher should <u>start</u>** (doing what?):

    _____

    _____

    _____

    _____

2. In order to manage us students better, **our teacher should <u>stop</u>** (doing what?):

    _____

    _____

    _____

    _____

3. In order to manage us students best, our teacher **should <u>keep using</u>** some methods that already work pretty well (like what?):

    _____

    _____

    _____

    _____

I sure hope this helps out:

_____

Student signature

GOTCHA!

You forgot to enforce
a Class Rule!

GOTCHA!

You forgot to enforce
a Class Rule!

GOTCHA! GAME

This coupon worth
3
Bonus Points

Added to your next regular assignment.
Sign below and return with your
written work.

_____

Lucky Student

*Note: Some restrictions may apply. See your teacher
for complete details and expiration date.*

GOTCHA! GAME

This coupon worth
3
Bonus Points

Added to your next regular assignment.
Sign below and return with your
written work.

_____

Lucky Student

*Note: Some restrictions may apply. See your teacher
for complete details and expiration date.*

GOTCHA! GAME

Official Rules Poster

1. Whenever this poster is displayed in the classroom, the rules of the game are automatically in effect.

2. The teacher agrees to strictly enforce the penalties on each of the target behaviors listed below. There are no exceptions or excuses.

> **Target Behaviors:**

3. Any time that the teacher forgets to enforce a consequence on any of the target behaviors, the first student to observe that should immediately:
   - A. Face the teacher.
   - B. Point an index finger at the teacher.
   - C. Say, "Gotcha!" in a clear voice.
   - D. Tell the teacher exactly which target behavior was ignored.

4. If the student used the exact procedure described above and the teacher agrees, or a majority class vote agrees, that there was an ignored violation, the teacher will gladly accept the following consequence.

> **Teacher's Consequence:**

5. Any student who falsely claims to see a missed enforcement will be given the same penalty that would have been assigned for the alleged violation. Teacher judgment or class majority vote may be used to determine if a false claim has been made.

True Lies About the Author

Barry Christian has had adventurous dual careers as a clinical psychologist and school psychologist. He lives with his wife, Lillian, on a green mountaintop with views of the Gila Wilderness and beautiful Silver City, New Mexico. Both the kids are finally in college. Barry fancies himself as some kind of amateur gold prospector and southwestern historian. He has also written some mostly true articles for western treasure magazines. As might be expected, he requires many 504 accommodations to support his gainful employment in the local school district.

While we're telling all, here's a timely response to our #1 FAQ: The ideas for OBM were blatantly lifted from the writings of Dr. Milton Erickson, the pages of *Mad Magazine*, a collection of *Far Side* calendars, and a half-dozen syndicated detective shows. Somehow all of this artful subterfuge was mixed with the author's clinical training in applied behavior analysis. A pinch of "attitude" was added, and poof! ... OBM was spawned. *At least that's our current spin.*

Finally, Dr. Christian and the entire R&D staff at the OBM Institute send their best regards as you try to make some sense of the handbook.

Barry T. Christian, PhD
School Psychology Services
P.O. Box 4023
Silver City, NM 88062
redhill@signalpeak.net